Edwardian London

Volume 2

Titles available from The Village Press are:-

The London Library:

Hardback
Village London Volume I
Village London Volume II
London Recollected Volume I
London Recollected Volume II
London Recollected Volume III
London Recollected Volume IV
London Recollected Volume V
London Recollected Volume VI
Village London Atlas
Besant's History of London - The Tudors
Besant's History of London - The Stuarts

Paperback
Village London Pt. 1 West and North
Village London Pt. 2 North and East
Village London Pt. 3 South-East
Village London Pt. 4 South-West
Village London Atlas
Old Fleet Street
Cheapside and St. Paul's
The Tower and East End
Shoreditch to Smithfield
Charterhouse to Holborn
Strand to Soho
Covent Garden and the Thames to Whitehall
Westminster to St. James's
Haymarket to Mayfair
Hyde Park to Bloomsbury
Belgravia, Chelsea and Kensington
Paddington Green to Seven Sisters
Highgate & Hampsread to the Lea
Edwardian London (4 Volumes.)

Other titles published are:

The Village Atlas - Birmingham and The West Midlands
The Village Atlas - Manchester, Lancashire & North Cheshire
The Village Atlas - North and West Yorkshire
The Village Atlas - Derbyshire, Nottinghamshire & Leicestershire

Edwardian London

Volume 2

The Village Press

First published in 1902 by Cassell and Co. Ltd.,
under the title Living London in 3 volumes.

This edition published by:

The Village Press Ltd.
7d Keats Parade Ltd, Church Street,
London, N9 9DP.

June 1990

British Library Cataloguing in Publication Data
Edwardian London.
    Vol. 2
    1. London, 1901-1910
    I. Sims, George R. (George Robert), 1847-1922 II. Living London
    942.10823

    ISBN: 1-85540-012-X
    (Series ISBN: 1-85540-029-4.)

Cover Artwork by Active Art, Winchmore Hill, London.

Printed and bound in Great Britain by:
J.W. Arrowsmith Ltd, Bristol.

CONTENTS.

CONTENTS.

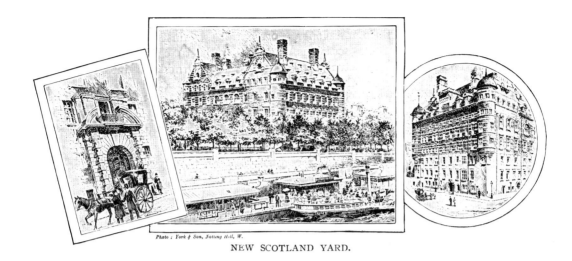

NEW SCOTLAND YARD.

LIVING LONDON.

NEW SCOTLAND YARD.

By MAJOR ARTHUR GRIFFITHS.

PROTECTION is the keynote of the London police system. To secure the comfort and safety of the people, to shield and safeguard personal liberty, to protect property, to watch over public manners and public health — such are the aims and objects of the vast organisation which has its heart and centre in New Scotland Yard.

The work of a police began, as its name implies, when men gathered together to live in a *polis* or city, and an essential part of good government was to empower a few to shield and defend the many. Despots used the weapon of the police to enslave and oppress ; in these latter days a fussy and too paternal authority, moved by the best intentions, may tend to lessen the self-reliance of law-abiding citizens, but the latter are taught, and they have learnt the lesson, that the policeman, according to our modern methods, is their best friend. His more serious functions, coercion, repression, vindication, are, as a rule, kept in the background ; most people rely upon him rather than fear him. It may be his painful duty to arrest you and lock you up if you offend, but he much prefers to be your guide and champion, to help and stand by you at every turn. His eager and unremitting guardianship is everywhere constantly on view : at the crowded street crossing, when with uplifted finger he stays the multitudinous thunder of the traffic ; in the lonely night watches, when he tries every door and window and, if needs be, rouses the careless householder to look to his fastenings, or, later, risks his valuable life against the murderous burglar. See the trustfulness with which the lost child trots beside him, hand in hand, securely confident of the kindness of this great man, who has babies of his own at home ; see him again amidst the turbulent East-Enders, giving short shrift to the ruffianly wife-beater, or in Hyde Park at a stormy Sunday meeting, or at a fire, or after an accident. With gentle or rough, he is always the same, civil-spoken, well-mannered, long-suffering but sturdy and uncompromising servant of the public.

The constable on his beat, with the law at his back, possessing and exercising power and responsibility, is the outward and visible sign of the ruling authority. He stands at one end, the Chief Commissioner, who only wears uniform on State occasions, at the other The former is in actual contact with people and things; the latter inspires and directs him, acting through him as the unit that distributes the current, so to speak, of concentrated authority through all the ramification of the colossal machine. The Chief Commissioner is subject to the

trusted to him, the muzzling of dogs, the precautions against contagious disease; he has the right to check gambling, and may send his myrmidons into a house to break up any coterie collected to play games of pure hazard. Crime, its prevention, pursuit, and detection, are, of course, primary duties devolving upon the chief of police, and he has at command the *personnel* of the force, a magnificent body of men, a finer *corps d'élite* than any army has ever owned or any general has ever been privileged to handle in the field.

TESTING CAB AND OMNIBUS DRIVERS.

Home Secretary as his superior, and in that sense is not supreme, but within certain limits he is practically an independent autocratic ruler. He has great statutory powers, and it would take pages to give them in any detail. He really holds all London in the hollow of his hand. The streets and thoroughfares, the routes and arteries through the town, are subject to his regulations, so is every driver of any kind of vehicle, from the state coach of an ambassador to the automobile car. The 'busmen and the cabmen come to him for their licences, and to be tested in their skill in driving and knowledge of the streets; and one of the most curious sights is to see the police examiner at work, seated with his pupil on the box of a prehistoric 'bus, or old-fashioned waggonette, starting on the test journey, when practical proof of competence must be given.

The Chief Commissioner rules, too, at all times of rejoicing and equally of disturbance, preventing obstructions and maintaining order both on shore and on the Thames; the abatement of public nuisances is en-

All this and much more appertaining thereto would be beyond the personal ken of a single individual, and the chief has three principal assistants at his elbow to relieve him by a judicious division of the great mass of business that must be transacted day after day. These, the heads of the police hierarchy, are men of mark, having very distinctive qualities and gifts, and all of them public servants of approved value.

There is little at first sight to associate the Chief Commissioner with the police officer and the stern duties he is called upon to discharge. Gentle, unobtrusive in manner, soft-voiced, of polished courtesy, he seems more fitted to shine in society than as the strict disciplinarian, the master of many legions, the great prefect of the greatest city in the world. Yet he is a leader of men, strong and purposeful, ready to take a decided line and never weaken in it under pressure either from above or below. The old saying that the nation is happiest which has no history applies to the Metropolitan police, which, after some periods of discontent and unrest, has long been quietly and peaceably governed. The three Assistant Commissioners for general duties are long-tried officials, constantly engaged; and in addition there are four Chief Constables. India has always been a favourite recruiting-ground for our police officials, and many of the best have been obtained from there.

Even if armed with the best credentials, it is not an easy matter to gain access to these chiefs. Constable-messengers meet all visitors to New Scotland Yard, subjecting them to strict inquiry and detention before ushering them in. Not only must the superior officers be spared interruption in the midst of business, which is incessant— for all matters, those even of minor importance, come before the departmental heads—but there may be danger, certainly inconvenience, in admitting strangers. In the worst days of the dynamite terror a daring ruffian got some way inside with an infernal machine, and irresponsible persons come who may be mischievous as well as importunate. The police are worried to death with callers on all errands, and on none more foolish than the desire to make spurious confession of some notable crime. One day a lady arrived in a cab with several children and a heap of baggage, clamorous to see the Chief Commis-

sioner, and determined to go straight to gaol with all her belongings as the murderess of a soldier whom she declared she had killed, cut up, and buried. It was all nonsense, of course, but she was only got rid of by an ingenious ruse. Her chief terror was lest she should be separated from her children, and she was told this would not happen and she might remain at large if she would sign a paper promising to appear when called upon.

Divide et impera. To parcel out authority and pass it on through various branches is an essential condition of a great public office. Decentralisation is constantly kept in view at police head-quarters, and executive business is done for the most part locally at the twenty-two "divisions" or units of administration into which the Metropolis is divided. But the lines all centre, the threads are all held in New Scotland Yard, from which all orders issue, to which all reports are made, to which all difficulties are referred. This gives supreme importance to the telegraph-room department, the great department with its army of operators continually manipulating innumerable machines. Every division is in direct communication with headquarters; every item of news is flashed along the line, and the Chief has his fingers at all times upon every subordinate in every part of London. The unity of direction thus conferred is obviously most valuable: New Scotland Yard knows all that is going on, and can utilise at will and almost instantaneously its whole wide-reaching machinery. On one occasion this was amusingly illustrated when

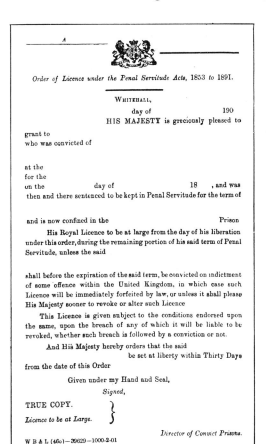

Order of Licence under the Penal Servitude Acts, 1853 to 1891.

WHITEHALL,

day of   190

HIS MAJESTY is greciously pleased to

grant to
who was convicted of

at the
for the
on the   day of   18   , and was
then and there sentenced to be kept in Penal Servitude for the term of

and is now confined in the   Prison

His Royal Licence to be at large from the day of his liberation under this order, during the remaining portion of his said term of Penal Servitude, unless the said

shall before the expiration of the said term, be convicted on indictment of some offence within the United Kingdom, in which case such Licence will be immediately forfeited by law, or unless it shall please His Majesty sooner to revoke or alter such Licence

This Licence is given subject to the conditions endorsed upon the same, upon the breach of any of which it will be liable to be revoked, whether such breach is followed by a conviction or not.

And His Majesty hereby orders that the said
be set at liberty within Thirty Days
from the date of this Order

Given under my Hand and Seal,
Signed,

TRUE COPY.
Licence to be at Large.

Director of Convict Prisons.

W B & L (460)—39629—1000-2-01

CONVICT'S " LICENCE."

the French police appealed for help in the arrest of a certain fugitive. The emissary came over with a photograph and full description, and the latter was at once disseminated through London. That same afternoon a constable stopped the very individual in Regent Street, and at a second call in the afternoon the prisoner was handed over to the French police officer. There was good luck in this, of course, but some good management, and it serves to show how extensive is police control. It may be added here that our police are by no means despised by their French *confrères*, although our

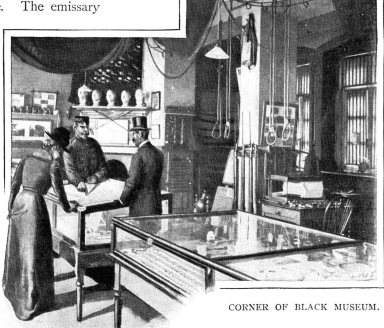

CORNER OF BLACK MUSEUM.

Photo : Thankfull Sturder, St. John's, S.E.

peculiar ideas, by exalting the liberty of the subject, greatly limit the powers of our authorities.

New Scotland Yard is kept constantly informed of the state of crime in the Metropolis. Every morning a full report of all criminal occurrences during the previous twenty-four hours is laid before the third Assistant Commissioner, the Director of Criminal Investigation. He sees at a glance what has happened, and decides at once what should be done.

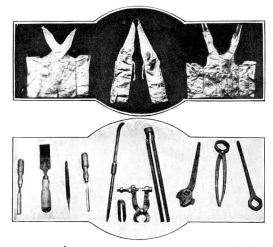

BURGLAR'S POCKETS FOR HOLDING THE TOOLS
SHOWN BELOW THEM.

He has many expert subordinates and specialists within reach—men who have handled detective matters for many years with unerring skill. The best advisers are called into council when serious and mysterious crime is afoot, local knowledge also, the divisional detectives being sent for to assist those at headquarters. From the Director's office, after anxious conference, the hunt begins, any clue is seized, and the scent cleverly followed, until, as a rule, the game is run to ground.

Detection and pursuit are greatly aided by other branches at New Scotland Yard. There is first the "convict office," at which all ex-prisoners discharged from penal servitude are obliged to report themselves, and, if sentenced to police supervision, to record their intended place of residence and proposed way of life. The conditions upon which release has been accorded before the expiring of sentence are plainly stated on the "licence" or document which is issued to all as their credentials or permission to be at large, and it must be produced at all times when called for. Often enough, it is to be feared, the perpetrator of a new crime is to be found among these old hands. The predatory habit is strong, and the shrewd detective on the hunt almost always looks first among the

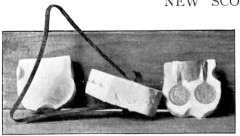

COINER'S MOULDS (SHOWING SPRING TO
HOLD THEM TOGETHER).

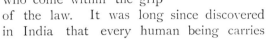

SKELETON KEYS.

however, more prompt and infallible methods of identification coming into force —for instance, the system of measurements after the plan of M. Bertillon for recording unchanging personal characteristics; and now the record of the "finger prints" is being more largely applied to all who come within the grip of the law. It was long since discovered in India that every human being carries a distinctive mark in the impression of his five finger tips on a white surface after they have been duly blackened. All we need now is a greater accumulation of these

licence-holders or ticket-of-leave men who are known practitioners in a particular line or "lay." It is no uncommon thing to take a man for a small matter and find he is the very one wanted for a greater. The chance "stop" or pick up of a suspicious - looking character leads to his identification as the author of a big job not yet brought home.

LIFE PRESERVERS.

When an arrest has been made, it is usual to pass the prisoner with as little delay as possible to Brixton Prison; but now and again a person suspected of mysterious or political crimes is taken to New Scotland Yard for examination of a special kind. There are many aids to identification, to stimulating recollection, at police headquarters. The stored archives, the records

PICKLOCKS, VICE, AND
CENTRE-BIT.

records, the extension of the system to all criminals in custody, and the legal power to enforce the "printing off" on all arrested persons. Comparison can then be instituted between the new and the old as classified in the central office, and certain identification must follow. At present, photographs, tattoo marks, and recognition, the latter carried out at Brixton and applied to all under suspicion, are among the chief guides.

KNUCKLEDUSTER.

The detective police officer, anxious to improve himself professionally, will find much

and registers and photographic albums are most useful. The search may be long and tedious, for there is a strong family likeness in the dangerous classes, the criminal brand brings features to one dead level, but many a dark horse has been revealed by his portrait in police hands. There are,

BURGLAR'S FOLDING LADDER.

COINER'S IMPLEMENTS (INCLUDING
RACK FOR HOLDING COINS DURING
PLATING PROCESS, MELTING POT,
LADLE, POLISHING BRUSH, ETC.).

useful information in another branch at New Scotland Yard, the well-known Black Museum. This is more than a collection of grim and ghastly curiosities, the relics of celebrated crimes, such as those pictured on the two preceding pages. It is a school wherein the intelligent student may learn lessons to serve him in the conduct of his business. The methods of criminals are revealed to him here ; he may judge from the implements and tools of the craft how top-sawyers succeeded in it. Here are the " jemmy," the screw-jack, the rope ladder (Peace's), light and easy of carriage under an overcoat, the neat dark lantern made out of a tin matchbox, the melting pot and ladle of the coiners, with mould and other apparatus used by them ; together with relics that reveal the more elaborate processes of the banknote forgers, such as copper plates, burins, lithographic stones, and so on. There are many deeply interesting relics in the Black Museum, such as the chisel, on which the syllable " rock " was scratched, that led to the detection of Orrock, the Dalston murderer ; the rope with which Marguerite Dixblanc dragged the corpse of her murdered mistress into the scullery ; and others.

There is another museum at Scotland Yard of a less gruesome kind, in which the exhibits are constantly changing. The Lost Property Office is an institution which has its humorous side, bearing witness to the carelessness of the public, and at the same time to the general honesty of its servants. Some forty thousand articles are about the average annual crop of things dropped or forgotten in cabs and public carriages, or mislaid, and the harvest is a strange one. All manner of property is passed across the police counter, brought in by cabmen and others, and handed back to its owners on proof and payment of the necessary fees ; and among these are found such diverse articles as bicycles and perambulators, rabbits, cats, jewellery, umbrellas, and sewing-machines.

The Metropolitan Police is a mighty engine worked, happily, for good. It has been so admirably built up, so slowly and completely perfected, exercises such far-reaching and extensive functions, that it is well for the people of London it is ever devoted to their good, and acts primarily in their best interests. An organisation so powerful in the hands of despotic authority would make life a daily burden, and the word " liberty " would be an empty sound. But it is—as we may congratulate ourselves—the servant, not the master, of the public, and we need only blame ourselves if it should ever become the latter.

IN THE LOST PROPERTY OFFICE.

SUNDAY MORNING EAST AND WEST.

By A. ST. JOHN ADCOCK.

A SUNDAY morning in the height of summer. The Trafalgar Square fountains flicker and flash dazzlingly in the sunlight, and the air is so quiet that from the edge of the glowing pavement you can catch the cool tinkle of the water as it showers back into the basins.

This time yesterday morning the roar of life was at its loudest here : a busy, innumerable crowd billowed restlessly into the Square and out of it on every side ; carts, cabs, 'buses, carriages, rushing incessantly to and fro in the roadway, made the crossing difficult and even perilous. But to-day an obvious tourist, abetted by his wife, is leisurely erecting a camera to photograph the Nelson Column, and looks lonely in the middle of the road.

Nobody is in a hurry this morning. Most of the passers-by wear such an aggressive air of being out for pleasure, and not on business, as you may have noticed in schoolboys playing truant. There is a faded old man on the rim of one of the fountains hunched in an attitude that suggests years of bending over a desk in some dull office, but now he is reading his Sunday paper instead of writing in a ledger ; and on the benches round about more or less seedy loafers are basking in drowsy contentment.

From the direction of St. Martin's Church a char-a-banc crawls hesitantly by the kerb, and a narrow board on the side of it indicates that it is prepared to take excursionists to Kew or Hampton Court. A straggling procession of similar vehicles is slowly approaching down the Strand : most of them have a few holiday-makers, male and female—emancipated shop-hands, steady-going clerks, and visitors from the country—already seated under their striped awnings, and the drivers and conductors are keeping an alert look-out for more.

For nearly an hour past a shiny, yellow, smart private brake has been standing opposite one of the hotels near this end of Northumberland Avenue, and now you are warned by the stiffening of the groom at the horses' heads that those it waits for are at length in sight. A very gay, very elegant party of Americans streams out of the hotel, making a sudden brightness in the shadow of the huge, sombre building : Papa, glorious in a blindingly white waistcoat, a Panama hat, and loose white trousers ; Mamma, very stout, rosy and good-humoured, gowned in pink under a pink parasol ; three young girls, one of them evidently her daughter, and a middle-aged lady youthfully dressed, all four a bewildering shimmer of white and blue and crimson ; and with them are three young men and a middle-aged one clothed in summery tweeds and serges. As there is only room for eight inside, one of the young men reluctantly climbs up beside Papa, who is taking the reins ; and away they go, whirling airily across the Square, a many-hued bubble of laughter and merry chattering, that switches off into Pall Mall, and is beyond sight and hearing at once, as if it had burst at the corner.

A little way down the Strand, where all the shops are asleep and the pavements but thinly peopled, if you look in under the wide archway of a certain hotel you shall see, against a background of loungers in basket-chairs, with iced drinks on spindly tables at their elbows, spruce cabs and carriages waiting for their owners or hirers ; and conspicuous amidst them the dandy black and yellow coach that will presently start for a run to Walton - on - Thames. Its dapper, white silk-hatted coachman stands deferentially discussing his four horses with a prospective passenger ; and from the long wicker sheath hung by the back seat protrudes the brazen horn that by-and-bye, when the full coach rattles gallantly on its journey, will waken jolly echoes in sober suburban streets and green lanes by the riverside.

By this time the bells are ringing for morning service, and the out-of-door population is leavened with an increasing proportion of church- and chapel-goers, of both sexes and all ages, carrying red or gilt-edged books. Wandering west, along Pall Mall into Piccadilly and through the stately byways of Mayfair, you meet with more and more church-goers, more fashionably dressed, and more aristocratic of look and bearing. Generally there is one exquisitely groomed male to every two ladies, but now and then the ladies are unescorted ; and occasionally, armed with the inevitable red or gilt-edged volumes, two or three of the sterner sex are stepping churchwards together, with no petticoated accompaniment to persuade them thither.

There are church-goers, too, in some of the few carriages that are rumbling demurely among 'buses and excursion vehicles down Piccadilly ; and dashing past them, with a jaunty levity that has a spice of wickedness in it, comes a hansom carrying a blissful man in boating flannels. Beside him is a pretty river nymph in a sailor blouse,

FOUR-IN-HAND.

smiling out from under the sauciest straw hat that was ever made. The glimpse you have of them, and of the sly luncheon hamper on the roof, gives you such a vivid momentary vision of sunny, rippling water and two in a boat that you can almost hear the cool plash of the dipping oars.

Whichever way you take, there are cyclists everywhere—women and men, alone, in pairs, and by the dozen. Turning back and up Regent Street to loiter for a while at Oxford Street corner, you see how the tops of outward-bound 'buses are bubbling and frothing over with gossamer white hats and dresses, and laces and ribbons ; and occasionally, embowered among all this finery, you may pick out the mother of a family nursing the youngest, the father nursing the dinner-basket, and overheating himself with saving less manageable members of the family from tumbling off into the road.

Panting and snorting and bumping, there goes a motor-car ; four knickerbockered men inside it, and the back of it bristling with golf-clubs. Here comes a dog-cart with a smart looking party out for the day ; followed presently by a glossy, high-stepping steed drawing a natty trap, wherein is a large man, keenly conscious of his own dashing aspect, of the elegance and loveliness of the lady who sits by him as brilliantly arrayed as a very butterfly, and of the tremendous effectiveness of the white-breeched, top-booted footboy perched with folded arms at the back. Comfortable people are out sunning themselves in landaus ; expected guests are spinning off in cabs to pleasant little luncheons in Suburbia ; and all the time there are more cyclists, by ones, by twos, by threes ; and yonder, spreading and thinning out and winding among the traffic like a flight of birds, comes a party of nearly a score, a flutter of feminine drapery here and there lending a touch of grace and gallantry to it, to say nothing of colour.

And now the pavements grow temporarily populous with pedestrians homing from church ; and sprinkled among them are nursemaids returning from the Park, wheeling in dainty perambulators aristocratic infants who slumber deep in soft frills and laces under lace-edged canopies. Entering the

AWHEEL.

Park at Marble Arch, and passing the usual agnostic, the usual prophet, the usual social reformer thundering to half-bored, half-amused audiences near the gate, you advance round Rotten Row, and are very soon mingling in the church parade of a highly fashionable, highly decorous crowd that grows denser at every step you take into it, until your walking perforce slows down to the gentlest possible foot-pace.

For under the trees here all the beauty and fashion of the West hold high carnival in the hour betwixt coming from church and going to luncheon ; but the whole vast multitude is toned to such well-mannered harmony that there is no crush anywhere, no unseemly excitement, no haste—only a stately pacing this way and that, murmuring of sedate voices, and rippling of politely modulated laughter. On the garden seats down the centre of the broad path and at the side, and on the green chairs closely scattered between the seats and more closely across the grass behind them, one half of the crowd rests and looks on at the other half which is in motion. Members of Parliament, retired military officers, financial princes, men of title and rank, pompous, indifferent, affable, dignified ; gay old gentlewomen quizzing the throng through their glasses, severe old gentlewomen disregarding it all with petrified stares ; blushful maidens, callow swaggering youths, matured imperturbable maidens and bored men of experience, matrons and dames, and fussy or stolid

old heads of old families, all talking and flirting and bowing and smiling and strolling and meeting and turning, and meeting and passing again, or pausing to shake hands and chat for a minute of last night's ball, or to-morrow's play, or this evening's little dinner.

Across the other side of London at this same hour, and from several hours earlier and for several hours to come, there gathers another crowd as vast as this, but differently composed and in a vastly different environment. In place of the grass and trees on one side of the road, and the gorgeous, neatly ordered flower beds on the other, you find two rows of squalid shops, wide open and roaring alluringly for customers ; in place of the garden seats, here is a confusion of overloaded stalls fringing the pavements to right and left from end to end of the long, narrow thoroughfare ; and, in place of the unimpeachable carriages and equestrians in the roadway and the polite gathering on the footpath, here the sun glares down through a dusty, malodorous atmosphere on a loud, surging, struggling, closely - packed mob, elbowing and shouldering hither and thither sturdily, and on eager shopkeepers and stall-keepers bawling and gabbling in diabolical concert. For you are in the East, and this is Middlesex Street, unofficially known as Petticoat Lane.

Arriving in Bishopsgate Street Without a little before eleven, you might have seen the tide of well-dressed or decent church- and chapel-goers at the full, and have heard the church bells ringing placidly as they rang in the West ; but the moment you plunged into the " Lane " their pealing would have been inaudible in the nearer clamour of human voices. This tall red building is the Jews' Free School, and the droning of scholars at their lessons floats out at the open windows and mingles with the howls of the fish salesman, the wail of the lemon seller, and the raucous patter of the cheap jack. You pass from a clothier's stall to a butcher's, to tinware, crockery, toy, fruit, hat and cap stalls, confectioners' stalls, boot stalls, more cheap jacks, more fish stalls, more clothiers, and pretty well all of them

Jews. Now and then you collide with a man who, having no stall, careers about in the crowd with a stack of trousers on his shoulder, and flourishing a pair in his hand implores you to take your choice from his stock at " a dollar a time " ; you meet men and boys adrift in like manner with braces, handkerchiefs, socks, boots ; an old bearded Hebrew hovers at the corner of Wentworth Street with a huge bowl of gherkins steeped in a yellowish liquid, and reiterates drearily, " All in winegar—'apenny each ! "

Opposite an earnest man in his shirt sleeves bellows over a glass tank, " 'Ere yar ! The champiun lemin drink—'apenny a glass. 'Ave yer money back if yer don't like it ! " And close alongside a gramaphone is all the while reproducing a sharp, jerky imitation of the voice of a popular music-hall star singing a comic song. Just beyond it a clothier mad with zeal has leaped upon his stall, and is frantically waving a coat before the eyes of the crowd. " As good as it was the day it was made ! " he shrieks. " Look at it for yerselves. It'll stand it. Look at it ! " He hurls it at the simmering mass, and it completely extinguishes two heads, the owners whereof casually disentangle themselves from it and toss it back to him. " Worth 'arf a guinea," he insists. " It's goin' for eight bob—seven—six—five—three an' a tanner, an' not a farden less if I—— Now then, Sam, 'elp the genelman try it on." He pitches it to a paunchy, shirt-sleeved partner, and the next moment the customer, a weedy youth and shy, is trying it on. " 'Ow's it fit at the back ? " the partner demands of a friend who is with the customer. " Bit loose, ain't it ? " " Loose ! " interrupts the partner furiously. " Young fool—where is it ? 'E'll never 'ave no better fit than that,

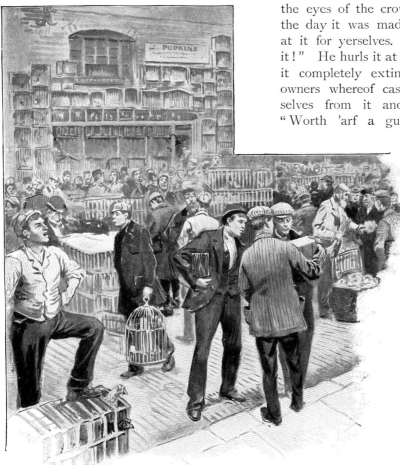

BIRD FAIR (SCLATER STREET, BETHNAL GREEN).

not at any price." He pats the customer encouragingly on the shoulder, has his money in a twinkling, and sends him shuffling off with his old coat under his arm.

The fair overflows all the streets branching from Petticoat Lane, and diverging to the west you may penetrate to Cutler Street and Phil's Buildings, which are wholly given over to clothiers; going farther east by

doors and in the gutters hutches and cages, towering one above another, swarm with rabbits, fowls, pigeons, ducks, cockatoos, parrots, thrushes, canaries, and such smaller birds in amazing variety; and the sellers bawl against each other, and the birds crow, coo, quack, scream, and sing against each other deafeningly. Men without shops or stands roam in the crowd carrying a cage or two and crying their wares; men and boys waylay you in the crush or on the skirts of it with wriggling heaps of rabbits at the bottom of small sacks, and offer you the pick of the bunch for six-pence.

OFF TO CHINGFORD.

Escaping through Cygnet

way of Wentworth Street, which is as rampant and as congested as the "Lane" itself, you emerge on Spitalfields, where the Market is half open, trafficking with coster-mongers, whose trucks and donkey-carts are huddled outside it.

This turning by the church brings us to Brick Lane, and Brick Lane leads to Sclater Street, locally known as Club Row, where you will find Bird Fair in full blast. It is Petticoat Lane over again on a much smaller scale; with next to no Jews, hardly any women, less diversity, no side-shows (unless you count the betting tipster and refreshment stalls right out past the limits of the crowd); no frivolity in short, but strict attention to business.

Most of the shops in Sclater Street are kept by bird dealers, and their outer walls up to the first floor have all broken into an eruption of bird cages. Beside the shop

OUT FOR THE DAY.

Street, you stumble into a smaller, quiet market in Bethnal Green Road, for the sale of cycle tyres and second-hand accessories; and meat and vegetable stalls are moderately busy for some distance past it. Noon being gone, as you follow the Bethnal Green Road and Cambridge Road to Mile End Gate, people are coming away from Sunday morning services, many in Salvation Army uniforms, and loafers gathered at street corners are yearning for the public-houses to open.

SUNDAY MORNING IN HYDE PARK (CHURCH PARADE).

Photo: A. B. Hughes, Fulham, S.W.

SUNDAY MORNING IN MIDDLESEX STREET, WHITECHAPEL.

A drab, dingy, squalid neighbourhood; and yet you come upon Romance flowering in the heart of it. You will not see a carriage stopping every day in front of that grimy old house sandwiched between the shops yonder; and you may easily know why it is there now by the rose in the driver's buttonhole and the white ribbon bow on his whip, and by the sightseers who form a double line from the carriage door to the gate of the house, and include two frowsy women with babies, several small children carrying smaller children, and one unwashed infant who, propelled by a bare-footed sister, has arrived in considerable state in a soap box on wheels.

Whitechapel Road presents a very different spectacle from that to be seen at this hour in Oxford Street; and yet it has at least one point of resemblance, for all the 'buses and trams running away from London are packed with happy fugitives who are running away from it too. But here is no Oxford Street equipage, this coster's barrow racing and rocking towards Chingford under the weight of its owner and some friends, the former in his shirt-sleeves and the feminine members of the party in all the pride of bright dresses and big-feathered hats. Some little distance behind them a substantial family group jolts soberly along on chairs and boxes in a greengrocer's cart; and overtaking and passing them whirl a dozen of Epping-bound cyclists—factory lads and artisans, mostly in their working clothes—who will return under the stars to-night, tired perhaps and rather rowdy, with green branches and blossoms wreathed round their handle-bars.

Night is half a day off yet, however. It is only just luncheon hour in the West, where the gongs are calling pleasantly select gatherings to shady interiors of Belgravia; and here, in the East, the loafers have disappeared from the corners, for the public-houses are open, and you are meeting shirt-sleeved men and bare-armed women going for the dinner beer, and men, women, and children hurrying home with steaming dishes from the bakehouses—some one or other of the hungry urchins pausing, maybe, at a safe corner to raise the cloth from his dish and thrust a finger in after a well-browned, succulent potato, wherewith to propitiate his appetite by the way.

SUNDAY EXCURSIONISTS PASSING DOWN PICCADILLY.

SEARCHING A CHINESE SEAMAN'S CHEST.

HIS MAJESTY'S CUSTOMS.

By E. S. VALENTINE.

HARD by Billingsgate, stretching for a matter of one hundred and fifty yards or so along Thames Street, rises a large grey stone building, inhabited during business hours by three hundred clerks. It may be not inaptly termed the "King's Toll-Bar for London." It is the Custom House. Here is the home and centre of the revenue collection of the greatest port in the world. It is the headquarters of a small army of blue-coated and brass-buttoned functionaries familiar to merchants and mariners, tourists and travellers: all, indeed, whose business or pleasure leads them to foreign parts and home again to the heart of the British Empire.

But it must not be supposed that these numerous emissaries of the Custom House are ever gathered together within its four walls. They are distributed in batches—all save the actual clerical staff—and often many months may elapse before they so much as set eyes upon the chief establishment.

For instance, if you wend your way along the banks of the river east of the Tower of London, you will, at intervals, amidst the mass of closely-packed tall buildings and high walls, come across small, unpretentious structures, inscribed with the legend " His Majesty's Customs." Outside, maybe, an officer will be standing with his gaze bent upon the Thames, where his comrades are in a boat. These are the water-guard, whose duty it is to board ships coming up the river, and to superintend the unloading of such as carry bulk cargo. A group of officers and searchers taken at the Tunnel pier is shown in the photographic reproduction on p. 289. The men serve long hours—twenty-four at a stretch. If your curiosity impels you to peep into their quarters, you see in one room a couple of chairs and a desk littered with the latest official orders and notifications. Tobacco or brandy is expected to arrive carefully done up in the form of cheeses, or a large consignment of pirated English copyright works is to be seized. If you glance into the other room of these water-guards, your nostrils may be assailed by the aroma of ham or beefsteak, which our Customs officer himself is preparing against the return of his comrades.

"Oh, yes, we mess for ourselves," says your host, in response to a query on this head ; "Government furnishes the utensils, and we do the rest—that is, when we're ashore. When we're out on the river we carry our lunch with us, or mess on board ship."

Each group of the water-guard consists of four only, and the land-guard men make up most of the outside service.

They are vigilance incarnate, these Custom House men. It is no use trying to evade them. Day and night they are on the watch, waiting at the docks, rowing in the middle of the Thames, strolling about the railway stations, ready to pounce upon the incomer, whether he be master of a merchantman or merely proprietor of a modest portmanteau, with the query, "Anything dutiable?" or "Anything to declare?"

Every year it grows harder to elude or cheat the Customs. Yet the system in vogue to-day is infinitely simpler than it used to be. As has already been said, the "outside" staff of the Custom House is made up of a land-guard and a water-guard. There are no longer any "tide-waiters" or "land-waiters," such as appertained twenty or thirty years ago. At each of the great docks there are from forty to eighty officials. It is the duty of some of these to look after the cargo, while others inspect the effects of passengers and the crew. While this process is going on aboard ship, the master of the vessel is sending a report of her arrival and an account of her cargo to the Custom House, which he is obliged by law to do within twenty-four hours from entering port. Not a box or a bale may be landed until the master's declaration and that of the consignee have been compared by the indoor clerks at the Custom House, and what is known as the "entry," or warrant showing the duties on such goods as are dutiable to have been paid, is in the hands of the Customs men at the docks.

The process of examining luggage by the Customs inspectors at the docks is a sufficiently familiar one to all who have ever travelled out of this kingdom. The general air of bustle and excitement ; the impatience and oftentimes the annoyance of the travellers at the delay ; the occasional protestations on the part of nervous ladies ; the grim determination of the inspectors to probe to the bottom of every mystery ; and once in a way the discomfiture of a detected smuggler, unaware of the enormity of his or her offence ; the strange apparition of cigars in the middle of steamer cushions, and of brandy or perfume dexterously concealed in under garments : all this forms a twice-told tale. Rigorous attention, too, is required and given to the heterogeneous luggage of the aliens who land upon our shores.

Sometimes foreign—and, alas, British—members of the crew exhibit an ingenious pertinacity for smuggling. The officer who is told off to visit their quarters is usually acquainted with their devices ; for it seems pretty hard to Jack Tar that he may not

CAUGHT IN THE ACT.

bring his friends and family tobacco and spirits which he has bought "dirt cheap" in foreign parts.

But, as might be expected, by far the cleverest and most obstinate smuggler is the Chinaman. As an instance, a couple of Chinese seamen on board an Indiaman were imprisoned for concealing four pounds of tobacco and refusing to pay the fine upon detection—that is to say, treble the value of the goods with the duty added, which in

impertinences which occasionally distinguish countries where a tariff wall has been carefully reared. The business here, be it said to the credit of our Customs officers, is often done with an adroitness which a conjurer might envy. Presto! and your largest trunk is "inspected" to its innermost depths, and a tiny cabalistic chalk mark affixed which enables you to pass the barrier with an air of conscious rectitude—forgetful, perhaps, of the two or three smuggled volumes of Tauchnitz,

LUGGAGE AWAITING EXAMINATION BY CUSTOMS OFFICERS (CHARING CROSS STATION).

their case amounted to £3 13s. each. There are always some amusing cases of this description, especially on the arrival of a large vessel from the East whose crew has never before been subjected to a Customs examination.

At the railway stations, such as Charing Cross, about the hour that the Continental express is due, the little group of Customs officials are on the alert to examine such goods and luggage as have come through in bond, so to speak, from the port of Dover. England being a free-trade country, the returned tourist or the foreign visitor or immigrant misses, as well he may and with gratitude, those too assiduous attentions and

plainly marked "not to be introduced into the United Kingdom," reposing in the folds of your pyjamas.

One mighty department of the Customs consists of the bonded warehouses beneath, above, and surrounding the docks. Herein are stored the vast quantities of wine, spirits, tea, tobacco, etc., not required by the importer for the present, the duty being therefore unpaid. These vaults and warehouses are guarded day and night, they are under Crown lock and key, and none may enter them for the purpose of removing goods unless he carries with him a receipt from the Long Room of the Custom House showing that the King's fee has been duly paid. The bonded warehouses at St. Katherine's Docks can hold 110,000 tons of goods, those of London Docks over 250,000 tons, and the Royal Albert Docks have accommodation for an even larger amount. All the tobacco imported into London is stored at the Victoria Docks. There it stands, piled in huge casks, often millions of pounds' worth, with £100,000 worth of cigars in chests. The wines and spirits are in vaults at the London Docks; tea and sugar being distributed amongst various bonded warehouses. It is at the London Docks that one's eye catches sight of a door in the east angle inscribed "To the Kiln." This leads to a furnace in which adulterated tea and tobacco, pinchbeck jewellery, and other confiscated wares were for many years burnt.

"We burn few things here now," remarked one of the Customs officers; "most of what is done takes place at Deptford. The tobacco is given to the asylums, especially those for the insane, throughout the country."

"I suppose you destroyed a good deal of contraband merchandise in the old days?"

"I only wish I had a shilling for every hundred pounds' worth I've burnt. I've thrown a bushel of paste diamonds, 600 hams, 4,000 pirated novels, 2,000 pairs of gloves, and 150 pounds of tobacco into the kiln in

BEADLE.

the course of a day. I've burnt six crates of condemned pork-pies, fifteen dozen infected undershirts, and forty boxes of cigars during a morning. If you happen to be a smoker or a snuff-taker, it goes very much against the grain to see good material going to waste; but if importers won't pay the Customs dues they must, of course, be taught a lesson. Yet I, for one, am glad the Board has to a great extent abolished the old plan of burning."

And now, after having taken a brief survey of the character, numbers, and duties of the outside staff, let us return to headquarters in Thames Street, at which as yet we have only glanced.

As you cross the threshold into the wide corridor you are confronted by a gorgeous beadle in a scarlet cloak and cocked hat.

"The Long Room?" echoes the beadle, marvelling that anyone could by any possibility be ignorant of the precise whereabouts of that mercantile emporium, "Upstairs to the left." And he waves his arm in the direction of a crowded staircase, by which twoscore Custom House frequenters are ascending and descending Half-way up the staircase a long

OFFICERS AND SEARCHERS (TUNNEL PIER)

row of placards, proclamations, and official announcements, affixed to the wall, invite

is here, at the section marked " Report Office," that the master of every ship entering the Thames from foreign parts must deliver an account of her cargo. It may be a simple document (if the cargo is of a single article and consigned to but one person), or it may consist of several

ALIENS AND OTHERS AT THE DOCKS : AFTER LUGGAGE EXAMINATION.

the attention. Mariners are notified that there is a wreck in the river which they are cautioned to avoid ; there is an announcement concerning the sugar duty ; John James is requested to take his goods out of bond ; William Smith has been promoted to a first-class inspectorship ; and so on, each fresh notice as it is pasted up commanding a due amount of respectful attention.

At last we have gained the Long Room, far famed wherever the merchant flag of Britain floats, which has given its name to a hundred and more so-called "long rooms" in Custom Houses all over the kingdom, rooms which are only long in respect of time, and often not even in that. But this —the original Long Room of the Port of London—justifies its name. It is really a huge apartment—190 feet in length by 66 in breadth, and of majestic height. Eighty clerks are seated behind the continuous counter which runs round its four sides. This is the department where the bulk of the documents required by the Customs laws are received by the King's officials. It

papers, and be somewhat intricate (if the cargo is a mixed one and belongs to several persons). It is the business of the Customs officials to compare the master's report with the one presented by the consignee. If they agree, all is well ; otherwise an explanation is demanded. If the items of the cargo are of a dutiable nature, the duty must be paid ; after which the consignee's papers, or "entries," are signed by the Long Room officials, and serve as a warrant to the Customs officers at the docks to release the cargo.

Sometimes, just before the announcement of the annual Budget in the House of Commons, the Long Room of the Custom House presents a very animated scene indeed ; as, for instance, when a rumour got abroad, in the spring of 1901, that the Government had decided to impose a duty upon sugar. It so happened that the very day when the duty was to come into effect a ship arrived in the Thames laden with many hundreds of tons ; the captain made the utmost haste up the river, and then despatched the fleetest messenger obtainable to reach the Custom House and report his cargo. Alas! the messenger flew at top speed, but he was not quick enough. He arrived in Thames Street a few minutes too late—the Custom House had closed at four o'clock. Had the captain's emissary been a quarter of an hour sooner, or his ship a faster sailer, the consignee would have been saved a trifle of £4,000 duty. Where the goods are in bond—that is to say, stored in the Government warehouses, as sugar now is —the business of removing it must still be transacted at the Custom House.

The Customs duties levied here amount to £10,000,000 a year, or, in other words, about half the Customs of the kingdom are paid at the Port of London. To accomplish all the work that the collection of this vast sum entails there are no fewer than 170 rooms in the Custom House, besides the Long Room. But there is very little that is interesting in any of these; unless, perhaps, the Board Room, where oil portraits of George III., George IV., and Queen Victoria adorn the walls.

But on the ground floor of the big building in Thames Street is an extensive warehouse, where confiscated goods which are not destined to undergo the ordeal of the flames await the annual sale in Mincing Lane. This is the King's Warehouse; and is simply but bountifully packed with the most singular and fantastic *omnium gatherum* of merchandise from the four corners of the globe. Cheek by jowl with a dozen boxes of raisins and a couple of cameras will be an imitation grand piano containing a hundred gallons of brandy, a couple of tons of chocolate, a hundred dozen bottles of perfumery, five hundred flagons of liqueurs, thousand of prunes, and figs and tea *ad libitum*. The sale of confiscated articles usually brings in a matter of £2,000 per annum, even though some of the merchandise goes for a mere song to the fortunate purchasers who foregather in November at the official mart in Mincing Lane.

THE LONG ROOM.

IN BATTERSEA PARK.

FOOTBALL LONDON.

By HENRY LEACH.

THERE is one section of London's vast population which doesn't care a jot for football, another which goes simply mad over it, and there is every reason to believe that the latter is increasing considerably. And these two sections, be it remembered, are not merely and respectively the old and the young. Whilst there are ragged urchins kicking paper balls in back alleys in Fulham and Whitechapel, there are top-hatted, frock-coated gentlemen with grey beards, who sorrow over the passing of sixty winters, but who yet on this same afternoon are kicking the boards in front of them on the stand at Queen's Club, so high and so uncontrollable is their excitement as they watch the fortunes of a great match. Only in the brief half-time interval, when the players are being refreshed, is the nervous strain the least bit slackened. A football ground, after all, is one of the best places in the world for the observation of raw human nature.

There have been many eras of London football, and of such stern stuff is the London football enthusiast made that for a period of adversity, extending over nearly two decades, he could still keep his mind steadfastly fixed on one great purpose and work unceasingly for its accomplishment. So in 1901, when Tottenham Hotspur won the English Cup, the equality of London with the rest of the football

SCHOOLBOYS AT PLAY.

world—not to say its superiority—was re-established.

Football in London rouses itself from its summer's sleep less readily than it does in the provinces, where they keep a vigil on the last night of August that they may the earlier kick the ball when September dawns. In London we are not so precipitous, and we recognise the right of King Cricket to prolong his life for a few more days if he may. Nevertheless, when the autumn comes football is in the air, and the great professional clubs lose no time in the commencement of their business. Even in August, when the sun is hot o'erhead, and when, according to football law, no matches shall be played under pain of

the threshold of the season's campaign. And that other one is eight months in advance, in the last days of March and the beginning of April, when the proven stalwarts of the season close together for the final bout in which the honours at last are the laurels of absolute and undisputed championship.

It seems to me that few modern pastimes

Photo: Russell & Sons,
Baker Street, W.

A RUGBY "SPRINT"
(BLACKHEATH CLUB).

can so conjure up in one's mind a vision of the games of old as this practice football, when the qualities of the players are being tested, and when every mind is on the strain as to how the best possible team shall be selected. Every individual of the crowd round the rails has an interest in the result. Either he pays his half-guinea for a season ticket or his admission money every Saturday, and if the team is not to his liking he will want to know the reason why. Nominally the committee is the arbiter and it actually makes the choice of men ; but no committee of a professional club in the metropolitan area or anywhere else would dare to neglect the force of public opinion to any substantial extent. You see, it takes some thousands a year to run these professional clubs, and those thousands have to come from the men who are shouting round the green.

TAKING THE FIELD (BLACKHEATH CLUB).

the most grievous penalties — yes, even in this warm, mellow month, if you come with me down to Woolwich or to Tottenham I could show you crowds some thousands strong. And these would be criticising, praising and condemning, hoping and despairing, but all of them yelling, as they watch the first practice games of the season in which old and new players are weighed in the balance and accepted or rejected for the League team as the case may be. This is a time for nervous excitement for all concerned, and indeed in this respect there is only one other period which may be properly likened unto this one upon

And so it happens that when Sandy

McTavish, the new forward, who has come all the way from Motherwell, Dumbarton, or the Vale of Leven for four pounds a week, strips himself and bounds into the ring for practice and for judgment, his feelings on analysis are found to be much the same as those of the gladiator in the glorious days of Rome. Sandy skims down the wing like a bird in flight, such are his ease and grace and skill ; and at the right moment—thud ! and the ball has whizzed into the net, a splendid and most excellent goal. Sandy thus has made his mute appeal. The crowd is appreciative, it

give me the practice games in the early days when the law forbids a real foe.

And when the season opens, away bound the professional teams like hounds unleashed, and every camp is stirred with anxious thoughts. There is Tottenham Hotspur, who vindicated the South after the period of darkness. Enthusiasm always runs very high at Tottenham, where the bands play and the spectators roar themselves hoarse when goals are scored, and betake themselves in some numbers to the football hostelries when all is over to fight the battle once again. It is a football fever of severe form which is abroad at Tottenham. Again, at Plumstead, where the Woolwich Arsenal play—a club of many achievements and many possibilities. The followers of the Reds, as they call them from their crimson shirts, are amongst the most loyal in the land, and Woolwich led the way in the resuscitation of the South. League clubs came to Plumstead when Tottenham was little more than a name. Over at Millwall is the club of

ON THE ROOF OF ST. PAUL'S CATHEDRAL CHOIR SCHOOL.

screams its pleasure, the latest Scot is the greatest hero, and—it is thumbs up for Sandy. But what if he fumbled and fell, and, perhaps through sheer nervousness, did nought that was good upon a football field ? None would know so well as Sandy that his fate was sealed, and that no mercy awaited him. There are scowls and murmurs of discontent from beyond the touch-line, and, most cutting of all, there are derisive cheers. Poor miserable Sandy knows full well that thumbs are down, and a vision of the second team, with a subsequent ignominious transfer to some other club, comes up in his tortured mind. Yes, for the human view of it, for the strenuousness, the excitement, the doubt, and the stirring episodes of London football,

that name, which has likewise had its ups and downs, though they call it by way of pseudonym the Millwall Lion.

In the meantime, whilst these great teams, and the others which are associated with them in London professionalism, play the grand football, there are no lesser if younger enthusiasts by the thousand in the streets and on the commons and in the parks, and their grade of show ranges from the paper or the rag ball of first mention in this article to the full paraphernalia of the Number Five leather case and the regulation goal posts and net. And don't think this is not the most earnest football. If you do, stroll upon some Saturday in the winter time into Battersea and Regent's Park, and there you will see the youngsters striving for the honours of victory and for the points of their minor Leagues. The London County Council makes provision for no fewer than

struggle between the Corinthians—the most athletic gentlemen in London — and, very likely, one of the strongest League teams from the country. There is certain to be a very big crowd, which is second to none in enthusiasm, but there is this difference between the congregation these matches draw and most others, that it is a trifle more cosmopolitan, a trifle less fanatical, that it breathes a little more of the spirit of amateurism and the 'Varsities. And up at another great amateur head-

A "CUP-TIE" FINAL (CRYSTAL PALACE).

eight thousand of these football matches in its parks in a single season. And at our London public schools great homage is paid to King Football under widely varying conditions. At one institution— St. Paul's Cathedral Choir School—it is even played on the roof, as the illustration opposite shows.

And then there are two other continuous features of London football that I must note. The one is the great and noble element of amateurism which must always flourish. Go to Queen's Club, Kensington, one of the finest football arenas in the world, or to Leyton, and there you will see a

Photos: Russell & Sons, Crystal Palace.
A CORNER OF THE CROWD (CRYSTAL PALACE).

quarters, Tufnell Park, you should see a game between the renowned Casuals and the London Caledonians or "Caleys." That is the game to warm the blood of a football follower. And at that historic spot which is known as the "Spotted Dog," you will find the great Clapton team disport themselves. These representatives of amateurism are indeed great in their past, great in their traditions, even if they are not great in the eyes of the Leagues.

The other notable and enduring feature of London football is its Rugby section. It has a story all its own, and the Rugby enthusiast never could see anything in the "socker" game. It is admitted that "rugger" is a cult, a superior cult, and though it has its followers by thousands in London, it is not the game of the people as is that played under the rival code of laws. Yet London has always held a glorious place in the Rugby football world, and the public schools and the 'Varsities supply such a constant infusion of good new blood, so that when the fame of Richmond and Blackheath fade away, we shall be listening for the crack of Rugby doom.

And so the eight months' season with its League games, its Cup-ties, its 'Varsity matches, rolls along, we round the Christmas corner with its football comicalities, and we come in due course to the greatest day of all the football year, when the final tie in the English Cup competition is fought out at the Crystal Palace. It cannot be an exaggeration to say that it is one of the sights of the London year when over 100,000 screaming people are standing upon the slopes of Sydenham, and with quickened pulses watching the progress of the struggle. How the rail-

In Loving Memory
Of   , who died whilst fighting for the English Cup against   at
on
———
Boldly to the fray they went,
But got beaten to their sorrow;
They were put to sleep by a better team,
And the funeral's to-morrow.

A DEATH CARD.

way companies get them all there from the city is a mystery, and it is another, though a lesser one, as to how quite half that crowd has travelled up from the country towns and cities in the small hours of the morning. On his arrival, the country Cup-tie visitor, whether he comes from Manchester, Sheffield, Birmingham, or any other of the great centres, lets all London know of the fact, so much is he badged and bedecked in the colours of his favourites.

At night, when the greatest battle has been won and lost, he swarms over the West-End with his pockets full of the many football editions, and a death card of the losing team in proper black-bordered "In Memoriam" style tucked away in his pockets as a memento. In both these paper goods is a great trade done. Football journalism is a profession in itself, with all its own editors, specialists, and reporters.

The Cup day passes, and now the season nears its end. For still a week or two it holds up its tired, nodding head; but at last there comes the first morning of May, and all is over. And even the football Londoner is not sorry for that.

HALF-TIME REFRESHMENTS.

TABLE LAND IN LONDON.

By J. C. WOOLLAN.

COME with me now and see one of the most strangely human sights that the world can show. It is that of the biggest city there is, and the one containing most varieties of human life, being fed during an ordinary day. Very likely it has never struck you that there is anything remarkable in this process. But when you come to know or reflect that there are some hundreds of people breakfasting in the city at four o'clock in the morning, that—so it has been calculated — there are nearly a million people lunching in restaurants within a few miles of the Strand every day, and that each evening some thousands of dinners are laid on West-End restaurant tables which, with wine, cost an average of a sovereign each, whilst, on the other hand, there are far more Londoners who live each day—and live not at all badly either—on a single shilling each — when you come to think of all this, and hundreds of other facts of a more detailed and more interesting character which could be adduced, you will begin to perceive that the Table Land of London must indeed be one of the biggest wonders of this glorious Metropolis.

We must set out very early, when three-quarters of London is asleep, and we must stay up very late, when half the sleepers have done their day's work and gone to bed again, if we would see but a little of the abundant variety of this Table Land. So the night air still gives a ciammy

touch to the cheek when we turn out to see the beginning of the feeding of London. In the West there are still cabs crawling near the doors of clubs to pick up the few who live by night and sleep by day, but the chefs of the West are now all asleep, dreaming perchance of hundred-guinea dishes they would serve to kings at tables in Walhalla. To-night we will come back to the West; but now, for the opening of the day of food, we must hurry away to the East, for the doors of Pearce and Plenty and Lockharts and others are already ajar. Wonderful institutions are these, dotted up and down in this part of London, where folk of inferior means abound. Even while they remained closed, but when the men-servants within were astir and boiling gallons of water and giving their mugs a rinse, there were some hungry loafers outside who had dozed throughout the night in doorways and on benches, and whose stomachs had moved them betimes to spend the two or three coppers earned or begged the night before.

Tattered and unkempt they enter now;

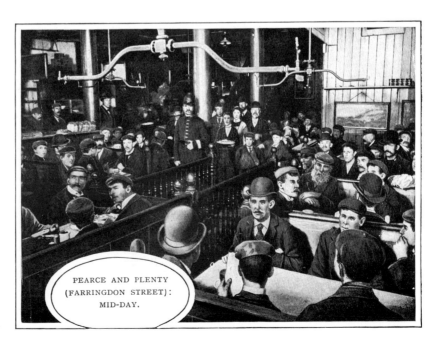

PEARCE AND PLENTY (FARRINGDON STREET): MID-DAY.

ALEXANDRA TRUST
RESTAURANT (CITY ROAD):
BREAKFAST.

that the average cost per meal per person at these places is not above threepence. Pearce and Plenty alone supply forty thousand meals a day, and in their case the average cost to the diner works out at less than twopence. We must hasten from here to the quarters of the city which begin their work at nine o'clock, and soon need feeding; but still, while we are carefully noting the food expenditure of the working poor, we may carry the examination a little further, for it will serve to show us what a vast business this one is.

The purveyors with the alliterative and euphonious names use up in a year thirteen tons of cocoa and twenty-six of tea. They require for their business of this period as many as 900 tons of flour and 1,000 tons of potatoes. A thousand oxen, a thousand sheep, and more than a thousand pigs are slaughtered for them; they need a hundred

for a halfpenny they get a mug of steaming tea, and for another a piece of bread and butter, and, satisfied with their penny breakfast, they loll a while, and then they go their way again. Carters and lorrymen, always amongst the first astir, take their places, and then there come the workers whose working day begins at six o'clock, and who breakfast here for twopence as a preliminary. By eight o'clock these restaurants of the poorer people are all as busy as can be, and so they remain throughout the day and well on into the evening. The two-penny breakfast gave way to the fivepenny and sixpenny dinner —we call it dinner here at midday—and that in its turn to the twopenny tea, and that to the twopenny supper. Here and at the Alexandra Trust restaurant in the City Road, as well as at the Red House, Commercial Road East, the sixpence provides for the people a substantial meat meal. It is tolerably certain

AERATED BREAD COMPANY'S DEPÔT (LUDGATE HILL): MID-DAY.

thousand gallons of milk; and, as a cap upon all these astounding figures, they sell a million and three-quarters of eggs! So great is the business of feeding these literally twopenny-halfpenny diners, and such are the style and quality of these latter when seated at their tables, that a hundred mugs and cups are broken every day, and on an average about forty thousand plates and saucers every year.

under its full title and dignity as an Aërated Bread Company's depôt, or a B.T.T. as one of the British Tea Table Company's establishments. These places, with their long galleries of tables and their neat and uniformly-clad female attendants, are really, when you come to think of it, one of the foremost institutions of London, and are peculiar to London. How the Metropolis could get on without them nowadays is not

SLATER'S RESTAURANT (PICCADILLY): AFTERNOON.

We have been rather anticipating the feeding of the day in the above; but at any rate we have finished with the third-class restaurant, and shown of what it is capable. So we may move on, as we proposed, into the heart of the City, into Cheapside, Fleet Street, and the Strand. It is now the turn of the A.B.C. depôts, and the Lyons' tea-houses, which are found in every direction. Those known by the names of Express Dairy, Golden Grain, B.T.T., Mecca, and other distinctions are all busy with their various customers. The Londoner is always partial to abbreviations, and would hardly recognise an A.B.C. house

to be imagined. Some few of them have been busy before we stroll their way at eleven o'clock, but now they are all hard at work. City clerks and business men, who could not breakfast before they left their homes, or who did not do so sufficiently, turn in for their coffee and rolls at fourpence or fivepence a time.

A gradual transformation scene takes place, and in an hour or two these depôts are thronged with the ninepenny luncheon crowds, who lunch lightly from tea or coffee and eggs or cold meat. At half-past one every seat is metaphorically at a small premium; but an hour later the crush is

TABLE D'HÔTE AT THE TROCADERO.

over, and preparation is made for the lighter business of afternoon-tea. An institution indeed! Do you know that one of these firms of caterers in all its depôts dispenses two million loaves, a million rolls, and five million buns and cakes in one year? And in the same period they use up nearly half-a-million pounds of tea, coffee, and cocoa, and 350,000 gallons of milk! Multiply these vast figures, and you will have approximately some idea of the heavy contribution which the tea-shops make to the Table Land of London.

And these are only the light lunchers. The City and the Strand district, and now the West-End, have been pouring their tens of thousands into every grade of restaurant, from the humble sausage shop to the aristocratic Prince's. There are the restaurants such as Slater's, the Cabin, and the Piccadilly "Popular," for the people of modest incomes, and there are the luncheon bars like those of Sweeting's and Pimm's, where men, whose limit is about fifteen minutes, stand up and eat good food from a marble slab; nor must Crosby Hall be forgotten. And, in the Strand, we now find Gatti's—the famous Gatti's—in full harness. In the long Adelaide Gallery here a rare study is always to be obtained of cosmopolitan human nature, taking its soup and meats—carved in full view—and sweets and cheese, and drinking, perhaps, for choice, its lager beer, which is as good in this place as anywhere. The Gallery picture is even brighter and more human in the evening, when the dinner dishes are served, and later on, when ladies in low-cut bodices and men in immaculate evening attire file in from the theatres and the music-halls for supper. Gatti's in its way is not so much of London as of England and the world.

Still farther West the thoroughly fashionable restaurants are now gay with luncheon parties; yet this is hardly the time for a proper study of these resorts. Rather would we wait an hour or two and drop in to Slater's, in Piccadilly, for tea, or saunter down Bond Street, and discover here and there several cosy tea houses whose main object is the accommodation of the ladies of society who often find themselves in this neighbourhood on a summer season's after-

noon. Or, perhaps, instead, we might go on to Claridge's in Brook Street, where for a surety there will be many lovely women and brave men of the highest degree. For Claridge's, itself in the heart of the society quarter, is unique, and when you tread upon the india-rubber frontage and notice, on entering, the high superiority even of the servants, you instinctively realise that this is a place for royalty and ambassadors; and so it is. But it would only be to meet a friend, who happened to be staying there, that we should venture to take tea in such a social capital. When you come to think of it you can ring any number of changes on afternoon tea in the West-End, and the searcher of experiences will, if a lady, and a lady with a man friend who glories in the M.P. affix to his name, assuredly not neglect one which is different from all others. I allude to the popular society pastime of taking tea in summer on the Terrace of the House of Commons; and, lest you should imagine the adjective to be unjustifiable, let me tell you that the returns for a single session indicate that during that period the lion's share of forty thousand teas were served on the little strip of promenade which lies between our noble Parliament buildings and the murky waters of the Thames.

In the evening, when the electric glow illumines the western area, we return again to peep at a few places in a fairyland of evening dress and epicureanism. This is the reign of the chef. For some time in advance he and his serfs have been hard at work in the planning and execution of such rare dishes as their restaurant is famous for. The chef is a high dignitary whom the curious may seldom see. He is an artist, a genius whose mind is constantly at work in the performance of some new feat in culinary science which will bring a word of approval from the lips of the most exacting gourmet who places faith in him. Of what he is capable is not to be told in print, for he does not even know the limits of his own ambition. The possibility of making delicate soups from old boots does not appear so fantastic to him as to his clients. A good chef and a good waiter—and if you treat the London waiter fairly you find him an excellent servant — are as indispensable to true epicureanism as the appetite itself. The chef's tools must be perfect, and so of course they are.

The kitchens of the big restaurants between five and nine of the evening are a revelation to those who only eat, and think nothing of

GATTI'S (ADELAIDE GALLERY): MID-DAY.

the preparation. Here is a great army of cooks in many grades of rank, all attired in spotless white, and engaged in the deft manipulation of silvery utensils. The raw food stuffs come to them, they have their instructions, and in good time there pass to the flower-bedecked, glistening realms above such dishes as are triumphs of the culinary art. You can see that the scale of high-class meal-making is here a very grand one; but you would hardly guess, all the same, to what these raw food stuffs aggregate in quantity in the course of a year. Come into the manager's office of one great and fashionable restaurant, which is not a hundred miles from

KITCHEN SCENE AT THE CARLTON.

Piccadilly Circus, and look at his record. Really! Nearly 500 tons of meat! Poultry —150,000 head! More than a hundred tons of fish! Thirty tons of potatoes! About a thousand pounds of butter! As a sample of dessert, nine or ten tons of grapes. And, though one of the largest, this is yet only one of the score or two of high-class, famous restaurants in the quarter of high life.

Where shall we dine? must, under all the circumstances, be always a perplexing question. One can do it to so much the same effect at so many different places; yet each has in its way its little distinctions. A purse containing at least a guinea and a half—for that is about the price of a really first-class dinner with a bottle of wine—is assumed. Soho has a reputation all its own, for in numerous little places here you may feed on six courses of a French menu for a single half-crown or less. For pure luxury, however, we may go to the Carlton, at the corner of the Haymarket and Pall Mall, which the King himself, as Prince, was known to patronise in its earliest days. Here we may see the greatest men in society, in art, in literature, in commerce, and the fairest women of the day toying with an entrée and chatting amidst a scene of soft splendour and the sweet, low strains of music. Or at Prince's, or the Cecil, or the Savoy, or one or two others. Then there are a score more, each with its distinctive fame. There is the Café Royal, the Continental, the Criterion, and the beautiful Trocadero, with a *table d'hôte* and accompaniments which the experienced London diner has often praised. There is Simpson's, noted for old English fare; the Bohemian Romano's; the Imperial and Verrey's (with its "Persian Room") in Regent Street; and Pagani's in Great Portland Street, where there is an "artists' room," on the walls of which many celebrities—Mascagni, Paderewski, Melba, and others—have scribbled or drawn something or other; there is, too, the well-known Monico, and one must not forget Frascati's winter garden, where one seems to dine among the palm trees, and can study the great variety of human life to be encountered here, and wait for yet another solo from the cornet player in the band; so dallying with the hours till one realises that the dinner-time is past, that supper-time is coming along, and that— heigho!—a long day is far spent.

A CORNER AT PRINCE'S.

IN A MEWS.

GARDENING LONDON.

By WALTER P. WRIGHT

GARDENING is the most intensely human pastime, short, perhaps, of fighting, that the Londoner indulges in. When a man spills the contents of a watering-pot over himself, the veneer of civilisation fades away, and nature comes through. It is not meant to convey by this that he flies into a fearful temper and uses heroic language. No! On the contrary, he beams seraphically on the world at large, and wonders why people make a fuss about so trifling a thing as Fry's last century, when he, the horticulturist, has struck a cutting.

The student of character has not completed his education until he has made a round of London to study its gardens and gardeners. The odds are that he will find he has opened up a new field—one unexplored either by the fictionist or the philanthropist. The first thing that will strike him is the astonishing diversity of conditions under which people overcome by the love of flowers manage to grow them ; and if he be a professional horticulturist his astonishment will be the greater instead of the less. There are certain conditions which the latter looks on as essential to success, and lo! the

cockney cultivator sublimely ignores the whole lot of them, yet scores all along the line. He is informed that the plants must be watered regularly, so he floods them twenty times a day, and the first-floor, who dries his underclothing on the window ledge, goes frantic as an earthy, worm-tinctured mixture pours down. They must be stimulated? Why, surely! There are dregs of beer, and lees of tea, and ashes from knocked-out pipes, and match ends, and chimney scrapings. Don't make any mistake, those plants are not going to starve.

Of course, there is no phase of London gardening which interests the student more than window culture. Societies exist on purpose to encourage this sort of thing. If a Londoner, male or female, has the inspiration to grow plants on the ledge, you may rest satisfied that a cactus, or a petunia, or a begonia will be found there soon, in some receptacle or other. And it really need not create very much surprise if the quality of them is as good as those which grace the balcony or porch of a West-End mansion, where the work has been done by a florist, under contract, very likely, to the

IN PORTMAN SQUARE.

a vegetable corner, a stuffed donkey. This animal was a real work of art, and its expression was one of mingled envy and admiration. I divined that its presence there had some deep and subtle meaning, and at length it dawned upon me that it was intended to convey a delicate compliment to the owner's carrots, which were sweet to it even in death.

Vain the attempt to gauge the happiness, the solace, the contentment which this window and forecourt gardening brings to those who indulge in it. Think of the lives they lead—the lives they are bound to lead! These toiling, moiling thousands are in the grip of the octopus of London slumdom, and they do not recoil from the monster in hate and terror ; they just twine flowers round its choking limbs, with that marvellous patience, that inexhaustible courage, that odd, half-humorous, half-pathetic determination to make the best of things, which awaken at once the wonder and respect of observers.

Sometimes a young reporter on a weekly paper discovers a garden on a London roof, and clucks as loudly as a gratified cockerel over his first grub. Bless the reporter's innocent heart, there are gardens on hundreds of roofs in London. Many a Londoner can lie, anticipating his last long sleep—

> With his nose, and the tips of his toes,
> Turned up to the roots of the daisies."

And if they are not daisies, but vegetable

tune of a couple of hundred pounds a year. There is as much interest in the mews garden as in that in Portman Square.

The back-street window gardener does not usually rest content with a plain box or a simple row of pots ; he generally rigs up an archway, or a miniature palisade (the latter painted a very vivid green), or even something more elaborate still in the way of a tomtit green-house, the finial of which is graced with his country's flag. He is patriotic, let me tell you, as well as inventive.

The same spirit of ingenuity marks the gardener a little further out, where they have forecourts and back patches, like the Walworth garden here shown. I used to gaze with a speculative eye from a passing train on one back garden which contained, in addition to

A GARDEN IN WALWORTH.

I. FIREMEN'S GARDEN NEAR BLACKFRIARS BRIDGE.   II. ON A POLICE COURT ROOF.
III. AT THE TOWER OF LONDON.   IV. ROYAL HORTICULTURAL SOCIETY'S
SHOW OF COLONIAL FRUIT, ETC. (VINCENT SQUARE).

marrows, as in the case of the police court roof garden illustrated on the opposite page, it is no matter, since flowers come in somehow.

There is a garden, and a nice one, too, in the Tower of London, as the reader may see by another of our photographic reproductions. In years gone by the Beefeaters used to hold a show within the walls, where capital beetroot, and onions, and potatoes were exhibited. And although that has become a thing of the past, owing, I believe, to much of the ground having to be given up, gardening is still carried on.

The old soldiers have plots at Chelsea. As a youngster, it often fell to my share to go to the old Botanic or Physic Garden, belonging to the Apothecaries, near there, and a journey on to the *Invalides* of the Embankment led to many friendships with the veterans who gardened within its gates.

The firemen are gardeners, too. You will find many examples of their skill at the various stations in and around London, and there is one garden which anyone who visits the floating station near Blackfriars Bridge may see. Whether the firemen surreptitiously set the engines to work in order to water the plants is not known, but one thing is certain, the flowers look uncommonly fresh and bright. It would be hard if it ever fell to the lot of one of these floricultural firemen to mount to one of the windows which I have been talking about when flames were spurting forth. He would face the danger to his own life and limb calmly, without a doubt, but would shrink shudderingly from smashing up the canary creeper and the zinnias. On the other hand, what gusto he would display if he had to turn the hose on a slug-infested box of phloxes!

The suburban gardens are one of the glories of London. It is worth anybody's while to spend a day amongst them, and a compulsory round ought to be ordained for those who assert that the Londoner has no sense of the beautiful, that he has no soul for art. One of the most famous carnation growers who ever lived cultivates his prize flowers in a back garden at Clapham. Then look at the chrysanthemums! Hundreds of amateurs grow collections where you would not think that there was room to hang a clothes line. They have their troubles, of course, for the feline epidemic rages strongly in Suburbia; but when they can sally forth on the King's birthday with a flower of the size of a savoy in their buttonholes, none so happy.

Art is one of those little-big words which some men find tender morsels on the tongue. It means much, of course, if you have a weighty way with you, and nothing at all if you haven't. But if a man, untrained by any professor, takes possession of a mud-heap, on a site from which gravel has been taken, and on which discarded hardware has been left, and straightway makes it to blossom, he has a sense of the artistic not less true than the sense of the Little-Big. Well, such a thing happens thousands of times every year in suburban London, and examples are to be found by all who care to seek. The gardens in Nevill's Court, which you enter through a passage from Fetter Lane, are not, a friendly policeman told me, quite what they used to be in years gone by, but on a November afternoon I saw chrysanthemums there, and aucubas, as well as asters, marguerites, and rhododendrons. The fact is, most people gather their impressions of floricultural London from Covent Garden Market, which is very fine in its way, but is really not London gardening at all.

London flower shows are more numerous than most people are aware. They range from the slum display of pots of musk and ivy-leaved geraniums in dingy mission-halls to fashionable affairs held by the two great societies, the Royal Horticultural and the Royal Botanic. The former held really fine exhibitions every fortnight for a considerable number of years in, of all places, the drill hall of the London Scottish Rifle Volunteers, Buckingham Gate, Westminster. It was a bare, gloomy sort of hall in the early hours of a foggy morning, but when the costly and beautiful orchids from the great cultivators and the rare new plants from Kew came along, with all sorts of flowers, fruits, and vegetables, there was a transformation scene if you like. However, the Society has its own hall now—a fine building, with glass roof, in Vincent Square, Westminster, and the flowers and fruit are naturally seen to much better advantage than they were in the drill hall.

The professional horticulturists rather affect to sniff at the Royal Botanic Society, whose home is at Regent's Park. Being anxious to popularise itself it started a series of promenade fêtes and the like. The people like these very well—the professionals don't. Give the horticulturists a chance of seeing an odontoglossum with a spot half an inch broad on its snow-white petals instead of one only

The people round the parks look out for the beginning of the summer bedding, and they look out for the end of it, too, for when the beds are cleared a large number of plants are given away. This is the slum gardener's opportunity. It is all very well for that superior jobbing gardener who comes and worries you to let him muddle up your place to say, as he often does, that the authorities take good care to keep all the decent plants, and only give away the rubbish, but the back-street horticulturist does not believe in looking a gift-horse in the mouth. He takes what he can get, and makes the best of it—a very good best, too, sometimes, believe me. With these acquisitions, and perhaps a few bulbs

three-eighths of an inch across, and they will troop eagerly to the spectacle, but the sight of Lohengrin in his car in a children's procession has no interest for them, though knight and swan be decked never so gaily with flowers. *Addio! bel cigno canor!* the horticulturist has gone.

There is one thing that the much-maligned London County Council must be blessed for. It has enormously improved the London parks and public gardens. It really does not matter very much what part of London you are in, without going any great distance you can find a pretty park or garden-like enclosure. Most of these are very admirably kept. They have their displays of hyacinths, tulips, and daffodils, then after a sort of spring cleaning they blossom out towards the end of May with the summer bedding.

AFTERNOON PROMENADE FÊTE IN THE ROYAL BOTANIC SOCIETY'S GARDENS, REGENT'S PARK.

picked up at a stall near the Smithfield Meat Market, followed up by some odd roots bought from a costermonger's barrow in the spring, he does wonders.

When he has set up friendly relations with the park gardeners by accepting their plants, he feels, so to say, one of themselves, and drops in to enjoy all the features. He could tell you, for instance, all about that magnificent sub-tropical garden at Battersea Park, where great broad-leaved castor oil plants, and palms, and other plants with handsome foliage, are grown out of doors. And it is surely unnecessary to say that he is in close touch with the beautiful chrysanthemum shows which are so great a feature of nearly all the parks in October and November.

These chrysanthemum displays are perhaps the very best thing that the London County Council does in its parks. And it must not be forgotten that the doors of the chrysan-

MUSIC AND FLOWERS (VICTORIA EMBANKMENT GARDENS).

themem houses open at that period which is of all others the dreariest in London— when the autumn rains and fogs bring depression. On grey November days the glorious flowers are wonderfully cheering, for their colours are as rich as their shapes are quaint.

You may, of course, hear good music in the parks and gardens during the summer months, as well as survey beautiful flowers. Thus, in the Victoria Embankment Gardens, near Charing Cross Station, the jaded Londoner can smoke his pipe with the cool air

from the adjacent river blowing around him, and have ears and eyes tickled by sweet sounds and sights, at eventide. He does not get a chair for nothing, nor is free refreshment brought round, but he is a hopeful soul, and he looks to the future with confidence.

Hyde Park, with its magnificent series of flower beds running parallel with Park Lane, is perhaps the queen of public places for gardening. Regent's Park has glorious beds of bulbs in the spring, but the workers' enclosures of the L.C.C. cater nobly for the masses.

While there is life in London's gardens there is life in all the city. The gentle art of floriculture brings into the lives of the toilers daily joy and refreshment. The people are healthier, happier, better, for the work they do among their plants. Gardening is the sweet handmaid of ennobled humanity. The scent of flowers comes to each and all of them with the sweetness of an old song's echo—

"The lilt of an olden lay."

IN HYDE PARK (NEAR PARK LANE).

A CORONER'S INQUEST IN LONDON.

By A. BRAXTON HICKS and C. DUNCAN LUCAS.

IT is a strange scene—a scene of infinite pathos—and one which, although it is enacted each week-day of the year, brings into play every emotion known to man. We are in the Coroner's Court. A few days back at midnight a woman went over London and it was a girl who tried to hold him back. And, as we watch, the police with the ambulance bring in yet another " case."

Outside the mournful drama is just beginning. The waiting crowd is agog with excitement ; for the evening papers have

OUTSIDE A CORONER'S COURT.

Bridge. Eighteen hours later the Thames police discovered her body attached to the hawser of a collier lying off Vauxhall. All that is mortal of her is resting in the iron container in the mortuary at the rear of the Court. On a slab close by are the clothes she wore. The once gay hat with the faded pink flowers, the cheap blouse, the torn skirt, the mud-stained underclothing — they are hardly dry yet. The vengeance of the great river is complete.

Two others are in the house of death : an old man with a bullet wound in his back, and a young one—he jumped in front of a train,

made the best of the latest sensation, and a haggard-faced man has passed in with an officer on each side of him. A dozen constables with an inspector or two are standing by. The burly man with the papers under his arm is the Coroner's officer —a kindly soul. On him has fallen the duty of inquiring into these deaths. In search of evidence he has visited the relatives of the dead in their homes and found them too ill to tell their tale. He has combated those who desired that the affair should be hushed up : he has sifted the true from the false. He has also summoned the jury and the

POLICE AMBULANCE ENTERING MORTUARY.

cantankerous class who decline to agree to any sort of verdict: in which event the whole terrible business would have to be commenced over again. These jurors receive two shillings a day for their labours and are chosen from the Parliamentary voting lists, the occupants of each street being tackled in turn. They cannot be considered overpaid, for their attendance can be enforced for the entire day if needs be, and if eight inquests are on the list they must return eight verdicts.

Let us take another glimpse of the Court. At a large table are seated the reporters; in the centre is the witness-box; while at the back are rows of chairs which are occupied by members of the public—dishevelled women, curiosity-mongers, and the like—and those witnesses who are able to control their feelings. Witnesses who are inclined to be hysterical are confined in the waiting-room—if there happens to be one—until they are required to give evidence. The Coroner, who can trace his office back a thousand years and more, has sworn the following oath on his appointment:—

witnesses, and issued the Coroner's orders to the doctor to attend and perform three post-mortem examinations in return for the sum of six guineas—two guineas per body.

But to the business of the day. The Coroner has alighted from his cab and steps silently into the mortuary. Having glanced at the deceased the representative of the Crown enters the Court preceded by his officer and followed by his clerk.

"Gentlemen, the Coroner!" exclaims the officer, and every one rises to his feet. At the far end the Coroner seats himself at a raised desk, and below him sits his clerk. To the left are the jurors—twenty-three of them. It is sufficient if twelve men return a verdict, but an important affair and one which may have to be adjourned has to be investigated, and the extra number has been summoned as a precautionary measure. Were only twelve to sit when the hearing of an adjourned inquest was resumed one juryman might be absent owing to illness, and another might belong to that

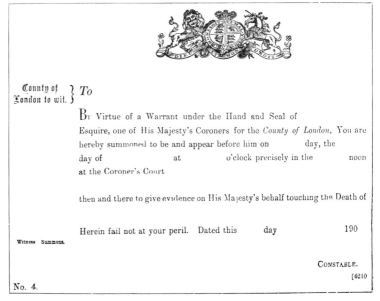

County of London to wit. } To

By Virtue of a Warrant under the Hand and Seal of
Esquire, one of His Majesty's Coroners for the *County of London*, You are hereby summoned to be and appear before him on   day, the
day of   at   o'clock precisely in the   noon
at the Coroner's Court

then and there to give evidence on His Majesty's behalf touching the Death of

Herein fail not at your peril. Dated this   day   190

Witness Summons.

CONSTABLE.
[6210

No. 4.

WITNESS SUMMONS.

"I solemnly, sincerely, and truly declare and affirm that I will well and truly serve our Sovereign Lord the King and his liege people in the office of coroner for this district of   , and that I will diligently and truly do everything appertaining to my office after the best of my power for the doing of right and for the good of the inhabitants within the said district."

The Coroner serves the King by inquiring into all violent or unnatural or sudden deaths of which the causes are unknown, and any deaths that occur in the prisons in his district. In addition, when gold or silver coin or plate or bullion is found concealed, the owner being unknown, the Coroner holds an inquest on them. Like dead bodies they are "sat upon," and if the verdict is "treasure trove" they become the property of the Crown.

This, however, *en passant*, for the Coroner is in his Court. With a number of docu-

JURORS PROCEEDING TO VIEW A BODY.

ments before him he signals to his officer, who in these words, addressed to the jury, proclaims the opening of the Court :—

"Oyez, Oyez, You good men of this district summoned to appear here this day to inquire for our Sovereign Lord the King when, how, and by what means Maria Black, James Spindler, and William Fowler came to their deaths, answer to your names as you shall be called, every man at the first call, upon the pain and peril that shall fall thereon."

This done the Coroner, reading from his list, calls out the names of the jurors, and each man present answers, "Yes." Now and then an objection will be raised. There is one to-day.

"Sir," cries a meek-looking man with a flowing white beard, "my presence here is useless. I am stone deaf."

In a low whisper the Coroner answers : "Then you may go."

With surprising alacrity the deaf one hastens to depart, but the strong hand of the officer, at a sign from the Coroner, is placed on his shoulder and he is ordered to resume his seat.

There is one absentee. A juror has been summoned imperatively to the City on business. The Coroner knows that business ! And when the missing one

TO WIT.	Information of Witnesses severally taken and acknowledged, on behalf of our Sovereign Lord the King, at	

in the parish of   on

the   day of   1   , touching

the death of

before   , Esquire, one of His Majesty's Coroners for the said County, on view of the Body of the said Person then and there lying dead.

on oath deposes :—

I am

I live at

I identify the body now lying dead as that of

IDENTIFICATION FORM.

returns to the bosom of his family on completion of his business, he discovers that his morning's recreation has cost him forty shilling pieces.

But though a few perhaps have given a little trouble, these jurymen to-day are honest fellows—mostly.

The following is the oath administered to jurymen :—

"You shall diligently inquire and true presentment make of all such matters and things as shall be here given you in charge, on behalf of our Sovereign Lord the King, touching the death of —— ——, now lying dead, of whose body you shall have the view: and shall, without fear or favour, affection or ill-will, a true verdict give according to the evidence, and to the best of your skill and knowledge, so help you God."

The oath taken, the jurymen leave the Court and file into the mortuary chamber, where they view the dead. Some look at the bodies intently ; others pass through the abode of death as swiftly as possible. On their return to the Court the real business begins.

"Walter Black," says the Coroner, calling the first witness.

A man of forty, hollow-eyed, white and trembling, palpably a hard drinker, quits his seat next to that of a crying woman—a sister of the dead woman on whose body the first inquest is to be held—and steps into the box. The thoughtful officer advances, clutches the right arm of the witness to support him, and administers the oath :—

"The evidence which you shall give to this inquest on behalf of our Sovereign Lord the King touching the death of Maria Black shall be the truth, the whole truth, and nothing but the truth. So help you God."

The man kisses the Testament and the Coroner examines him :

"You are Walter Black, and you identify the body of the woman which you have seen lying in the mortuary as that of your late wife, Maria Black, who, I understand, was a German, speaking very little English ? "

"Yes, sir."

"You last saw her on the morning of Wednesday, the 13th inst. On the Friday following you heard that she had been seen by William Presence to jump off the parapet of London Bridge. As she did not return home on the Wednesday, did you inquire as to her whereabouts ? "

At this question all eyes are focussed on the figure in the box. The jury lean forward : the clerk waits pen in hand.

"I beg your pardon, sir," says the witness, and the Coroner repeats the question.

"N-no, sir," the man stammers at length.

A CORONER HANDING BURIAL ORDER TO HIS OFFICER.

"The fact is, sir, I was not anxious about her."

"Not anxious about her ! " repeats the Coroner sternly. "What do you mean by that ? I won't have anything kept back, you know."

"Well, sir," says the witness, toying nervously with his fingers, "my wife was in the habit of going away for two or three days. On this occasion I concluded that she had gone to visit a friend."

"When she left you, had you quarrelled ? "

"Oh, no, sir."

"Were you both sober ? "

"Yes, sir."

"The fact is, you didn't care what became

of your wife. Have you anything to ask the witness?" says the Coroner, turning to the jury.

The answer is in the negative. Walter Black steps down, and William Presence takes his place.

William Presence, stout and florid, relates how he saw the woman gazing at the muddy water below the bridge—she was standing on one of the stone ledges as Big Ben tolled the hour of midnight.

"You are not going to your death, surely," he observed.

Then thinking that he might possibly be mistaken, and being in a hurry to catch his last train home he walked on. An instant later he heard a splash and dashing to the parapet he saw a body engulfed. He hailed the police, a boat at once put off from the stairs below, but Maria Black had gone to her doom with the tide.

John Learoyd, blue-eyed, bronzed and stalwart, is the third witness. He is of the Thames police, and was out in his launch in the neighbourhood of Vauxhall when he espied what seemed to him to be a mass of ragged clothes clinging to the anchor chain of the collier *Maude*, of Tynemouth. He put his helm to starboard and found a body —"the body, sir, I have seen in the mortuary."

John Learoyd is followed by Martha Watchwell. The Blacks were her lodgers, and she saw Maria Black when she left the house for the last time. She was drunk, and so was Walter Black, though he swore he was sober.

"They used to go on the drink for a week," she explains.

Constable 124 ZZ is sworn. At five o'clock on Monday afternoon he met Maria Black clinging to a lamp-post, drunk and incapable. He escorted her to the police station and she was placed in a cell.

"Inspector Toogood," says the Coroner.

The tall man tells his story. He went on duty at eight o'clock, and finding the prisoner sober at ten he let her out on her own recognisances.

'How is it you didn't keep her?" asks the Coroner.

"Well, sir," says the officer, "we generally let the drunks out when they're sober if they haven't been disorderly. We get a good many drunks about our parts."

"Had she time to get from the station to London Bridge by midnight?" queries the Coroner.

"Plenty of time, sir."

"And I suppose she could have procured more drink on the way."

"Certainly, sir."

The cause of death demands no further elucidation. A brief summing-up by the Coroner, and the jury are asked for their verdict. They return it without the least hesitation. In less than sixty seconds the foreman replies:

"Suicide whilst temporarily insane."

The form is made out, each juryman signs his name on it, and another inquest is over.

Walter Black gives a sigh of relief, but there is not a tear in his bloodshot, bleared eyes. Five minutes later you may recognise him at the bar of the "Crown and Thistle" round the corner—fifty yards from the spot where the body of his dead wife lies—with a glass of brandy before him. He is one of Nature's reptiles. And in half an hour you will see him standing within the precincts of the Court—in a dark corner for choice, for the cockney crowd has not taken kindly to him—waiting for the order for burial, which must bear the Coroner's signature.

The demon drink—what a part it plays in these Courts! The rôle is difficult to describe, for in the midst of tragedy there is comedy. There is no comedy in the Court to-day, but take a typical case. A man has perhaps died a violent death, and a post-mortem examination has disclosed the fact that he was a hard drinker.

"Was your husband a temperate man?" asks the Coroner of the widow in the witness-box.

"Oh, yes," is the frequent answer, "he was a teetotaller."

The Coroner then adopts a different course.

"Are *you* a teetotaller?" he asks the woman.

"Oh, no," she replies. "I drink beer—a couple of glasses a day."

"Well, what did your husband drink?"

"He drank nothing but brandy, sir," is the answer, "but he was a *perfect* teetotaller."

A CORONER'S INQUEST.

BIRTHS AND DEATHS REGISTRATION ACT, 1874.

CORONER'S ORDER for BURIAL.

To be given by the Coroner to the Relative of the Deceased or other person who causes the Body to be buried, or to the Undertaker or other Person having charge of the Funeral.

I, the undersigned, Coroner for the_____ of _____

Do hereby authorise the Burial of the Body of _____

aged about_____which has been viewed by the Inquest Jury.

Witness my hand this_____day of_____.

_____ Coroner.

*** **The Coroner must not issue this Order except upon holding an Inquest.**

The Undertaker or other Person receiving this Order must deliver it to the Minister or Officiating Person who buries or performs any funeral or religious service for the Burial of the Dead Body ; or, in the case of a burial under the Burial Laws Amendment Act, 1880, to the " relative, friend, or legal representative of the deceased, having the charge of, or being responsible for the Burial "

(443Js)

Let us return to the Court. The jury are now about to decide as to how the old man, whose body also lies in the mortuary, met with his death. The crowd outside are swarming at the doors, and twenty constables are employed in keeping them back. The deceased was well known in the district as a generous man. A slender figure arrayed in black advances towards the box. It is the widow. Gently assisted by the Coroner, she describes in a broken voice how her nephew called upon the deceased and demanded money. He had had ten pounds the week before to go to Canada but had spent it in riotous living. The interview was a stormy one, a quarrel arose, and the next thing she heard was the report of firearms.

That is all the woman can relate. Becoming hysterical she is conducted to the waiting-room to regain her composure, and the inquest is adjourned. In half an hour she is brought in again and proceeds with her evidence. Little by little the Coroner extracts every detail of the ghastly tragedy.

"John Space," calls the Coroner. "I understand he wishes to give evidence."

There is a movement at the rear of the Court, and a man—with dissipation written large on every feature—comes forward in charge of two officers. The Coroner cautions him, for being under arrest he need not speak unless he wishes. But he is thoroughly self-possessed, and intends to save his neck if he can. Duly sworn he informs the Court that the death of his uncle was the result of an accident. The latter had threatened him, had snatched up a loaded revolver which was lying by—had pointed it at him, in fact. A struggle followed, the weapon exploded, and the old man fell.

"But the deceased was shot in the back," remarks the Coroner.

"I know nothing about that," is the reply.

The views of two other witnesses are different. The doctor declares that the deceased could not have shot himself: while a dealer in second-hand articles identifies the prisoner as the man who purchased the revolver of him a week before.

There is a murmur in the Court which is instantly suppressed, and the jury consider their verdict. Ten minutes later they declare that John Space is guilty of murder.

The Court clears at once. There is a rush for the front of the building, and with the utmost despatch the prisoner is bundled out. An angry sea of faces greets him as he emerges, curses are hurled at him from right and left, but fortunately for him, as he goes towards the waiting cab, he has the protection of the police. The cab door closes, a savage yell goes up, the crowd presses closer and closer, but Jehu whips up his steed and one more man is off to Brixton prison. A missile is thrown at the vehicle perhaps, a youngster or two cling on behind, and the mob disperses.

When the third inquest has been held the Coroner's labours are practically over. All that he has now to do is to give the doctor his fee, the jurymen their two shillings apiece, fill in the necessary forms relating to the business of the day, and pay the expenses of the inquest. This last he does out of his own pocket, but he is reimbursed ultimately by the local authorities.

This, however, has been an easy day. On occasions a Coroner will hold as many as nineteen inquests, and to obtain a fair idea of his work one must spend a day in his office. He is remunerated on a basis of thirty shillings per inquest, but out of his income he has to keep a clerk and pay all his travelling expenses. The expenses of a Coroner may be reckoned as from one-third to one-fourth of the salary.

Then let us consider the responsibilities. The Coroner must get at the truth, the whole truth. His Court is the Court of the People. To separate the facts from the lies is no easy task. A favourite trick of suicides is to leave behind them a note accusing of a crime some person against whom they have a grudge. The accuser being dead it is impossible to ascertain what foundation there is for the charge. And then there are the letters of suicides—letters sent to the Coroner, and which he is bound to read. One of these communications was spread over five quires of notepaper, and all that was intelligible in it was that the author intended to destroy himself because he was dissatisfied with his features.

And what shall we say of suicide in general? Suicides often show much method in their madness. We recall the case of a doctor who one night had a hot bath. While he was in the water he drew a razor across his throat, placed it on the side, and died quietly. He didn't want a mess. A certain chemist, desiring to create as little fuss as possible, opened a vein in his arm, and holding it over a basin bled silently to death. Strange, too, was the death of a constable who, wishing to make doubly sure of destruction, tied a rope round his neck and attached the other end to a rail of one of the bridges spanning the Thames. He was both strangled and drowned.

Over eight thousand inquests are held in London every year, and about four hundred and fifty of these are cases of suicide. Probably in every instance the victim was of unsound mind when he committed the deed. *Felo de se* may be said to be practically unknown.

REMOVING A PRISONER.

BILLINGSGATE : LANDING FISH.

ROUND LONDON'S BIG MARKETS.

By ARTHUR RUTLAND.

PORTER WITH
EELS.

SOME time in the night, two steamers, fitted with ice tanks and carrying cargoes from fishing towns along the eastern and north-eastern coasts, come in up the Thames, and are moored under the flare of the lamps that burn till morning at the back of Billingsgate Market. No sooner are they moored, with the ripples flapping sleepily against their idle keels, than they settle into silence and somnolence, except for the lessening hiss of steam from their engines, and the unwinking stare of the lanterns that watch fore and aft until dawn rises over the river, putting out simultaneously the lights on anchored boats and barges and the stars in the sky.

If you go round to the front of the market, even as late as a quarter to five this summer morning, there is little or no life at all in Lower Thames Street; but just before the hour sounds from the neighbouring steeples a clatter of hoofs and grinding of wheels on the stony road jar through the stillness, and a ponderous railway van, heavily burdened, sweeps down Fish Street Hill and pulls up gallantly opposite the yet closed gates of the Market. You hear a similar van rattling after it; and nearer, making more sedate haste along Thames Street, glides a private brougham, which stops at the door of one of the crazy, tumbledown old fish shops, and a substantial, prosperous-looking merchant alights with a cigar in his mouth, and, calling a "Good-morning, Thomas," to the coachman, who touches his hat and drives off, lets himself in with a latchkey. You may see him presently, when his shutters are down, disguised in a white smock and a cloth cap, writing at his desk among trickling consignments of newly arrived fish and shouting lustily to perspiring assistants.

Directly Billingsgate unfastens its gates the streets in its vicinity are all alive. It is as if some wizard haunting the deserted spot muttered a cabalistic word, and, hey, presto! public-houses and coffee-houses are wide open; shops of

PORTER WITH COD.

fish salesmen and factors on Fish Street Hill, St. Mary-at-Hill, and Thames Street are stripped of their shutters, and high-packed vehicles, mysteriously materialised, are lining the kerbs before them ; the two railway vans outside the Market are rapidly multiplying into so many that the roadway is getting impassable ; fish porters innumerable hurtle, as it were, from the clouds and up from the earth, as if every paving-stone were a trap-door, and swarming everywhere in white smocks and round, iron-hard hats, designed

stream one after the other with boxes on their heads, lidless boxes crusted with ice that is melting and dribbling through on the bearers.

By this, the interior of the Market has lost its barren look. The stalls, each of which is merely a desk and a floor space, are becoming congested with stacks of boxes ; with barrels of eels, and barrels and loose mountains of lobsters, mussels, whelks ; with salmon and cod ranged on the stones or on raised boards, or, in the

A CORNER OF LEADENHALL MARKET.

to cushion heavy burdens, are deftly unloading all the carts. There are continuous processions of such porters trotting into the Market with oozy, trickling boxes on their heads, and there are continuous processions trotting out of the market, handing metal 'tallies to the carters by way of receipts, hoisting fresh boxes on to their heads, and joining one or other of the processions trotting in.

If you pass through the cool, dim, sloppy Market and out on to the wooden platform at the rear, you see the steamers here being unloaded in like manner. A broad iron bridge slopes down to them, and down one side of the bridge porters are hurrying empty-handed, and up the other side porters

shops that occupy the two sides of the market, on shiny, slippery slabs. There are bloaters from Yarmouth ; there are kippers from Peterhead and Stornoway ; there are all manner of fish from Hull, Grimsby, Milford Haven, Fleetwood—all manner of places round the British Isles that have any fish to send anywhere seem to have sent them here.

The bustling and shouting increase until by half-past six, or thereabouts, the tide of business is at the full, and beginning to turn. The railway vans have gone, and other railway and carriers' and fishmongers' carts that have been hovering in Eastcheap and other outlying streets, and the costers who have been clustering their barrows at

COVENT GARDEN : SHELLING PEAS.

the lower end of Love Lane, are swooping in to bargain and buy, or to carry away consignments of fish already ordered, and the Market is emptying as rapidly as it filled.

Noon is not more than two hours gone when Billingsgate is practically shut again; the fish shops round about look as if they had been looted by an invading army; fish porters lounge at street corners, or in public-houses and coffee-shops, and vast-booted men tramp clumsily inside the Market and in front of it, trailing snaky hoses and washing the stones.

Three minutes' walk east of Billingsgate, whence London gets most of its fish, and you are in Leadenhall Market, whence London gets a good deal of its poultry. Billingsgate does not start work in these days so early as it used to; but it is an hour ahead of Leadenhall, where as late as six o'clock the only sign of life is in the large centre arcade: here a covered van has just drawn up with a cock crowing derisively from somewhere inside, and the driver is making remarks to the policeman who stands under the clock gazing round as if he could not make out what had become of everybody.

In Leadenhall there are no stalls; it is a maze of attenuated streets, and every salesman has his shop. It begins later than Billingsgate, and it finishes later too. From seven to nine it is at its busiest, but it does not show any marked signs of slackness until after noon. Besides being greatly patronised by local hotel and dining-room caterers, it does an appreciable trade with thrifty City clerks and housekeepers who live within easy distances. Perhaps the requirements of these customers have broadened its ideas, for it is not so bigoted in its view of poultry but that it accommodates a butcher or two, a few fruiterers and greengrocers, a publican, and a newsagent.

But when all is said, in Leadenhall you come back to poultry. You may purchase select breeds of dogs there, it is true; on the pavement before two or three shops in cages one on top of the other there are puppies who intermittently romp together and stand adding their yelpings to the general uproar. You may purchase hares too, and rabbits, dead or alive. You may even acquire a swan, if your taste runs in that direction, for you will see specimens standing resentfully in large cages that are yet not large enough for them to stretch their necks. Also, there is one shop devoted to every variety of singing bird.

Nevertheless, the commoner class of poultry predominates. You see it naked and dead dangling from hooks and lying on shelves inside the shops; you see it befeathered and very much alive imprisoned in wicker crates and wooden cages piled about the pavements outside the shops, and there are moments when the combined crowing of cocks, clucking of nervous hens, and quack-

bulgy hampers in both arms, which contributions are accumulated in their vehicles until they have obtained what they came for, or as much of it as they can get, and are glad to be turning their horses' heads homeward.

Amidst all the uproar of the market, and whilst buyers are crushing and elbowing each other up and down the narrow alleys that run through the wilderness of miscellaneous produce gathered here to be sold, you come across, in summer, a group of women in a quiet corner behind a rampart of baskets, placidly shelling peas into sieves and cir-

SCENES AT PEDLARS' FAIR.

ing of ducks pretty well submerge every other sound.

Farther east is Spitalfields Market; to the south, just over London Bridge, is the Borough Market; but westward is Covent Garden, that surpasses these in their own line, and is, besides, the largest flower market anywhere in or near London.

So enormous is the amount of business done each morning at "the Garden" that it is impossible for nearly half the buyers going there to drive up within sight of it. The streets leading into it, and many that branch therefrom or pass the ends of them, are literally blocked with a tangle of greengrocers' carts, while the greengrocers, aided by regular or casual assistants, are momentarily struggling out from the hurly-burly of the Market, propelling barrow- or truck-loads of fruit and vegetables, or balancing columns of round baskets on their heads, or staggering along hugging

cular tins; and by-and-by, outside the building, among a litter of cabbage leaves and hemmed in by waiting carts, you discover a numerous company of other women similarly engaged.

They make two little islands of industrious repose in this welter of tumultuous trafficking. The only other spot that is as peaceful just now is the auction room over the road—a bare, spacious hall, with wooden-canopied, pulpit-looking erections placed at intervals down either side of it. There are no auctions in progress at present,

FRUIT AUCTIONS AT COVENT GARDEN.

but notices written on giant slates tell you that there are going to be several towards noon, and later.

When you come back to attend these, rude tiers of seats have been pulled round into three sides of a square before certain of the pulpits, in each of which an auctioneer's clerk sits writing busily, and an auctioneer stands lifting up his voice and bringing down his hammer with undeniable effect. Bunches of bananas swathed in basketwork and matting, long boxes of pears, of apples, of pineapples, are hauled in quick succession up on to the table immediately below the auctioneer. "Show 'em!" he cries mechanically. His porters tear open the matting or rip off the box lids, and eagerly eye the buyers and others perched row above row on the tiers, ferociously reiterating the auctioneer's cry of "Now then! Who bids?"

The bidding is prompt but cautious; nearly everything is bought, and bought cheaply; and money and goods change hands with such facility that another "lot" is put up, bid for, and sold before the previous one has been carried beyond the door.

Meanwhile, the Flower Market closes at nine, so, of course, you have been there before returning for the auctions. The view you get from either of its immense doorways is like the first bewildering glimpse of the transformation scene at a theatre. Against a background of broad-leaved palms and multitudinous flowerless plants, billowy clouds of snow-white blooms mingle with stretches of skyey blue, shot through here and there with flaming reds and yellows and purples, all in a lavish setting of every shade and tinting of green.

The blended fragrances within are suffocatingly sweet; the aisles of vivid, varied colour dazzle the eye almost as sunlight will; and, strangely contrasted with their surroundings, the salesmen, buyers, and porters might be merely scene-shifters preparing the transformation scene, and the flower-girls flocking about the cut-flower stalls might be blowzy, bedraggled fairies not yet dressed for their parts.

Some of them are very old flower-girls,

and some of them very young; they are all keen bargainers, and go off with armfuls, or basketfuls, or apronfuls of scent and loveliness that, within an hour, they will have wired into penny and twopenny bunches, and be selling to spruce City men coming into town to their offices.

Nothing could be much farther removed from the beauty and delicacy and fragrance of that floral mart than the unloveliness and comparative squalor of the Cattle Market at Islington.

Two mornings of every week, winter and

SHOWING THE DONKEY'S PACES (CATTLE MARKET).

summer, before the world at large is awake, from lairs at Hackney Wick and Mile End, and from railway termini that have received them after long journeys out of green country places, droves of sheep and horned cattle, splashed with the mire of London roads and hungering for the fields, are shepherded through the iron gateways into the broad, paved Market square.

In company with a coffee-shop, a bank or so, some railway depôts, and a reading-room for drovers, the Market clerk has his office under the clock-tower in the middle of the square, and on one side of the tower sheep huddle patiently in their pens, and on the other bullocks fattened for the

NEAR SMITHFIELD MEAT MARKET.

slaughter and cows destined for the dairy farm stand in long rows tethered to the top rails of their stalls, and keep up a ceaseless, monotonous moaning, punctuated occasionally by a resounding bellow.

In and out among the sheep, and in and out among the horned cattle, go bronzed, farmer-looking men and florid, stolid, butcher-looking men, critical of eye and cunning with the forefinger, which they will dig knowingly into the ribs or flanks of beasts they have a mind to. And when a man has chosen his sheep a drover and his dog go off with them, and when he has chosen his bullocks a drover goes off with them also, the buyer sometimes whipping out a pair of scissors and snipping his initials in the hair on the animals' backs before he loses sight of them. Some of them are driven away along the roads to suburban grazing lands or slaughter-houses; most of them make a shorter journey of it to the neighbouring abattoirs.

On other days of the week Hay and Straw, and Pig and Poultry Markets are held here; and on Fridays there is a Market for the sale of horses and carts. Friday, too, is the great day of the Pedlars' Fair, when up the steps and under the roof of the Hide Market, and on the ample margin of stones round the cattle pens, you may enjoy reminiscences of Petticoat Lane with the yelling and hubbub all left out.

The Hide Market and that margin of stones are strewn and littered as if there had been a volcanic eruption near by, and the lava had come pelting down in the form of coats and trousers, and second-hand furniture, crockery, glassware, rusty stoves, odd door-knobs, indescribable salvages of ironmongery, ladies' dresses and children's toys, beds and bedding, carpets, doormats, window-curtains, so that as you pick your way through, you do not know you have missed the footpath till you find yourself astray in an impenetrable jungle of hosiery or cutlery, or stumbling over meat-screens and frying-pans, and amazing collections of decrepit tinware.

Simultaneously, the horse and cart fair is raging among the cattle-pens, and every few minutes spectators wandering thereabouts scatter suddenly to make way for a sprightly quadruped whose paces are being tried for the delectation of a possible purchaser. Neither horses nor carts are exactly new; and the "horses" include donkeys, and the carts anything from a coster's barrow to a dropsical four-wheel cab, or occasionally the haggard ghost of an omnibus.

Most of the sheep and bullocks that walk into the Cattle Market are carried later to Smithfield Meat Market (many Smithfield salesmen having slaughter-houses behind that wall which fringes the square); and at Smithfield they are in the greatest and, in some respects, the best-ordered of the London Markets. It covers such an immense area that there is space around it to accommodate all the carts and vans that go there: you see them backed in serried lines to the kerbs along three sides of the Market as well as under its archways, while their drivers or owners are inside doing business among mighty red and white groves and vistas of beef and mutton.

The early morning methods of the Markets are very much the same everywhere, the chief difference being in the nature of the commodities, the bulk whereof are brought up by one series of vehicles and taken away by another; but you may get more entertainment at Smithfield, as you may at Billingsgate or Leadenhall, out of the fag end of a Saturday's market.

Here, for example, this Saturday afternoon in Smithfield, now that more than half the stalls are shut, comes a staid, matured City clerk with his shrewd, economical little wife and their eldest son, a dapper youth who has himself just become "something in the City" and has met them by arrangement, but reluctantly, and in some fear of compromising his budding dignity. Depend upon it, the matured clerk has a large family, or they take in boarders to eke out his salary. The inevitable men, women, and children who hover about the gates to sell penny canvas or straw bags know them by sight as regular Saturday customers, and their experience stands them in good stead.

They do nothing rashly. Having inspected a dozen stalls, they go back to one they had passed, and secure a shoulder of mutton or a great piece of beef for remarkably little money. At the newer end of the Market, where they have now and then picked up a bargain in poultry, they buy several pounds of good cheap bacon and

MEAT VAN.

a formidable wedge of cheese. Then they go out and across the road to the Fish and Vegetable Market, where they get some fish for this evening's dinner or supper, and lay in a stock of fruit and tomatoes, supplemented by a selection of marrows and, possibly, a couple of cucumbers; so that, at last, when they shape their course for a penny tramcar home, the clerk is carrying two bags, his wife has her arms full of miscellanies, and their son, following them with a hang-dog, furtive air, eyes the passers-by loweringly, and, with the bag of shamelessly protruding meat in one hand and the basket of fish in the other, is secretly praying he may not be seen by anybody who knows him.

BAG SELLERS.

PENSIONERS AND "BLACK JACKS."

AT CHELSEA HOSPITAL.

By DESMOND YOUNG.

TO the average Londoner, Chelsea Hospital is merely a home for military "veterans battered in their country's wars." Rightly considered, it is more. It is, by means of its inmates, a bridge—the only accessible bridge—between the Army life of the past and of the present, between the battles of yesterday and those fought in the valleys of Abyssinia, on the burning plains of India, and in other parts of the world where the arts of peace have long held sway. For no man is eligible for its benefits under the age of fifty-five unless disabled by severe wounds or loss of limbs, and, as a consequence, its inmates, numbering about 570 all told, represent the pick of the oldest of our warriors.

Worn-out fighting material are they, as is evidenced by the pathetic fact that, though some men have rested in the haven for a quarter of a century, the average duration of life there is only about five years. As the last abiding place of the very cream of our superannuated fighters, then, Chelsea

Hospital is, and ever will be, the link connecting deeds of military glory separated by long intervals.

Many and varied are the circumstances that bring veterans together under the hospitable roof of the famous institution. Sometimes an old soldier marries a young wife, with the usual result—jealousy, quarrels, unhappiness. Taught in the bitterest of all schools, that of experience, that May and December will not mate, he seeks the shelter of the Hospital, sure that there peace and comfort will be his. Many an in-pensioner has a wife outside, but it is significant that she is rarely his equal in age. Seldom will a scarred and wrinkled warrior leave a helpmeet who has spent spring and summer with him, who has travelled with him hand in hand through life, who has shared his joys and sorrows since youth and hope were high. In other cases a broken-down veteran is alone in the world. The sole survivor of his race, he has not a single relation to whom he can look for assistance.

This being the case, what more natural than that he should bethink him of Chelsea Hospital ?

The unfilial conduct of sons and daughters is another prolific cause of soldiers relinquishing their pension. And what stories of such ingrates cluster round the case of unclaimed medals in the Great Hall !—a case wherein repose scores of war decorations bestowed on inmates dead and gone, some of them of considerable intrinsic value. Again and again have such insignia been applied for by persons who would not give their departed owners a shilling—nay, who played the parts of Goneril and Regan in the oft-acted tragedy of *Lear*. Other veterans there are—though these, happily, are in the minority—who "sup sorrow by spoonfuls" through business troubles as well as through the unnatural conduct of their children. Inheriting money, they embark in shopkeeping and the like, fail, and then enter the Hospital, there patiently to await the last summons.

Once an old soldier joins the establishment, he does not often leave it voluntarily, because, in addition to being comparatively well off, he can adapt things exactly to his liking. There are no irksome rules to worry and annoy him, and no duties to be performed. "We haven't to do anything," said one fine old soldier, "except attend church on Sunday." If a man chooses, he can remain out till nine o'clock every night in the week, and by getting permission—granted as a matter of course—he need not return till twelve. He can, too, go away on furlough as opportunity serves. There is practically no restriction on him.

Just the same degree of liberty is accorded him in purely domestic matters. Every man has his own cubicle, which is his "castle," and concerning which he has full power to use the words of a poet now beyond the reach of the interviewers and other animalculæ to whom he addressed them :

"No foot, if you please, over threshold of mine."

No other pensioner can enter it unasked. He is the lord and master of his little home. Here he is free to do as he pleases. He rises when he likes ; welcomes whom he likes ; goes out when he likes ; eats when he likes (for his food is put into his cubicle at stated times, and not served at a common table) ; does exactly as tastes and habits dictate without let or hindrance from anybody.

GARDENING.

That this absence of rule tends to make the in-pensioner more comfortable is plain in every ward. Even old soldiers, accustomed as they have been to that cast-iron, inflexible routine which stifles individuality and converts men into machines, have not all the same tastes and dispositions; and the great difference in the arrangement and decoration of the cubicles shows the wisdom of the governors in recognising this circumstance. While some are as plain as a barrack room —destitute of everything beyond absolute necessaries—others are embellished, externally as well as internally, with pictures from the illustrated papers, tobacconists' show cards, and a wealth of similar odds and ends. Nor is this all. In a few of the cubicles a marvellously elaborate scheme of decoration has been carried out on a shelf over the bed. The centre-piece is a loud-voiced clock, which is flanked on either hand with tiers of fancy cigarette and tobacco boxes, match boxes, photographs and pictures given away with packets of cigarettes, and other trifles. All this does not sound very promising material as a substitute for such wall ornaments as plaques and oil paintings; but it really brightens up a cubicle to an amazing extent, and truly remarkable are the perseverance, ingenuity, and taste displayed in making the most of it.

Half of each cubicle is taken up by a bed; the other half is for sitting and eating purposes. Such things as boot cleaning are done outside in the ward—where the necessary appliances are close at hand—and for reading, writing, and companionship, the Great Hall, with its collection of weapons, its old leather drinking vessels, known as "black jacks," and other interesting contents, is available. There, with a congenial comrade, and his memory stimulated by the objects around him—the portraits of Britain's famous fighting sons, and still more by the tattered fragments of flags taken from the enemy in war that hang over them—the pensioner can drive the hours along by fighting his battles over again.

Or, if the weather is fine, he can go out into the spacious grounds and mix with his fellows, or take an airing on the seats in the piazza, with his back to the memorials of British heroes—a number of mural monu-

ments as appropriately situated as they are inspiriting.

Once a week there is a full muster in the Great Hall. Pay is given out there every Saturday morning, and the pensioners, all dressed in their best, turn up in full force to receive it. For many years the money allowance was only one penny per day, but now it is twopence, each inmate receiving fourteen-pence per week. Although this is not a large amount, it is sufficient to provide the indispensable tobacco, which is almost the only commodity that the old soldier need buy. Food, clothing, beer (a strictly limited quantity), firing—these are all free. So that he does not really require much pocket money. No doubt he could spend more than he gets; but that is a very widely distributed capacity.

Besides owning a cubicle, some of the pensioners have also proprietary rights over a plot of land. At one corner of the hospital grounds, between the disused cemetery and (strange juxtaposition!) the site of that vanished scene of so much uproarious jollity, Ranelagh Gardens, is an enclosure divided into 148 allotments about twenty feet square. Each of these is supposed to be the freehold of a separate inmate, though, as a fact, some men have two or three plots. Whether from a sense of life's impermanence—for a pensioner often sows and another reaps—or from ignorance of one of the oldest of arts or some other cause, applications for an ownerless plot from those who do not already possess a garden are sometimes lacking. There is no demand for it; nobody seems willing to have it at a gift. And in this case it is transferred to a man who already cultivates a slice of the land.

Like the cubicles, these duodecimo pocket estates bear the impress of their owners' hands. Not one is so small but that it reveals something of its proprietor's idiosyncrasies. Some are filled with old-fashioned flowers—pinks and stocks, lupins and hollyhocks; and in the autumn groups of the plots are gloriously radiant with the many-hued and queenly dahlia. More architectural than anything else are the decorations of other squares. On one stands a miniature castle of pebbles and cement about five feet high, surmounted by a battlemented tower, and

I. THE CHAPEL.   II. A GARDEN SCENE.   III. THE GREAT HALL.

with door windows, and all complete. Here and there, again, a contemplative old soldier has built him an arbour, and when it is clothed in green and the days are warm he sits in it for hours at a stretch, puffing away at his pipe and musing over the far-distant past.

"Practical" is writ large on yet another class of allotments, since they contain a cucumber frame, a few score lettuce or rows of onions, two or three beds of radishes, a sowing of mustard and cress—"something worth looking after," as your severely utilitarian gardener says. There is an obvious reason for the growing of such crops. They can be turned into money, especially on Sunday, when the shops are closed, and when people living in the neighbourhood cannot go to their usual sources of supply for a "bit o' green stuff for tea."

What more can an old warrior want than a cubicle and a bit of garden at Chelsea? Nothing; and the generality of those who enter the Hospital recognise it and are contented accordingly. Many, indeed, become so attached to the place that they cherish one of the most common delusions of old age—

that when "something happens" to them the whole institution must inevitably collapse and fall into nothingness. Ever since the days of the first grandfather the same fallacy has been current.

While, however, most veterans who gain admittance to the institution do not leave it till the end, some discharge themselves in a huff and go back to their old pension. A man may, for instance, get in a coterie where he is chaffed, and may ultimately vow in his haste that he will not stand it any longer. That done, he feels bound, repent his words as deeply as he may, to take his departure. But, whatever the cause may be, very few leave who do not wish to go back again.

That is not impossible. In fact, some men do return. They send in their application, and, if there is nothing against them, their names are put on the list and they await their turn—wait till the forty or fifty men having prior claims on the institution have either died or been taken in—and then they pass through the gates once more, to remain as long as life lasts.

MEMORIALS IN THE PIAZZA.

LONDON'S HOMES FOR THE HOMELESS.

By T. W. WILKINSON.

HOUSE OF CHARITY : TABLET ON WALL.

"NO man need beg, starve, steal, or commit suicide." Characteristic alike in wording and "display"—for the Salvation Army believes in hitting between the eyes —the placard has been read by thousands of sceptics in the Blackfriars shelter. Some of the *habitués* of that institution certainly would not endorse the proposition as a whole (they would jib at "beg"); but, whatever the professional "dosser" may think, there is less temptation now for a poor houseless wanderer in London to beg, steal, or take his departure to the next world by the cheapest route—*via* the river Thames — than ever there was. Never before was the Great City so rich in homes for the distressed. Never before were so many hands extended to raise the man in the gutter.

When De Quincey, ill and faint from hunger, turned from Oxford Street into Soho Square, and sank exhausted on a doorstep, refuges for such as he there were none. Cross this same square now, and at the corner of Greek Street you face the oldest hospice in London. Here is a refuge founded specially for cases like the Opium Eater's. Without, it is not attractive: a large, smoke-begrimed, gloomy building, plainly labelled "House of Charity"; within, there is ample to draw the habitual "dosser" a thousand

miles if he saw a million to one chance of enjoying it. Solid, old-fashioned comfort—comfort of the Georgian and early Victorian era—that is the impression that the interior must needs produce. And the table side of the house—decidedly a weak point with many charities—accords with its fittings and appointments. The food is of the best, and is supplied without stint. The Soho Square refuge for the homeless, in fact, is in this respect unique.

Not altogether a blessing to the Council, and still less to the warden of the institution, is this distinction. For all the social wastrels in the Metropolis wend their way to Greek Street, primed with moving tales of unheard-of vicissitudes and armed with testimonials much more interesting than convincing. But against this drawback can be set the circumstance that no other charity of its kind in London benefits so many deserving people. From the connections of royalty to domestic servants, from University men to unlettered hinds—all come to Soho Square. One day—and these are actual cases—a countess gives a poverty ring at

HOUSE OF CHARITY : ENTRANCE.

the door, her pockets empty, her strength exhausted, her hopes and aspirations temporarily gone. On another the cousin of a duke ascends the steps, applies for shelter, and is admitted. The victim of a rascally solicitor—a man who had owned a prosperous West-End theatre—also seeks succour; and a lady who finds her way to the hospice in her hour of need proves to be the granddaughter of an archbishop. Barristers, solicitors, physicians and surgeons, profes-

the sandwichboard man's restaurant, the famous soup kitchen. Unlike many London shelters, it has a provincial reputation, because most of the round score of beds it can place at the disposal of the destitute are usually occupied by men who have come from the country in search of employment. Not that it refuses shelter to other unfortunates. No; destitute aliens it takes in, and penniless Londoners, too. But for many years the bulk of its beneficiaries have been "travelling

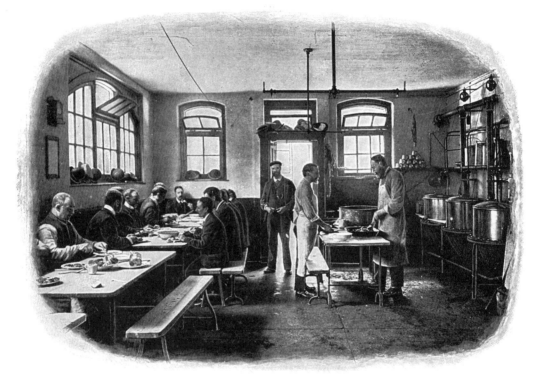

HAM YARD HOSPICE : THE SOUP KITCHEN.

sional men of all kinds, veritable "human documents" many of them, come in a never-ending stream. Tragedy, again tragedy, and yet again tragedy—the same thing is witnessed day after day in the House of Charity.

Since De Quincey took his nightly strolls in Oxford Street, too, a host of other refuges, intended for a different class of destitute people from that fed and housed in Soho Square, have sprung up all over London. Further west stands that admirable institution, the Ham Yard Hospice, and to the east is an equally excellent charity worked on somewhat similar lines, the Field Lane Refuge. The Ham Yard Hospice is above

tradesmen." Once an applicant is admitted, the streets, provided his references are satisfactory, have no terrors for him for a fortnight. He is boarded and lodged for that period, and allowed to go out daily in search of work.

At Field Lane much the same system is in force. For at least fourteen nights the man who is able to satisfy the superintendent of his eligibility for the benefits of the refuge is sure of a bed. As for life in the refuge, the ordinary course of events runs thus : After breakfast—" plain "—come prayers, at nine o'clock. Then, having meanwhile scanned the advertisement columns of the newspapers provided, the inmate makes a scour for work till noon. At twelve, if he cares to come in for it, is dinner—good meat soup and bread. Another prowl round the streets, and he is back, at five, for the evening meal, which consists of bread and meat and tea. Every day four men are told off in turn to fetch broken food from certain large City warehouses, and it is from this that the soup is made and the meat comes for supper. Other necessary work—as the cleaning of the dormitories—is done by the inmates; but ample time is allowed them for opportunities to work out their own social salvation. In the evening the "Field Laner" attends a meeting in the large room where the Ragged Church service is held on Sunday; and, finally, he is present, with his thirty-four companions in misfortune (the refuge has a capacity for thirty-five men all told), at prayers. The women are subject to similar rules, only they are not expected to be in at midday.

Of another class of refuges the Medland Hall, Ratcliff, and the Providence Row Refuge, Spitalfields, are the leading representatives. The first of these institutions, one of the several means by which the London Congregational Union is

FIELD LANE REFUGE : SUPPLYING COCOA AFTER THE RAGGED CHURCH SERVICE.

doing so much good work, is world-famed. Every place of this kind in London has its peculiarity. That of the Medland Hall is cosmopolitanism. Situated on the fringe of London's great waterway, and open every night in the year to all comers, with only such restrictions as are necessary to prevent its abuse, it is a focus for destitute men of all nationalities.

Deeply impressive is the scene in front of the hall shortly before six o'clock. Though everybody knows the time for opening the doors, men have been congregating from all points of the compass for a couple of hours, and now they are drawn up in a queue extending along the east side of the Horseferry Branch Road to Commercial

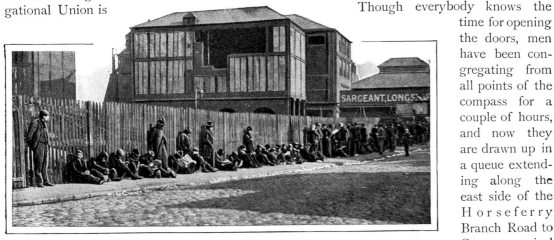

MEDLAND HALL : WAITING TO ENTER.

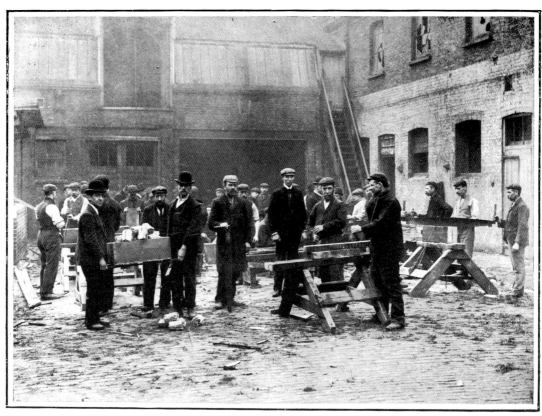

CHOPPING WOOD AT THE "MORNING POST" HOME.

MEDLAND HALL: INSIDE.

Road. Five or six hundred in number, they form a strange string of humanity—a strange string, truly. An unshorn outcast in a faded, rusty frock coat, unmistakably a clerk, one of the City's rejected, rubs shoulders with a burly son of the soil who looks as if he had stepped straight out of Mr. Thomas Hardy's pages. Propped up against the fence, silent and wondering, a negro takes stock of his neighbours, some dozen dockers. Further on stands a blue-bloused German sailor, accompanied by his two boys, on whose fair, innocent faces anxiety and curiosity are singularly blended ; and still nearer the door there is a Spanish seafarer. Other aliens there are in plenty, and as for the rest, who shall attempt to describe them, even in catalogue fashion? Take a fact that speaks volumes in this connection. Two bunks— only two—were occupied in a single year by 317 different visitors, among whom were Americans, negroes, English sailors, firemen, engine-drivers, clerks, blacksmiths, printers, grooms, coach-painters, bricklayers, shoe-makers, etc. One of the inmates was a well-educated young fellow from Cork. On the fifth night of his stay, having meanwhile written to Ireland, he received a telegram : " Money forwarded. Come home at once. Father dying."

Also included in the three hundred occu-pants was an old bluejacket who, when he drew his pension, walked along the file in front of the hall and gave each man a penny. This was an act of true generosity, and in the annals of the institution it does not by any means stand alone. The superin-tendent tells of a not less gratifying incident that deserves to be recorded to the credit of human nature—of a labourer who turned out at four o'clock in the morning to look for work, and who, having succeeded, returned a week later with three shillings " to help some other poor chap."

Pass now through the hospitable doors of the shelter. It is still a few minutes short of the hour of seven, and yet every one of the 343 bunks it contains has been allotted. Men with admission tickets—which are available for six nights, or rather seven, since Sunday is not counted—have been let in first, and the remaining space has been filled by the new-comers. All applicants, whether

admitted or not, have been given a substantial lump of bread-and-butter. Scattered over the building, the fortunate ones are making the most of their respite in the bitter struggle with cruel fortune. Some are wolfing their bread-and-butter with eloquent voracity, and, as Macaulay said of Johnson, "swallowing tea in oceans," to enable the men to make which beverage a prodigious quantity of boiling water is ready when the hall is opened. Tea? Something hot in many cases—something concocted from leaves already brewed and double-brewed in a cheap cook-shop. A few men are busy in another way. Here and there heads are bent over

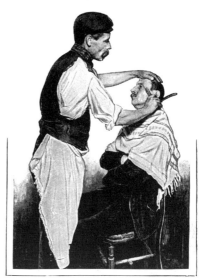

A "HALFPENNY" BARBER.

boots that seem beyond all possible redemp-tion, and trousers in the last stage of shock-ingness are being patched with infinite artistic care—an operation for which cloth cuttings are supplied gratuitously. But the majority of the men are so tired and footsore with perambulating the endless streets that they are already in their shallow bunks. A touching picture, and yet a pleasing one withal, for the poor fellows are temporarily contented, in spite of their past sufferings and of the darkness of their present outlook. As to the bunks, they are wooden frames in line on the floor and having inside a bed of dry sea-weed encased in cloth leather.

Brightness, comfort, perfect order, and system—these are the characteristics of the Providence Row Night Refuge, familiarly

PROVIDENCE ROW NIGHT REFUGE:
MALE AND FEMALE APPLICANTS.

presented by the *Morning Post* Embankment Home, in Millbank Street, Westminster. Supported mainly by the readers of that journal, it is managed by the Church Army on its usual lines, and differs essentially from most shelters open to the penniless in that it does not give something for nothing. All its inmates—and it has one hundred beds, a number of them in separate cubicles — are required to do some work in return for food and lodgings.

known as "The Dormitory," which owes its existence to the zeal and abounding charity of the late Rev. Dr. Gilbert. The doors are opened at five o'clock. Fifteen minutes later it is full; it has received its complement of about three hundred men, women, and children—not all out-of-works or the dependents of such, but unfortunates of many kinds.

At night the large building is one of the sights of charitable London. The men's sitting-room, with its inmates reading, smoking, and conversing as if the world went pretty well with them; the corresponding part on the female side, where women are knitting and sewing and their children are gambolling about the floor; the well-fitted lavatories (one in each section), in which there is every convenience for personal cleanliness, notably a monster foot-bath two or three yards long, and being used by a dozen inmates simultaneously—all this is delightful to witness, and differs essentially in some respects from ordinary shelter life. It is a cut above that. The food allowance night and morning—bread and a basin of capital cocoa —is also superior to that usually given in large institutions of this class. Yet an inmate can remain for three weeks.

A third class of shelters is admirably re-

Some are employed at their own trade; others are sent out window cleaning, sandwich-board carrying, etc.; others—the majority—are put to chopping wood, of which they are required to do an amount proportionate to the benefits they receive. The "task," however, is mere relaxation: three baskets for breakfast, six for dinner, and two for tea. And so a man may go on for weeks; for there is no hard-and-fast rule as to the length of time which he may stay, every case being dealt with on its merits. This is an excellent system. By its application in the *Morning Post* Home thousands of men have been given a chance of rehabilitation.

After a man has stopped in all the free homes for the homeless, as well as those in which he works out his keep—and these two classes, if he take them in the proper order, may provide him with board and lodgings for months—there are still the Salvation Army shelters between him and the street. At certain of these institutions twopence procures an itinerant, male or female, a bunk which is, in some respects, like those at Medland Hall, except that American cloth is used. Comfortable, as contrasted with an ordinary bed, it is not; but clean, free from anything that will irritate or harm—yes.

Getting into a bunk is like getting between two icicles, so little attuned is American leather to the human skin. Presently, however, owing to its non-porosity, it makes the body unpleasantly warm, and occasionally, moreover, sticks to it, with the result that the "dosser" may next morning carry away something like the remains of a porous plaster on parts of his frame where porous plaster was never voluntarily put by mortal man. And yet nothing could well take the place of American leather, which, let its faults be what they may, has one supreme merit. It is easily swept, washed, and disinfected. Besides, there is, after all, a way of preventing it from sticking to the body. Here is the "dosser's" recipe. Gather some paper, such as the contents bills of evening journals, while on the way to the shelter, and lay it between the American leather and your nobility.

But the cheapest shelter of the Salvation Army is the one at Blackfriars. Wonderful is the amount of spending in sixpence there. For an inclusive charge of fourpence supper, bed, and breakfast are provided ; another halfpenny will secure a shave at the hands of one of the two barbers, both of them "lodgers," not official Figaros ; and with the remaining three-halfpence tobacco, food, clothes, anything may be purchased. For among the *habitués* are a number of "merchants" who not only retail by halfpennyworths such commodities as broken pork pies, sausage ends, and the sweepings of the ham and beef shop counter, but sell "hard up," or cigars and cigarette ends gathered in the street, as well as boots, shirts, and other fruits of begging. Besides, a man can wash his shirt, and, indeed, do anything else in reason, free of cost.

A strange institution, this, at Blackfriars— the cheapest hotel in London, the resort of some of the most hopeless of outcasts, the finest training school in England for learning the arts and shifts of destitute life in a great city.

On the whole, then, the Metropolis is not ill supplied with homes for the homeless, and comparatively few of those who form its flotsam and jetsam are not benefited by one or other of them, while every year hundreds are by their aid given a new start in life. When a man once gets into the gutter in London it takes something very little short of a miracle to raise him up again ; but the annals of the city's shelters prove that the thing is done nevertheless.

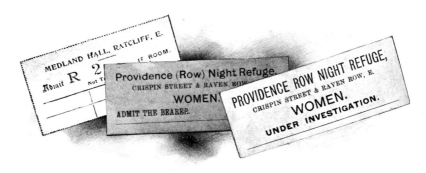

ADMISSION TICKETS.

LONDON'S DRESSMAKERS AND MILLINERS.

By ELIZABETH L. BANKS.

MADAME SMARTLY'S establishment is in the vicinity of Bond Street; Miss Stitchem's place of business is near Clerkenwell Green. At the entrance of the Bond Street apartment one sees the sign "Madame Smartly — Modes" engraved on a highly polished plate, very tiny and elegant in its inconspicuousness. In the window of the place near Clerkenwell Green, the legend "Miss Stitchem — Dressmaker" is painted in huge, uneven, black letters on a large piece of cardboard almost the size of the windowpane. At Madame Smartly's are mirrors reaching from floor to ceiling. At Miss Stitchem's the only looking-glass is a small one hanging on the wall.

At Madame Smartly's, Lady de Blank, when she is

JUDGING THE EFFECT.

trying on her new frock, can see her reflection from top to toe in the mirrors by simply looking. Indeed, she could see herself if she were twice the height she is—and Lady de Blank is a tall and willowy woman, too! Not only does she see her length, but she sees, without difficulty, her back, for the mirrors are so arranged that she can view any part of herself or all of herself without any trouble whatever. She has but to look and behold. At Miss Stitchem's Miss 'Arriet 'Obson, notwithstanding the fact that she is a diminutive young woman, less than five-feet-one in height, has all sorts of difficulties in arranging the glass so that she can see her face and the beginnings of her waist at the same time; and when she desires to see for herself just what sort of a "hang" Miss Stitchem has imparted to her skirt, Miss 'Obson mounts a chair, and thus is enabled to see the bottom of it in the glass, although, of course, she cannot then see anything of her face or her waist or her hips.

At Madame Smartly's there are thirty girls at work. Eight of these young women will have been employed, each in her turn, at her own speciality, on the wonderful Court gown that has been ordered by Lady de Blank. At Miss Stitchem's there will be only one pair of hands and one set of fingers at work on Miss 'Arriet 'Obson's dress. Lady de Blank, a day or two before the Court is held, will call on Madame Smartly, so that—preparatory to making her curtsey to the Queen—her gown may have the finishing touches put to it by one of the assistants. Surely it *is* an artistic creation, and well worth the bill of eighty guineas which Lady de Blank will receive some time during the year.

The silk petticoat is veiled with net, and over this is the cream-coloured French needle-run lace, with short satin strappings in the front and long strappings reaching to the bottom of the skirt in the back. There is also a paste trimming which sparkles among the lace. The silk bodice is covered with the lace, with pearl passementerie about the low neck, and the waistband, which is very high at the back, is of beautiful Parma violet satin. Then the train—which, later on, can be turned into a second gown —is of deeper Parma violet velvet, edged with lace, and lined with a pale Parma violet to match the waistband. Then come the feathers and the veil.

Miss 'Arriet 'Obson will not get a properly made-out bill at all. When she goes to Miss Stitchem's to fetch her newly-made frock away, she will be told that the price for making, as previously agreed, is five shillings, and that as she forgot to provide sufficient cotton for the sewing there is twopence-halfpenny more for that; and, oh! Miss Stitchem had to get two more yards of braid at a penny-three-farthings a yard, which makes threepence-halfpenny, and so she is owing Miss Stitchem in all just five shillings and sixpence; and Miss Stitchem will probably say, though she herself was the maker of the frock, that she never saw Miss 'Obson look to better advantage.

Madame Smartly is what is known as a

TRYING ON A HAT.

"Court Dressmaker"; Miss Stitchem lives in a street that is really so narrow you could scarcely call it a street, and so, I suppose, she might be called an "Alley Dressmaker." On one particular point I am positive, and that is that Miss Stitchem is the cheapest dressmaker in the Metropolis. At any rate, if there is one cheaper, I have been unable, in a search of many days, to discover her!

Not far from Madame Smartly's, Lady de Blank may stop her carriage in front of the millinery establishment of Mesdames Swagger and Swell. It is much easier to order a hat than a dress. On entering she sees one hat, or several hats, that she likes. She receives the bows of many good-looking young shop-women, and a special and particular bow from Madame Swagger, who is handed a hat by one of the young women and places it upon the head of Lady de Blank. Then a tiny exclamation of "Oh!" from Madame Swagger, and the hat comes off. Just a bend or something in it has made my lady's whole face look awry, because hers is not the style of face for the hat, and Madame Swagger sees directly what the defect is. Ah! here is another, which is tried on; but oh! that particular shade of pink, bordering on the magenta, will not go with Lady de Blank's complexion, and Madame Swagger hastily grabs a bit of rose-pink and holds it up to my lady's head, hiding the magenta.

"That is the shade for your ladyship," says Madame Swagger. True! So it is! Madame Swagger is an artist—just as much of an artist as the painter who depicts on canvas a scene or a face in which the colours blend into each other to make the wonderfully harmonious whole. And Madame Swagger is not only an artist: she is an artist who has made her name. She takes the magenta velvet from the hat, substitutes the rose shade, and sends the hat to Lady de Blank with a bill for seven or eight guineas. Remember, please, there are ostrich plumes on that hat, gloriously curling, wavy plumes, which may be recurled twenty years hence! And then, Madame Swagger must be paid for knowing that Lady de Blank should not wear magenta, and she must be paid for her name, too.

While Lady de Blank's carriage is rolling along Piccadilly, come you with me down Shoreditch way, and I will show you where Miss 'Arriet 'Obson can buy a hat for three shillings and sixpence-farthing. There it is, in the window of a little shop, across the doorway of which you may read, " Headway and Topling—Ladies' Hats and Bonnets." But do you say that Miss 'Obson might do better to buy a naked hat and the trimmings separately and trim the thing up herself? But why should Miss 'Obson take all that trouble when here, in this very shop window, there is a notice which says, " No Charge for Trimming Hats and Bonnets, Materials of which are Bought Here." So into the shop let Miss 'Obson go, and she will find a rather pretty brown straw hat for sixpence three-farthings. Three yards of another shade of brown ribbon—a shade that will harmonise nicely with the brown straw—she will get for threepence a yard. It is satin on one side and cotton-back. She will find four " ostrich tips " for threepence three-farthings apiece, and three sprays of flowers with leaves at twopence three-farthings each. There's a sparkling buckle for three-half-pence, and the hat lining to go inside of the crown will be a penny three-farthings. A young woman trims the hat while Miss 'Obson waits; and Miss 'Obson, paying three shillings and sixpence-farthing, carries her hat home in a paper bag.

From the contemplation of Miss 'Obson and her paper bag, let us go back again to the West-End and into our carriage and away to the house of Mr. Fitly.

Mr. Fitly is a man dressmaker. Does not Shakespeare say that " the apparel oft proclaims the man?" Well, that is the way with all the garments that are made at the house of Fitly: they oft—or, rather, they *always*—proclaim the man dressmaker. Mr. Fitly's windows are large, but he tells you, with adroitness and shrewdness worthy of a woman, that his creations are shown inside, not outside! That is right—Mr. Fitly is an artist. He sometimes spends hours and hours in designing his gowns; and why should he put them in a window to be badly copied by would-be rivals?

When our carriage stops before Mr. Fitly's door, a boy in livery, with " Fitly " on his hatband, turns the handle for us and escorts us into the presence of the great dressmaker. He leads us into a large room, presses a button, and immediately we seem to be surrounded by duchesses—handsome, tall, graceful, stylish. They approach us, then float away. They toss their heads, move their arms and elbows aristocratically, look beautiful and self-possessed. Ah! if Mr. Fitly could only make us like unto those duchesses! A wave of the hand, and the duchesses disappear. They are but model-girls, employed by Mr. Fitly to spend several hours a day in putting on and off his gowns for the inspection of his patrons.

If we like any one of those model dresses, he will build us one in exactly the same style, or bring about such alterations as our particular make-up demands. His cheapest tailor-made gown will cost twelve guineas; but he does not confine his genius to tailor-mades—he will manufacture any sort of frock that the heart of woman may desire. Seated at a table is a young lady who is a lightning sketch artist, and will design a gown on paper in three minutes. If it is a handsome reception gown it may cost us forty guineas, but when we get it on, it will to all and sundry " proclaim the man," *i.e.* Mr. Fitly, and to have it known that one is dressed by Mr. Fitly is supposed to make any normal woman reasonably happy.

FINISHING TOUCHES.

What do you say? You have the most beautiful twelve-yard bit of crêpe-de-chine, with your linings, etc. etc., that you desire made up? Come with me by 'bus to Madame Suburbia (she is really an Englishwoman), who does business at Walham Green. She is one of the "ladies'-own-materials-made-up" dressmakers, and very smart and clever

establishment where you will find a limited company, ready to take your order for dinner, fish, fruit, salad, meat and all, on the ground floor, and then, a flight or so up, which flight you take in a lift, you will find seated at a table the firm's own special artist, who will render you valuable assistance in the ordering of your next week's "party

MODELS BEFORE A CUSTOMER.

she is, too, for she spends one day of every week going about "stealing styles," as she vivaciously puts it—that is, looking into the West-End shop windows to see what is the very latest, and then going home and copying the things for her customers at the price of thirty shillings or two guineas, they supplying their own materials.

Are you in a great hurry to order a dress and to-night's dinner at the same time? Jump into a hansom, and come to an

dress." What would this smart young woman suggest for, say, twenty-five guineas?

"Ivory white lisse, tucked from the waist down, frills at hem of lisse and satin mingled, headed by jewelled embroidery. Might not the corsage be of tucked lisse to correspond with berthe of jewelled embroidery? Lined with very good silk, of course, madam; and you say you have some lace of your own? Yes, madam, we *could* do it for twenty-two guineas! I would advise you, madam, by all means to have the tucks running in the way I have said, because you are not tall. They will add greatly to your height!"

Ah! This particular young woman is an artist, just as was Madame Swagger, the milliner, who knew at a glance that Lady de Blank must not wear magenta! She has quickly noted that you are short, and she uses her wits in designing a gown to make you look tall. It is for these "little things," which are, after all, such very big and important things, that one must pay.

Here comes the costermonger girl, aspiring to a new hat and dress for Derby Day! She will not patronise Miss Stitchem, of Clerkenwell. Not she! She belongs to one of the "Clothing Clubs" of the East-End, paying her shilling or shilling and sixpence every week, till there comes the time when she desires twelve yards of purple velveteen and a glorious ostrich feather. Think you she will wear the threepenny three-farthing tips which delight the heart of 'Arriet 'Obson? No, indeed! If she has not already put enough money into the "Clothing Club" to cover the cost of the velveteen and the plume, she can get them just the same, promising to continue paying in her weekly instalments. So for the velveteen she considers two shillings and a penny-ha'penny a yard not too

much; and for the plume, what is twenty-five or thirty shillings? They will put it in the hat at the "Clothing Club" for her, or she can do it herself, and then she goes in search of Miss Cutter, who, perhaps, resides near Tottenham Court Road, and will make up the purple velveteen for fifteen shillings and sixpence.

Your house-parlourmaid and cook will not pay quite so much for dressmaking as will the coster-girl. They find dressmakers in the East-End and the West-End who consider ten-and-sixpence or twelve-and-sixpence a satisfactory reward for the time and trouble they spend upon a dress to be worn on an "afternoon out."

What money it costs, what time it takes, what work it gives, this clothing of the female portion of Living London! Even dowager-countesses find pleasure and profit in the millinery business, and the modern Madame Mantalini may frequently be seen nowadays in London, keeping up appearances for her devoted, dependent Mr. Mantalini out of the profits of dressmaking! Thanks to them all, from Madame Smartly near Bond Street to Miss Stitchem of Clerkenwell, the women of London may all be clothed, most expensively or most cheaply, or for a moderate price.

IN READINESS FOR DERBY DAY.

THE PARROTS' AIRING PLACE.

THE ZOOLOGICAL GARDENS.

By RICHARD KEARTON, F.Z.S.

KING VULTURE.

HIDDEN away in the green recesses of Regent's Park, where a stranger might consider himself in the country were it not for the dull roar of Living London, the Zoological Society has its magnificent collection of between two and three thousand animals in palaces, pens, and ponds, scattered over a space of thirty odd acres of land. This enormous crowd, representing the wild life of every corner of the earth, gives employment, direct and indirect, to more than one hundred persons, and is visited annually by considerably over half-a-million people.

The Society was founded in 1829, and now consists of something like three and a-half thousand Fellows and Corresponding Members, the former of whom are able to exercise the privilege of free admission to the gardens during any day of the week, and are in addition supplied with a liberal number of tickets for the use of their families and friends.

Sundays are reserved exclusively for the benefit of Fellows and their friends, and during what is known as the "London Season" the Zoo forms one of the favourite resorts of fashion and beauty. The hot dusty days of July and August, however, work a complete change, and, as soon as the class whose pleasant lot it is to bask by the sunny sea or drink in the heather-scented air from the purple mountains of the North has taken its departure, Sunday tickets are handed over to servants and others.

Monday is the great day of the week at the Zoo. The price for admission is then lowered from one shilling to sixpence for adults; and cockneys and countrymen alike take advantage of the concession and jostle shoulder to shoulder in one gazing, wondering, happy crowd.

The keepers start work at six o'clock in the morning during the summer months, and an hour later in the winter. Sweeping out the yards and houses, as shown in the illustration on the opposite page, and preparing the day's rations for the animals are amongst the early morning duties of the men. Animals intended for food are slaughtered in the gardens, and great care is taken that all such creatures shall be in a healthy condition and capable of walking to the shambles.

Some idea of what it costs to feed such a huge menagerie may be gathered when it is stated that the meat and forage bill for one year mounts up, according to the Society's annual report, to over £4,000. It would be even greater were it not for the amusement visitors derive from feeding many of their favourites. For instance, the Bear that is here shown on the pole and its companion are seldom fed by the keepers during the summer months, and at the time our photograph was taken the larger of the pair of bruins occupying the pit was too fat to climb the pole. He was extremely selfish, however, and, when he saw his companion getting what he evidently considered more than his share of buns, flew into such a wild paroxysm of rage that he bit himself until the blood flowed down his shaggy coat.

Bears are the most arrant cadgers, and one old Grizzly, dwelling next to the Polar Bear's den, has learnt a trick which does great credit to his intelligence. He has discovered that one of the bars of his cage has a little play in its fastenings, and when he sees a visitor coming along he slips a paw beneath it and by gently working the piece of iron up and down produces a loud tinkle, which hardly ever fails to attract attention or earn a share of the buns and biscuits so much beloved in Beardom.

AT THE BEAR PIT : REACHING FOR A BUN.

The liberality of visitors armed with paper bags full of provisions often far outruns their knowledge of the feeding habits of the creatures on whom they attempt to confer a dietary favour, and it is laughable to watch a grown and apparently educated man gravely offering a Golden Eagle a penny bun or a Kestrel Hawk a milk biscuit.

It is sometimes difficult during the dark winter months to induce many of the feathered members of the collection to take an adequate amount of nourishment. They will not feed unless they have sufficient daylight to do so by, and when a London fog suddenly enwraps the Metropolis in its inky folds many of them mistake it for night and retire to roost.

If any of the animals are taken ill they are not, as might be supposed, removed to some building in the nature of a hospital, for if they were, the effects of removal and new surroundings

SWEEPING OUT THE WILD GOATS' YARD

READY FOR A MEAL.

by saying that the photographer was a dentist engaged in measuring the Hippopotamus for a new set of teeth.

Animals have their little moods just like human beings, and very small happenings will ruffle their tempers. The old Hippopotamus referred to above is a very fickle jade. In the ordinary course of things she will, when lying under water in her tank, come up to breathe every two minutes on an average, but if any alterations or repairs are being done close by she "turns nasty," as the young keeper puts it, and will remain under water for more than double that time. The elder keeper says that he has known her disappear absolutely for as long a period as twenty minutes.

The most popular animal in the menagerie is undoubtedly the Elephant, whose wonderful

would retard rather than expedite recovery. The sick creature is, therefore, coaxed by all sorts of ingenious devices to take its food.

If a specimen dies and its dissection is considered likely to lead to anything in the nature of an enlightening discovery in regard to the disease which has proved fatal, its body is straightway conveyed to the Prosector's operating chamber, and, in the case of a large animal, opened by a staff of experienced assistants. When the Prosector has made his *post-mortem* examination, which sometimes lasts three or four days, he communicates the result of his researches to the members of the Society in the form of a lecture.

The greatest feat in dentistry probably ever performed on a huge animal was accomplished by the late Mr. Bartlett, who removed one of the upper tusks of the old male Hippopotamus, the father of the one shown in the above illustration. To obtain this picture my brother, Mr. Cherry Kearton, was obliged to accompany the keeper into the yard whilst I stood outside listening to the remarks of a much puzzled crowd of men and women, who could not understand why the monster's mouth was being photographed. By and by a brilliant idea struck an old woman at my elbow, and she explained the situation to the satisfaction of her friends

CHIMPANZEE AND KEEPER.

trunk, great size, strength, docility, and intelligence appeal powerfully to the youthful imagination. What child could go to the Zoo and come away happy without having had an Elephant ride? It would be *Hamlet* with the Prince of Denmark left out; and some idea of the extent to which this amusement is indulged in can be formed when it is stated that a single animal has been known to carry eleven hundred children upon its back during the course of one day. I stood

incidents of history weighed heavily on her. Not far away a shaggy-maned monster, such as we are accustomed to see in pictures typifying Britain, lies stretched on his side fast asleep with an admiring crowd of schoolboys gazing proudly at him. A Tiny Tim, all there but the long scarf, perches on his father's shoulder at the back of the crowd and says, "Yes, that's 'im, dad, that's 'im what bit Livinstin' in my book," and the momentary gleam in his sickly little

AT TWOPENCE A TIME.

by one afternoon whilst the Elephant walked ponderously between the landing stages with its freight of passengers, and was amused at a youngster who refused to quit his seat until one of a crowd of admiring aunties had bought him "another ticket." He had already indulged in four Camel rides and his second or third on the Elephant, and was still gaily extracting twopenny tickets from his feminine relatives when I left.

In the Lion House the great members of the Cat-tribe dwell. Here is Kruger's Lioness, looking sad and solemn as if the chequered

eyes testifies his satisfaction at having met an old travel-book friend in the flesh.

Nearly all maneless Lions are mistaken for Lionesses, and the signs of sex on the name-card fastened in front of each den are not understood by one person out of every hundred, judging from the remarks overheard whilst standing by. It is here one sees the budding Landseers at work. An artist told me that whilst engaged upon a life-sized picture of a tiger's head, the animal caught sight of its finished eye on the canvas, and after gazing with rivetted attention upon it for several seconds flew into a great rage. And from my knowledge of the peculiar influence exercised over wild animals by anything in the nature of an eye, I do not think the gentleman was exaggerating the verities of his brush. It is not every artist, however, who, after setting up his or her easel in the Lion House, can paint an animal like the gentleman in question, and, judging from what one occasionally sees, some of them are deeply guilty of the eternal human weakness of trying to dodge the elementary drudgery of their craft and attempting to paint before they have learned to draw.

The Lions, Tigers, Leopards, Jaguars, and other animals are fed during the summer months at four o'clock in the afternoon, and just before that hour visitors may be seen streaming from all quarters of the gardens to see the great cats gnaw their meat and listen to the deafening roar of the king of beasts who gives tongue by way of grace. Two other interesting scenes are the feeding of the Pelicans and the Sea-lion.

The Monkey House supplies the real fun of the fair at the Zoo, and it is here one sees the supreme happiness of childhood—especially if someone has eluded the vigilant eye of the keeper and succeeded in surreptitiously smuggling a reel of cotton into one

MUZZLING A VICIOUS ALLIGATOR.

of the large cages tenanted by a number of small monkeys. On such an occasion I have heard the building ring with peals of delighted laughter at the droll tricks the nimble little fellows in the cage played with each other and the unravelled thread.

In the Ape House, where the far-famed Chimpanzee "Sally" used to dwell, is found the highest degree of animal intelligence, and often the dryest of human wit. One day I heard a little boy exclaim whilst looking at an Orang Outan, "Oh, ma, isn't he like a working-man?" and an elderly lady express a wish that she might be able to "stay for ever with the dear creature."

Here I have seen poor old Sally make a bouquet of straws and place it in the button-hole of her keeper, and later on a successor feed "the baby" (a younger member of the species living in a cage close by) with a spoon for the edification and amusement of an admiring crowd.

HUNGRY PELICANS.

The King Vulture—of which a photographic reproduction is given on p. 344—attracts a good deal of attention during the summer months (when he and his companion are on view) by reason of his beautiful fawn or cream colour, which renders him the handsomest bird of his family. This species is a native of tropical America, and when at home lives upon snakes and carrion, from which it drives all other species.

The stock of specimens is constantly being replenished from four sources—gift, purchase, a number of Parrots are given an airing outside the house devoted to these birds.

The head keeper told me one day, in answer to an inquiry, that the animals are wonderfully quiet at night time. During the autumn months the birds listen to the cries of migrants flying over lamp-lit London on their way to the sunny South, and cock their heads on one side as if trying to detect their friends passing high overhead. During his nocturnal rounds of inspection, this gentleman once had the great satisfaction

FEEDING THE SEA-LION.

exchange, and breeding ; and it is surprising when one comes to examine the history tablets on the pens and dens how many of the specimens have been born under our dull English skies.

On rare occasions animals have succeeded in escaping from their cages in the Zoo, and in one instance a monkey that had gained its freedom had to be shot because it terrified the Antelopes to a point of danger which rendered this drastic course necessary. Small feathered specimens have from time to time been stolen from the Parrot House, and on one occasion a Bell Bird was abstracted by some cruel miscreant who wrung its neck. During suitable weather of discovering how the Giraffe disposes its abnormally long neck whilst it sleeps, namely, by lying it along its side, and resting its head in the hollow between the front of the thigh and the ribs.

Some of the specimens in the collection are very spiteful towards their fellow captives, and the best places to witness the bullying cowardice of the strong when their interests clash with the weak are at the Wolf Lairs and the Reptile House. Old Alligators sometimes turn vicious and kill younger and weaker members of their species. They have in consequence to be muzzled and put under restraint, as shown in our illustration on the opposite page.

LOADING UP AN ANIMALS' VAN.

About twenty years ago, when Regent's Park could shake hands with the open country, numbers of Reed Warblers bred every summer in the Gardens; and the unwelcome visits of Wild Duck rendered it difficult to keep the species on different ponds pure bred. A Raven and a Magpie have voluntarily come to live in the Gardens. In the spring-time the latter goes forth in search of a mate, and upon returning builds a nest close by the Zoo. The former bird in all probability escaped from a private cage somewhere in the Metropolis.

A list of duplicate animals for sale is kept at the Superintendent's office, and the illustration above shows the keepers hard at work in the early morning sending away a vanload of superfluities to the docks to be shipped for Calcutta. New animals that have just arrived after a long voyage are often taken in while the average citizen sleeps.

The keepers are without exception the most amiable set of men I ever met in my life. In spite of the Secretary's admirable "Guide to the Gardens," and the plans and printed notices scattered up and down the grounds like daisies on a village green, the poor fellows are pestered to death by questions which are fired off at them incessantly from early morn till dewy eve. When a man can answer with pleasant politeness the same inquiry half a dozen times in as many minutes, and the question contains a strong element of absurdity, I reckon he has succeeded in chaining down a great part of the old Adam within him. A strange thing is that visitors will repeatedly ask for something which was removed before even they themselves were born from where they expected to find it.

When the summer is over and gone, the military bands cease to play in the grounds on Saturday afternoons, the Elephants and Camels discontinue giving happy children rides upon their backs, many of the waitresses are discharged by the refreshment contractors, and a sense of forgottenness, so far as the public is concerned, settles down upon the great menagerie.

A SIESTA.

STUDENTS AT DINNER.

WIG AND GOWN IN LONDON.

By HENRY LEACH.

THERE is nothing in all London or in London life which is so essentially of itself and of naught else as Counseldom, the small uneven area on the boundary of the City where stalk in sombre wigged and gowned dignity the men of higher law. The Middle and Inner Temples, Lincoln's Inn, and Gray's Inn are the Legal Quarter in a fuller and more complete sense than that in which any other little piece of the great Metropolis is claimed by any other profession.

We talk of the machinery of the law, by which we usually mean not so much the minor engines which work the police and county courts and bring about the conveyance of property in good and proper order, as the greater, heavier, slower, and more rattling instruments which drive the King's High Courts of Justice. Then, every little pulley, every ounce of steam, every drop of oil, which make this machinery work, are manufactured here in this Legal Quarter. Parliament and the people supply the raw ingredients; the Inns do all the rest, and do it in a grandiose spirit of autocracy. They supply the judges, from the great Lord Chief downwards; they supply the King's

Counsel, and the barristers of lesser and lesser degree, to the humble, patient, and often weary " devil," and they are breeding up always within these their own preserves a new brood of the wigged and gowned species, who in good time will themselves carry on the great work of judgment-making at the standard rates of anything up to a thousand guineas a time—or more.

For nothing must be held so intact as the conservatism of the law. Great movements of reform must be held back from the

INVITATION TO A " GRAND NIGHT."

ponderous wooden gates of the Inns of Court; and, within, the whole legal family must in a very large professional sense lead the recluse life. Counsel may indeed be born in the Inns, they may grow up in the Inns, often enough they live altogether in and make the Inns their home, and they have been known upon occasion to die in the Inns, and thence be gathered to their legal fathers. Thus may they run the whole gamut of the life of law amidst the dirty bricks and tiny dusty windows of these strange old-world places.

The four Inns—the Inner Temple, the Middle Temple, Lincoln's and Gray's, as aforementioned—all amount to pretty much the same thing at the finish, standing in somewhat the same relation to each other as do the Universities. The student of law may enter his name at any of them and rise to the Bench. A man chooses his Inn, pays a guinea for a preliminary certificate, and, with or without a preliminary examination, according to circumstances, he is "admitted." Enter now the student into the life of the Inns, and into the study of all the forms and customs which appertain to the legal dinner.

A TEMPLE DOORWAY (2, PUMP COURT).

It is evident that one of the first principles of the law is the proper preservation of self, and it is instanced in the dinners of the Inns. It is their theory and their practice to turn from labour to refreshment with a soul-satisfying regularity, and there is a suggestion that any preponderance of attention should be on the side of the refreshment. The dinners of the Inns are the life and soul of the Inns; in fact, the dinners are the Inns. The rest at a pinch may pass. So the student is taught to dine in hall to begin

A TEMPLE FLOWER SHOW.

with. He must go on eating and eating, till in the fulness of time he becomes, almost as a natural consequence, a barrister.

Dining in hall is somewhat of a stately if light-hearted affair. The hall itself is an impressive place. There are huge oaken beams and beautiful carvings and there is a wealth of space along and above which produce a great effect. Everything is old, solid, and of the best ; and one feels somehow that these noble apartments have gone on and will go on increasing in their splendid worth like wines of a rare and exquisite vintage. So he

and rise with age and wisdom along the hall, till at the end in presidency is the senior barrister of the evening. The mess customs differ at each Inn ; but perhaps the one which has preserved most completely the traditions of the remote past is Gray's, where the senior of the mess drinks to every gentleman present during dinner, mentioning each one by name, only the students being given the " Mr. " prefix.

In all the Inns except the Middle Temple each mess carves for itself. The fare is good, but not elaborate. There are soup, meat, sweets

GOSSIP IN THE COMMON ROOM.

who dines in the hall of, say, Lincoln's Inn, remembers it. The speakers' voices, revelling in such rare acoustic properties as are here, glide from front to back and from side to side, with the clearness and resonance of bells, floating in their course past the large and handsome paintings on the walls of the legal lights of other days, heroes themselves of a thousand triumphs in elocution at the Bar, eaters themselves of the maximum of dinners in hall.

Lo! the first entry here of the student—unsophisticated, eager. He comes on his first night and takes his place at the very last mess in the hall. Each mess consists of four students, ascending in seniority, so that when the students have run out, the barristers begin

and cheese. When there is no soup there is fish instead, and, in deference to the considerable Roman Catholic membership of the Inns, fish is served on Fridays. The meal costs two shillings or half-a-crown per student, the former price ruling at the Middle Temple and the latter at the Inner, and as each student is entitled to half a bottle of claret or port it cannot be considered expensive. Here it may be incidentally mentioned that on Call nights and Grand nights the allowance of wine is increased to the extent of two bottles per barristers' mess, and one bottle per students' mess. In the glorious days of old at Gray's Inn four bottles used to be allowed per mess on Great Grand Night—occurring in the

Trinity term—but reason was found for a reduction.

These dinner details are not irrelevant, for, as I have indicated, the story of the Inns and of the legal life is to be told in dinners eaten. Meanwhile, the student is reading, and perhaps attending a few lectures, and in due course of dinners and exams. comes the night which will be for ever memorable, the Call Night, when the student is the student no longer. At the Inns the ceremonies of Call Night differ; but in each case the men are "called" before dinner and before the Benchers of the Inn. In the Middle Temple they are "called" in wigs and gowns, but elsewhere in gowns only. It is a great night, and one which the young barrister bloods feel should be "kept up." In the Middle Temple they have the special privilege of asking their friends to a Call party within the hall itself after dinner. Where the Inn does not recognise the need for a comprehensive conviviality, it is safe to say that a Call party is almost invariably held in the chambers of some barrister friend in the Temple or north of it.

Of the glorious deeds which have been performed on these occasions, when spirits are high and discretion is at a discount, there are many stories told. Thus now and then, after such a party, it is noticed curiously enough that the knockers have been removed from the doors of every adjacent set of chambers. The barristers who reign within are mightily offended, and a report is made to the Benchers, who govern the Inns. But Benchers are very, very human. Dreams of days of their own when youth had its fling are conjured up, and a reflection is made upon all the possibilities of "judicial ignorance," as sometimes exemplified by that great master of it who was once Mr. Justice Hawkins. Therefore, say the benevolent Benchers, they do not know what knockers are, and as for Call parties, no such things are recognised by the Inns, and therefore no members of the Inn could have been guilty. With no knockers and no Call party the case of the complainants falls to the ground. The ex-students receive a gentle hint that the knockers should be put back, and then the peace and goodwill of old reign in the Inn once more.

The Grand Night is a grand and most popular institution. Then the Benchers and the highest dignitaries of the law foregather with the barristers and students in their Inn and invite outside guests to dinner, often the most celebrated lights of other professions. It is strange that only solicitors are barred, an exception being made in the case of the President of the Incorporated Law Society. The City Solicitor has also been a guest. An invitation to Grand Night should never be refused. The dinner is good, the wines are excellent, and a stately decorum mingles with happiness and goodfellowship as the Benchers sit after dinner and drink wine with their guests. And, best of all, there is a strict rule of "No speeches," broken, as far as one can remember, only once, and that was when the King as Prince of Wales proposed the health of the late Lord Coleridge, Treasurer of the year, as far back as 1888, a circumstance which prompted the eminent lawyer to say, in response, that David was right when he said, centuries ago, "Put not your trust in princes." On these occasions the students sing songs to the accompaniment of the band in the gallery; at Gray's we see the passing of the loving cup, and the quaint drinking to the toast of "the glorious, pious, and immortal memory of good Queen Bess" (good friend of the Inn that she was); and all is pleasantry and contentment.

The Inns are largely residential. The records show that between three and four hundred persons live in the Temple. One Member of Parliament has lived there for over twenty years, and there are several popular K.C.'s—and some married ones—who abide there during the week. Very few barristers live in Gray's Inn, which has become quite a solicitors' quarter. Chambers in the Temple are comfortable enough for the bachelor, and they are cheap as London chambers go, for two or three panelled rooms —not to mention quite a large number of rats—may be obtained for £60 a year. There are housekeepers to make small meals, and if the resident is a member of the Inn he may obtain lunch and often dinner in the Common Room. But not all the names one sees in rows above each other on each side of the doors leading to the gloomy stone steps and thence to the oaks of the occupiers betoken

A "GRAND NIGHT" TOAST, GRAY'S INN.

"To the glorious, pious, and immortal memory of good Queen Bess."

actual residence—for even that of the Lord Chief Justice may be found at 2, Pump Court. The fledgling barrister is frequently poor enough in the world's goods, and works by night in Fleet Street for the living that the law does not afford him. For the advantage of him and others there is often posted up in the side windows of those old-fashioned wig shops in the Temple, amongst the advertisements of chambers to let, one which indicates that a person may secure the privilege of having his name painted on a door for a comparatively trifling annual charge.

The tragedies of the Inns—the life stories of men who have come enthusiastic to the profession of the law, and have utterly failed— would fill as many pages as are contained in a complete set of Law Reports. There are about eight thousand barristers, and only about one in eight is making a living. Amongst the juniors £2,000 to £3,000 a year is a large income. The life of the successful counsel is, of course, a glorious one. He is an idol of his Inn, a favourite in the Courts, a lion in society, and, most likely, an occasional debater in Parliament. When there is a

vacancy on the Bench his name may be mentioned, and in the fulness of time, if he thinks the dignity of a judgeship is worth the price that will have to be paid for it in loss of fees, he may go up. Not every leading counsel can afford to be a judge at £5,000 a year.

So do students, counsel, judges, come and go, and so life at the Inns in wig and gown is lived and will be lived. Terms begin in a hurry of activity and end again, and the Temple sleeps through the Vacation. Like most other things it has its seasons, and its fairest is in the summer term, when ladies in light muslins may be seen flitting through the squares and alleys or along King's Bench Walk ; when athletic counsel indulge in tennis on the green lawns ; and when for a day or two the Temple Flower Show is one of the attractions of a London season. Then, too, the Americans and the country sightseers ramble about. They take their guide books with them into the rare Temple Church, and they wonder that there can be such a peaceful spot in the heart of London as where the fountain plays and the birds twitter in the trees round about, while loungers and nursemaids sit on the benches listening.

IN FOUNTAIN COURT.

LOAFING LONDON.

By ARTHUR MORRISON.

IT is in London that the loafer attains his proper perfection—even the perfection of specialisation. The country hand in most trades—cabinet-making and cobbling, as well as loafing—is commonly perforce something of an "all-round man," and because of that fact, though a practitioner of broader experience, he fails to reach the specialised excellence of the Londoner in a single department. Out of London the loafer is rarely amenable to classification: he loafs how and where the hour's mood may lead him, dependent on an inborn instinct to keep him within gentle hail of fluid refreshment; and he is apt to fail of interest because of a certain sameness and lack of character.

But in the capital the principle of division of loafing is carried far: the East-End loafer differs in professional style from the loafer of the West; the Fleet Street loafer, the park loafer, the theatre loafer, the sporting loafer, the market loafer—all have their departments, their particular manners, their views of the world and of their own vocation, craft, or, as perhaps one should rather say, mystery. It is a fact that may easily escape the notice of the casual observer, who is deceived by certain characteristics common to loafers in general—such as exterior grease

THE THEATRICAL LOAFER.

and a convergence toward fully licensed premises.

Few indeed are the loafers who carry the label of their department plainly and visibly upon them; but among them, perhaps, the theatrical loafer is chief. Not the mere loafer about theatres, who is but a variety of the general loafer, but the loafer with a pretence to the appearance of an actor or a music-hall performer. He is in fact rarely either, but commonly belongs to the class of loafers who attach themselves as parasites to divers trades and professions; having the secret of somehow extracting a precarious living from a calling without working in it. So that when the corner of York Road was the chief hiring market in the "show" business (it has fallen from its estate of late), and since, in many places near the Strand, it was easy to observe the theatrical loafer at his best. Indeed, a thoroughfare in the Strand district has been informally rechristened "Prossers' Avenue" in his honour; the substantive "prosser" being derived from the verb "to pross," which is to persistently obtain liquid refreshment at the expense of anybody but the "prosser."

The theatrical loafer may not be an actor

THE CLUB LOAFER.

—often is not one, in fact—but in that case he is at pains to look more like one than the real thing. No real actor has so blue a muzzle, so heavy a slouch, nor such an amazing cock of the hat; and no real actor —except a very young one—obscures his speech with so much "gagging" and "fluffing" and "ponging," and the like technical slang. By his talk—and he will talk as long as you will minister to his "prossing"—you will judge him a genius of astonishingly long experience on the boards, reduced to his present pass by disgraceful professional jealousy and unscrupulous oppression. He will talk familiarly of "Fred" Leslie, "Johnny" Toole, "Teddy" Sothern, and even, if he judges you green indeed, of "Alf" Wigan, "Bob" Keeley, and "Jack" Buckstone. Sometimes it is possible that he may have seen some of the men he speaks of thus companionably—may even be an old actor who, through long idleness, has degenerated into a loafer, and is well content to remain one; though it would be unsafe to assume anything of the kind.

It is at times a little difficult to distinguish the loafer from an unfortunate actor who is really looking for work; but he is, in fact, a far cleverer man. The poor actor works hard and cannot get a living from the stage; the loafer never works at all, and yet somehow he lives, and it must be conjectured that the living comes, in some obscure alchemic way, from the stage. I have sometimes supposed that he may be a theatre charwoman's husband, or perhaps a dresser's. In any case there he loafs and "prosses," blue-faced, greasy and seedy, but with an air and aspect not to be described; not smart, not knowing, though intended to be both; but always aggressively suggesting the stage he has never stood on.

There are two other sorts of loafers who have in many ways a likeness to the theatrical loafer—the art loafer and the Fleet Street loafer. The art loafer we see less of nowadays than we did. Painters keep to their studios more and leave taverns alone, so that the loafer finds access difficult. He was (and is, in his survivals) a harmless loafer enough, and I almost think he must have some little income or allowance. Perhaps he, too, has a wife to keep him. He is less of a sponge, I fancy, than most other loafers, and though he can neither paint nor draw, he can wear a shapeless felt hat, an uncombed beard, and a seedy caped cloak, and he can talk studio "shop"; which things seem to satisfy his ambition well enough. I think he is near extinction.

But for the Fleet Street loafer something like immortality may be predicted. He has no distinctive uniform like the art loafer's. He is easily distinguishable, however, from the dock, market, or average East-End loafer by the fact that his dress, deplorably worn, damaged and greasy as it may be, has in cut and material always some faint pretension to gentility, always some hint of better days. The tall hat may be badly gone at the brim, may show traces of old cracks and knocks; but it has been oiled or tallowed streakily for months, even years, and perhaps of late has been anointed with something cheaper even than oil or tallow; and, moreover, it *is* a tall hat, which means a great deal. The coat may scarce have a button left, it may be rent, tied with string, pinned high at the throat because there is no collar—perhaps no shirt—beneath it; but it is a frock-coat, once black, and it once fitted the wearer—perhaps not this wearer—without a crease. I think I am often disposed to regard the Fleet Street loafer with some indulgence, because I have known more than one, and more than two, who were not always loafers; who worked, and worked hard; and whose misfortunes were as much the occasion of their downfall as their faults. Some of them had faults, it is true; but so have several other people I have met, who are not loafers at all.

But it is not with exceptions that my business lies, and probably the average Fleet Street loafer is no better than the rest. He does not work, but he gets a subsistence—a poor one, I fear—out of Fleet Street by means partly as occult as those used by other loafers, though not wholly. There is a process somewhat akin to "prossing" which is called "tapping," greatly in practice among loafers, but more prevalent in Fleet

Street than in most other parts. When Mr. Montague Tigg said, "We now come to the ridiculously small amount of eighteen-pence!" he was attempting to "tap" Mr. Pecksniff. In plain words, "to tap" is to beg money under a pretence of borrowing it. The "tapper" is an artist of many grades, through which he descends with more or less rapidity, according to skill and plausibility. He begins with sovereigns, or even more—though this is not in Fleet Street—and sinks by way of the half-sovereign, five shillings, and half-crown—many hang on a long time at the half-crown stage—to the shilling, the sixpence, the "few coppers," and even at last to the mere pitiful single penny.

I have a theory that many of the Fleet Street loafers are decayed Pall Mall and club loafers. When their clothes were good enough they loafed in Pall Mall, on the chance of catching a friend leaving a club and "tapping" him for a sovereign or so. One of the briskest and most successful of the Pall Mall "tappers" I ever knew would proceed by a sort of breathless stratagem. He would rush on his victim eagerly, as though pressed for every moment of time, feeling the while in his (own) waistcoat pocket. "My dear chap, *have* you change

THE CAB-STAND LOAFER.

for a sovereign about you?" Probably the victim hadn't. "Dear, dear, what a pity! (and he really was sorry, as you will soon see). Come, lend me five shillings then, quick!"—perhaps with some hazy reference to a cabman waiting round the corner. The victim, thus taken with a rush, would weakly produce the coins, which the "tapper" would instantly seize, with hasty thanks, and vanish. On the other hand, if the change were forthcoming, it was better business still. "Thanks, awfully—eighteen, twenty—quite right. Why

are often very impressive with green young journalists, who regard them as veterans of the profession, and are "tapped" with great freedom; and their complexions are the product of external dirt and internal Scotch whisky.

The Fleet Street loafer is often observed to merge into the sporting loafer. There are many about the neighbourhood who are, or who call themselves, bookmakers' runners; though they are rarely observed to run. And there are many who are Fleet Street

THE MARKET LOAFER.

where—what—where did I put—oh, there, I'll give you the sovereign to-morrow!" And the "tapper" would be gone round the corner in a flash, leaving the "tappee" standing staring and helpless on the pavement.

This sort of thing cannot endure for long, and the growing seediness of hat and coat makes operations in Pall Mall increasingly difficult. Club porters get uncivil, too, and victims grow warier. So the loafer declines on Fleet Street, and smaller "taps." But of course there are Fleet Street loafers who have never loafed anywhere else. Some came years ago to take the profession of journalism by storm, but have not begun storming, or even journalising, yet. These

loafers by locality, but sporting loafers by predilection. Not that they are expert in any sport, unless the "tapping" and "prossing" already mentioned be called sports. But they frequent the neighbourhood of the sporting papers, and are learned in spring handicaps. They do not wear tall hats, old or new, and their clothing is apt to be tighter about the legs than common, and to show signs of original loud tints.

The sporting loafer is by no means confined to Fleet Street, and he is often identical with the cab-stand loafer. The cab-stand loafer is a dingy and decayed imitation of the cabmen upon whom, it is to be presumed, he lives. He is like most loafers, a parasite upon a trade practised by more industrious persons, some part of whose earnings he seems to absorb by an occult process presumably akin to what men of science call "endosmosis." His counterpart is to be seen at the great markets, where the loafer takes the external appearance of the most dilapidated of market porters; being careful, however, never to push the resemblance to the extreme of lifting anything heavier than a quart pot. At Billingsgate he may gather sufficient energy to fill a paper bag with shells, topped with a stale refuse oyster or two, and either try to sell you the parcel of "oysters" cheap, or press it on you as a gift, in return for which he is ready to accept the price of a drink, as he takes care you shall understand. But such an exhibition of energy and enterprise is unusual, and for the most part the market loafer, like the rest, is content to merely loaf.

Comparatively with the market loafer the railway-station loafer is rare, though of course he exists. He is rare perhaps because the bustle of a great railway station disagrees with his contemplative nature: perhaps (and more likely) because passengers do not remain long enough for an acquaintance to be ripened to "tapping" point: and perhaps (more likely still) because unsympathetic officials, unworthily misconstruing the ardour of his gaze on piles of luggage, move him on. Such as he is, he has no distinctive features. I remember one who loafed for years at a large terminus, hanging about under the great clock, and now and again walking over to watch the passengers leave a train. He spoke to nobody, did not drink or smoke, and, since he was tolerated, presumably he did not steal. So that I wondered how he made his loafing pay. But at length I learned that the poor fellow was weak in

the head, and was merely waiting for his little son—who had been killed by falling out of a railway carriage on that line, four years before, on his way home from a holiday.

The most industrious loafer I have ever met is the chess loafer. To speak of an industrious loafer is to use a contradiction in terms, and it seems, moreover, something of

THE DENUNCIATORY LOAFER.

an injustice to call an ardent chess-player a loafer. But it is a fact that there are a number of men in London reduced to something much like a loafing life by their devotion to the game of chess. They are honest men, and no cadgers; but while they are not playing they are loafing, and the game seems to have on them the extraordinary effect of unfitting them for any other pursuit. I could name once-prosperous tradesmen who have let their businesses go to ruin while they played, and who now loaf, keen as ever ; and there are other men who never have been prosperous, and never will, for the same reason. One cannot refuse sympathy to so disinterested an enthusiasm, much as one may deplore its results.

The laziest loafer of all is undoubtedly the park loafer ; he will not even stand up to loaf. Indeed he will not often even sit. He lies on the grass and sleeps, embellishing the best of the London parks with a sprinkle of foul and snoring humanity, in every variety of rag and tatter, and scaring away the little children who would like to play there. To the ordinary intelligence it would seem that nobody—except Nebuchadnezzar — could extract a living from loafing of this sort. But the park loafer certainly eats, and his food is not grass ; for he brings it in a greasy paper, and casts the greasy paper abroad to aid further in the adornment of his particular

THE RAILWAY-STATION LOAFER.

garden. I think he must be—in many cases, at any rate—the "unemployed" loafer whom we used to see at Tower Hill. Not that all the men at the Tower Hill meetings were loafers, of course ; but certain benevolent people sometimes sent shillings for distribution, and they were mostly the loafers who got those shillings. I remember one making a dolorous and pathetic speech in which he assured the crowd that he had been out of work for twenty-eight years ; and, as he seemed of such an age as possibly to have been released from school somewhere about twenty-eight years before, the statement appeared quite credible.

Although the demonstrations are over, the loafer who gains a peaceful living by the simple expedient of being out of work is still common enough in the East-End and in other busy parts of town. He does pretty well, too, in the midst of a hard-working population ready to sympathise with a man who can find no market for his labour.

There is a sort of denunciatory loafer who frequents public places wearing a dingy red tie, making speeches and passing round a hat. He is in some sort allied with the out-of-work loafer, but he is a trifle more active, and by so much the greater nuisance. He collects pennies for loud denunciations, and he denounces whatever he judges the best "draw": the Government, the "privileged classes," the police, the drink traffic, the teetotallers— anything or anybody. He is a noisy half-brother to another red-tied loafer, who makes no public speeches, but "taps" and "prosses" on democratic principles ; being impelled by his devotion to humanity to reduce the general average of degrading toil by abstaining from it entirely, and being deterred by no false pride from bartering his sympathy with the downtrodden for as many drinks and small loans as the downtrodden may be induced to yield.

The list might be extended ; notably in the direction of the trade loafers, for there are few trades unattended by some sort of loafing retinue. There is even the boy loafer, in his varied degrees, "training on" as the sportsmen say, into a grown loafer as useless and unornamental as the rest ; but as we go the examination grows monotonous, and the classes tend to mingle in the floating mass of general Loaferdom.

OXFORD STREET.

REPRESENTATIVE LONDON STREETS.

By EDWIN PUGH.

TIME passes over many of the world's great towns and seems to leave no trace behind, but London has always been in a state of transition : ever growing and ever changing, it is, in a sense, no abiding city. Streets that a century ago were sacred to chaffering hucksters and small tradesmen are now the humming centres of a world's commerce ; districts that were once the favoured quarters of our aristocracy are given over to a cosmopolitan mob of alien immigrants. Yet in this seemingly chaotic huddle of houses there is a certain plan and purpose that has grown inevitably out of the needs of a swarming population.

" The East-End " and " the West-End " are phrases indicative of more than mere locality. When we talk of " the City " we do not always mean, strictly, the entire area of London over which the Lord Mayor rules. We have come to apply these terms to communities. " The West-End " could by no stretch of imagination be said to include Ealing, though logically that is the truer west end of London. The City proper contains within its borders streets utterly commonplace and even squalid ; but they have no place in the mental picture that those words " the City " conjure up. London is, in short, not to be rightly understood by a study of particular neighbourhoods, but by the study of such of her streets as can be said to be truly representative of any one distinct phase of her daily life.

And if I were pinned down to the selection of one such street I think I should choose Oxford Street, only stipulating that I be allowed to add to the stretch of thoroughfare bearing that name its miles of continuation, east and west. This would give me a road bisecting London from Hanwell to Barking almost straight and clear save for a little kink or two where it strikes the City. There is no other road which leads directly through London as this does, or reveals so many of its diverse aspects. A journey from end to

PICCADILLY.

NEW CUT, LAMBETH.

end of it would teach the average Cockney more about his native home than years of residence in one circumscribed neighbourhood.

It attains its fullest expression at Oxford Circus. Here it is part fashionable, part commercial. The bold sweep of Regent Street curves southward, cleaving a way between the muddle of nondescript byways that culminate in Soho and the stately streets and spacious squares lying on either side of Bond Street as far as Park Lane in one direction and Piccadilly in another. There is little that is impressive in the aspect of Oxford Street itself at this point, however; the buildings on either side form a higgledy-piggledy of mean, bare houses, edifices frankly utilitarian, and ambitious structures that fail of dignity for lack of congruous surroundings. It is its traffic, human and vehicular, that redeems Oxford Street from the commonplace. All sorts and conditions of men and women, from the tatterdemalion newsboy, hoarse and dirty, to the opulent society dame in her furs and silks, beside her shrivelled lord, meet and mingle here; and every kind of conveyance from a donkey-shallow bound for Covent Garden to a four-in-hand off to the races.

To no other spot in London does this description apply with the same exactness. Piccadilly Circus has its peculiar characteristics to be found nowhere else; and so has that confluence of thoroughfares at the Mansion House. Even Charing Cross draws a special leaven from the Strand, Pall Mall, Northumberland Avenue, the recruiting ground opposite St. Martin's Church, and the National Gallery. Oxford Street alone relies on no extraneous aid of striking effects for its distinctiveness. It is representative of average London; it has a solid, middle-class look about it; its pavements are thronged with the normal types of Cockney. It is London crystallised at its most obvious. *Outré* London must be sought elsewhere. It may be found in another street, primarily a mart as Oxford Street is, some miles away in the Whitechapel district.

This is Wentworth Street — a street of ugly, featureless houses, all built alike. Each ground floor is a shop, and the kerb on either side of the road is cumbered with stalls. As you worm your way through the press of people it is easy to imagine that you are in a foreign city. On every side are un-English faces, un-English wares, un-English writings on the walls. The accents of an unknown tongue assail your ears. Your companions are mostly women, Jewesses, the majority wearing the black wigs of the matron over their own scanty locks. There are blowsy and haggard mothers of clinging families; and full-blooded girls with dark eyes, languorously bold, ripe red lips, and ebon tresses. The men are of two kinds, the frowsy and the flash. Fish and poultry are the articles of commerce in which trade is most brisk. At every step you come upon a woman carrying a fluttering fowl or two, or a slab of fish in a basket with *kosher* herbs. There is bountiful good-humour and good-nature, too, or the beggars would not be so numerous. This is on week-days. On Sundays Wentworth Street is overshadowed by its more famous neighbour, Middlesex Street, popularly known as "Petticoat Lane," then a seething mass of chafferers, but on other days ordinary enough.

Another mart of a different sort, such a one as is to be found, but on a smaller scale, in any poor district of London, is the New Cut, Lambeth. Here the stalls are restricted to one side of the roadway. Jews are here too, but not preponderating. The goods exposed for sale are of every conceivable kind—there is no end to their variety; but they are, generally speaking, of a poor quality, shoddy or tawdry or pinchbeck. If a bad thing is ever cheap they touch the nadir of cheapness, however. Perhaps the most striking feature of the street is the placarding of the shops. Nearly every window is criss-crossed with slips of paper; nearly every article seems to have been exposed to a hail of tickets. At night the "Cut" shines forth murkily resplendent under the smoky glare of countless naphtha lamps. The eddying crowds go back and forth, and the costers bawl, and the quacks harangue, until voices and wares and customers are alike exhausted.

Yet another mart. It lies between St. Paul's Cathedral and Fenchurch Street, and comprises Cheapside, Poultry, Cornhill, Lombard Street, Threadneedle Street, Throg-

CORNHILL (FROM FRONT OF
THE ROYAL EXCHANGE).

morton Street, and scores of other byways intersecting these. Here there is no vulgar bellowing of hawkers. There are shops in plenty and itinerant pedlars of penny trifles in the gutters ; but these have no part in the mart. It is under the shadow of the Royal Exchange, in small offices high up or far back in lofty tiers of flats, in counting-houses concealed behind the mahogany and plate glass of pompous outer offices, that the trafficking is done. Outward and visible sign of all this stress of business is patent in the towering warehouses of Queen Victoria Street and St. Paul's Churchyard, and the never-ending procession of carts and waggons that lumber up and down. Seething black-hatted, black-coated hordes jostle one another on the pavements to an unending stir and uproar of slithering feet and rolling wheels. There is an atmosphere of feverish pre-occupation everywhere prevailing. Cheap-side is all too narrow to contain the press of vehicles and men that pours into it the whole day long. The wires that score the sky in a very catscradle are all too few for the impatience of these dealers in untold millions ; the hours too short to permit them even to be healthy in their habits of eating and drinking.

At the Mansion House the conclave of moving things and myriad noises reaches a climax and forthwith declines. In the several streets that suck up the City's output and scatter it eastward there is comparative peace. The rigours of the game abate ; there is even a frivolous market-place where live things may be bought, and a Monument to amuse the simple-minded. Beyond the Monument the river flows behind the turbulence of Lower Thames Street, riotous with unclean odours, darkened by tall ware-houses, cranes dangling ponderous burdens overhead precariously. This wealth of wharves and shipping is symbolised by the solid bank buildings in the narrow congeries of streets about Cornhill, where a chinking of gold and crisping of notes go on from ten to four in a subdued atmosphere of ordered calm. These are the streets of finance that feed the streets of fashion : Piccadilly and Bond Street with their shops that seem only to condescend to be shops, but take a very real revenge for their humiliation, notwithstanding, out of the elegant idlers who patronise them.

Bond Street owes its good fortune to an accident of birth : it is a street of such high repute that it scorns all ostentation. It is rather narrow and warped. Its houses have neither form nor comeliness, as a rule. But its neighbour, Piccadilly, only just misses mag-nificence. On its northern side it is worthy of its world-wide reputation ; the buildings are, for the most part, solid and responsible-looking ; the Royal Academy strikes a firm, austere note. On the southern side it is marred by some tasteless ornamentation that looms forth ludicrously beside the handsome frontages of some great hotels and galleries. St. James's Street, however, presents a goodly side view, terminating in a peep of the dark, mediæval-looking St. James's Palace. And, yet a little way ahead, bordering the hill, the pleasant boscage of the Green Park throws a welcome shade on the raised side-walk.

But Piccadilly only prepares us for the true splendours of the West-End. At Hyde Park Corner Park Lane makes a paltry exit. To realise the beauty of Park Lane it is necessary to turn into it from the Park. Emerging from Stanhope Gate you confront an imposing mass of monumental masonry that is only excelled by the show of the great hotels in Northumberland Avenue. There is no prevailing scheme of architecture ; each mansion preserves an individuality ; but the general effect makes for a grandeur that is tenderly tempered by the bright greenness of the Park itself. This is Millionairedom ; but a few bijou residences are sandwiched in between the palaces for the delight of those mice in the temple of

Mammon who, though comparatively poor, are superlatively select. It is all rather overbearing, perhaps ; and not to be compared for an instant with the noble vistas of Kensington. There, London is at its best and bravest and most beautiful.

The ample main road winds gently along through a verdant avenue of trees, limitless on the northern side ; on the south chequered by grey courts of stately houses. Just at the beginning of Kensington High Street there is an ugly wry twist and a brief sordidness of shops and unlovely houses ; but thereafter the road flows wide and smooth once more, ever opening up new wondrous prospects of mingled houses and trees. Hereabout is the abode of fashion and rank ; life moves with a luxurious leisureliness. In the streets there is evidence of a polished, cushioned state of being in the sumptuous equipages bowling swiftly along, in the tone of courtliness of which we catch a casual echo now and again, and the nicely-ordered etiquette that allots two men and a boy to one man's work. At night the windows are softly aglow ; beauty regally adorned trips

CHEAPSIDE (FROM THE MANSION HOUSE).

from kerb to doorway on an aristocratic arm ; the air is subtly murmurous with music.

A far cry from here to the Borough High Street, where from numberless obscure by-ways a teeming people congregate in a raucous glare of shop-lights. Day in this neighbourhood discloses everywhere, trickling into the main road, a very plague of squalid alleys, eloquent of poverty most abject. The High Street itself is lively and exhilarating ; St. George's Church, standing out boldly at

monotony of the ravelled skein of roofs. The area these districts cover is immense, yet every house is congested with tenants. You may pass through slum after slum, and find them all essentially alike : narrow lanes, unevenly paved, between high, barren tenements, with parallelograms of door and window accenting their dreary uniformity of construction. The dwellers are, for the most part, stunted, deformed, sickly, without a thought beyond the satisfaction of the day's

HIGH STREET, KENSINGTON.

its southern end amid low-growing trees, lends a touch of grace to the scene. Such roads as this you will find traversing a score of similar districts round about—in Walworth, Bermondsey, and over the water, from White-chapel to Silvertown. They are like mighty rivers in a wilderness of misery and want. The horrid streets lie cheek by jowl in serried rows between them, dark, dirty, forbidding, differing from one another in no particular save the depth of their degradation. There are gaps in the universal drabness ; here and there church spires point the way to Heaven ; theatres, music halls, and halls of science, institutes, libraries, and hospitals for the healing of mind and body, break the deadly

needs. In these regions of famine hunger is a common bed-fellow ; pain and weariness and cold the companions of every hour. The people work joylessly, talk witlessly, play stupidly, employing earnestness only when they bicker or fight or sin.

How different these grim realities from the mimic life of the Strand ! Here are the haunts of the mummer and the garish temples in which he struts his hour ; here are such contrasted edifices as Exeter Hall, scene of religious congresses ; Charing Cross Station, key of the Continent, a world's centre to which all nations gravitate ; the frivolous Tivoli, and sombre Somerset House frowning on the academic calm of King's College. Coutts's, oldest of old-fashioned banks, lies within hail of the Cecil, one of the newest of new-fashioned hotels. St. Mary-le-Strand Church dominates the purview, a haven of rest, shadowing that bitter battle-ground of ignoble passions, the cloistral-looking Law Courts. And this jumble of contrasts is reproduced in the wayfarers who haunt its classic precincts. Every grade and every order of society are represented. The humdrum types to be met with in Oxford Street—that are so truly representative because they *are* so humdrum—

It is large enough to tolerate even Bohemia. But the permanent home of Bohemianism is far away : in Brixton, where music hall artistes congregate ; in Avenue Road, St. John's Wood, and Holland Park, favoured of painters and histrions ; at Hampstead, and in strange odd nooks and crannies everywhere. Perhaps the most typical Bohemian colony, however, exists in Bedford Park, a suburb of dainty, rococo villas, set prettily among trees. But there is no one district of London corresponding to the Latin Quarter of Paris. The average Cockney is a hard-

THE STRAND.

are supplemented here by notable additions. The noble and the famous ; the rich and the wise ; the successful and the submerged, all flock to this place. Faces that you have never seen before you recognise instantly and tack a famous name to. Other faces, bearing signs of kinship with these great ones, flit slinkingly by, the nobleness struck out of them by failure and disappointment. Art and the camp-followers of art, science and the drama, sport, and religion and law have their emissaries here. The Strand is a blend of such seemingly irreconcilable elements that it might almost be said to epitomise the national character of the English. It is serenely tolerant of all things and of all men.

headed, practical person of an unromantic turn of mind, who gets what he can out of life as cheaply as possible and does not bother about his environment so long as he is comfortable.

Suburbia is his ideal dwelling-place : that belt of Villadom which engirdles London, and is essentially the same at Peckham as at Hornsey. But Suburbia is not all villas. In every district it is dominated by great, wide thoroughfares, closely resembling one another, arteries of traffic, alive with crowds from morn to midnight, and eternally thunderous with a roar of business. These streets—of which Holloway Road is a typical example—are formed of the strangest jumble of buildings imaginable. Monster

47

emporiums, ablaze with light, break the crazy roof-line of a row of hovels ; the cat's-meat shop and the palatial premises of a limited liability company's enterprise stand side by side ; the latest thing in music-halls and the penny gaff confront one another, rivals for the same public favour. Such streets often extend for miles under various aliases ; at night they are brilliant with a pearly radiance of electricity. The Hooligan and the professional City man, the artisan and the clerk, promenade the broad pavements, taking the air. Young men and maidens, their day's work done, meet for mingled purposes of flirtation and horse-play. Running out of the road on either hand are quiet, staid streets, impeccably residential, each with its garden-patch, back and front. There are other streets that have come down in the world, but these are outside the pale of

recognition : they belong properly to that nebulous territory, " the East-End."

London contains many more streets that might loosely be dubbed " representative," but in reality they reveal only bizarre aspects of the life of the great City : Wardour Street, for instance, the immemorial resort of old curiosity-mongers, tortuous and frowsy and prematurely aged—a very miser among streets, with its vast wealth of hidden treasure, costly and rare. Saffron Hill, again, the Italian quarter, redolent of garlic and picturesquely filthy ; and the streets of the Soho cosmopolitan quarter, compact of beetle-browed, dingy dwellings, home of political refugees, blacklegs, cheap restaurateurs, and French laundresses : these and others. But, since they are unique rather than representative, they hardly fall within the scope of this chapter.

HOLLOWAY ROAD.

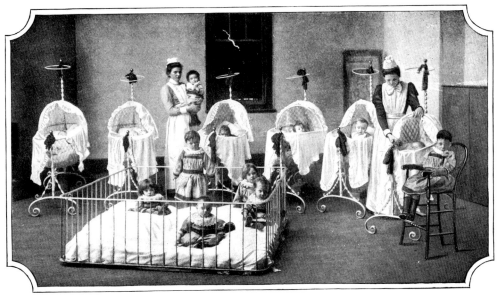

MARIE HILTON CRÊCHE: THE COTS.

CARING FOR LONDON'S CHILDREN.

By D. L. WOOLMER.

GODMOTHER London may be grave with experience, but she shows no sign of senile decay. Indeed, as her foster brood increases so she renews her youth, and as time brings her foster grandchildren and great-grandchildren she rises to the responsibilities, and conceives fresh and grand schemes for their use and benefit. Long before a call to the great and valiant nations of the earth to "take up the white man's burden" stirred up a spirit that developed in various enterprises, the heart of Great

MARIE HILTON CRÊCHE: MEAL TIME.

Britain throbbed with the discovery that a burden lay very near home. Like the giant Christopher, personified Benevolence responded to the voice of a little child whose only language was a cry in the darkness, and bent his shoulder to the task. What though the unexpected weight made him stagger, he would hold the small traveller aloft above the swirling stream or perish in the attempt. St. Christopher, struggling along in the centre of the current, making his last and best journey, might represent one aspect of London of to-day. The end of the story has yet to be written; the concluding chapters may or may not find their place in the library of posterity.

Numerous portraits of a St. Christopher of the eighteenth century, and various scenes in his life, form part of a collection of prints and pictures in the Foundling Hospital. A gentleman from wig to shoe-buckles, in the costume of an English sailor of the period, is considering the apparition of an infant lying in a basket at his feet. His poised walking-stick helps to indicate an air of general perplexity. Perhaps he shares the sentiments of the immortal Samuel Weller when he felt that "somebody ought to be whopped, only he did not exactly know whom." That baby is not the somebody, so, no one else being in evidence to suffer vicarious punishment, the stick is transformed into a shepherd's crook, and the child is conveyed to a place of safety.

A small guide, in the antique costume of dark brown jacket and trousers and scarlet waistcoat, engaged in conducting a visitor through the institution, readily lectures on the picture, and explains its meaning. That is Captain Thomas Coram, who picked up more than one little outcast, and determined to find a home for them and for other deserted infants in London.

A fragment of the eighteenth century has been well preserved within the gates of a green enclosure opening on Guilford Street. A constant stream of young life saves the venerable institution from decay. Childhood is always being born, and is always—sad to say—liable to desertion. The 550 children under the care of the authorities of the Foundling Hospital have all been forsaken by their fathers, and the burden of their maintenance has been undertaken by the governors in the hope of giving both the mothers and their firstborn a chance of supporting themselves worthily.

The light-hearted children playing in front of the only home that they have ever known show no consciousness of any burdens at all. The large family extends beyond the gates. Those who go out into the world still remain the institution's adopted children; while its infants are sent into the country, where they spend the first four or five years of their lives. Fresh air is a favourite gift of modern benevolence to London's potential citizens of to-morrow.

It is difficult to realise that in the great city a baby starts on its life march every five minutes. Thousands of little feet, destined to ache and bleed beneath their load, are bound to remain in the desert of bricks and mortar. Bands of love even more unyielding than rough apron-strings tie them to hardworking mothers, who for the sake of these atoms of humanity will keep a hold of life, hope, and respectability. To meet the need of the great army of women breadwinners, a crèche, or day nursery, now forms part of nearly all the organisations in town described as missions. The only private nursery of the slums is frequently a hotbed for seeds of the various ills to which flesh is heir, and calculated to produce wastrels and invertebrates who will by and by become a charge on the State.

Somewhere about thirty years ago two crèches for infants from three or four weeks old upwards, irrespective of creed or nationality, were started, the one in the East and the other in the South-west end of London. Mrs. Hilton's, in Stepney Causeway, is now known as the Marie Hilton Crèche, and is a part of the National Association for the Reclamation of Destitute Waif Children, which owes its existence to Dr. Barnardo. St. Peter's Crèche, Chelsea, extends its influence far beyond its own parish, and is double its former size. The East-End women toilers pay 1d. a day for each child. This fee covers not only the cost to them of food, but also of attendance if the poor little applicants are suffering from complaints that would shut them out of an ordinary day nursery, but which are yet not serious enough for their admission to a hospital.

One baby is sometimes pronounced a "handful." What is to be said of sixty-eight, all between the ages of three or four weeks and five years old!

"I sometimes think that a number together are more easily managed than one," the matron of St. Peter's Crèche answers to this remark ; "for they amuse each other. But sixty-eight are almost too many for this place. Our average for the year is forty a day, or between 11,000 and 12,000 attendances. The elder ones go to school, and come in for meals."

Let us take a peep inside a crèche for a moment. In the first room the younger inmates slumber in dainty white cots. A rosy-cheeked, curly-headed cherub opens a pair of blue eyes which fill with tears at the sight of strangers. He is lifted up and comforted, and exhibited by the matron as a "beautiful child." Near to him a bluish-white little ghost looks about him with an expression

IN THE FOUNDLING HOSPITAL GROUNDS.

A RAGGED SCHOOL UNION DINNER (CAMBERWELL).

of unnatural wisdom. Individuality is even more marked in the next room. A winsome child of three rises to her social duties, and plays the hostess gracefully. She runs to meet the matron and embraces her round the knees, and presents her hand with a smile of welcome to the visitors. Another of the same age is bent on proving that the newest rocking-horse is her own. When other arguments fail to convince a rival claimant for a ride she prepares to exercise the tyranny of tears. The favourite toy is a bone of contention which answers to the *Times* or the most comfortable armchair in a club for children of a larger growth. A sturdy, solid two-year-old stumps about in supreme indifference to the affairs of others, and one of his fellows is safely in pound—that is, within a large crib without legs, in which five children can take their siesta at one time.

The joys of "dining at my club" are not wholly at an end when the old age of childhood draws in amongst the slums. Poor children's dinners have become an institution. They were first organised by the Ragged School Union. The first of the autumn season of 1901, held under its auspices, may serve as a specimen of the entertainment given to thousands of underfed children throughout the winter.

"Camberwell Ragged School and Mission. Dinner twelve o'clock on Friday. Bring a spoon." The guests honoured with this invitation all belong to a neighbourhood described by a local tradesman as a "queer part," beset with danger for the inexperienced explorer. In all society it is convenient to classify acquaintances; on this occasion the master of the ceremonies has only invited the middle class on the visiting list. It is hard to realise that there is a set much lower than the seething mass at the doors of the hall. The same amount of crushing and squeezing would be attended with shrieks of pain or fright in a grown-up crowd; but the hungry children give vent to one cry only, that is for admission. Even after the tables are well furnished with 250 guests, there is no turning away of eager faces or lowering of outstretched hands until the sturdy caretaker disperses the crowd and shuts the door. When the last juvenile has clambered upstairs on all fours or been helped up by an elder, and all are seated at the long tables, a smile of expectancy expands the rows of faces. A slice of bread and a basin of soup thickened with peas and barley are served to each one, and they fall to with zest. In this and similar halls a dinner party, towards which the guests contribute a halfpenny each, is held throughout the winter once or sometimes twice a week.

London is said to be the maelström which surely draws to itself the wildest of modern nomads from the provinces. Ragged school and other missions are a means of saving the underfed children from being dragged into the criminal class. It is not always an unmixed evil when the young Ishmaels of society are cast off by their own people or cut themselves adrift. Tennyson asks:—

> Is it well that, while we range with
> Science glorying in the time,
> City children soak and blacken
> Soul and sense in city slime?

The street arabs need not be left to sink in the mire. The blackness of night in dark corners, under sheds or railway arches, is periodically pierced by a dazzling beam. It shoots from a vigilant eye, none other than a bull's-eye. Scurry like the flight of frightened rabbits ensues, but one urchin remains in the firm but kindly grasp of a policeman. " I ain't doing nothing," cries the wriggling captive; but his captor knows what he is about, and will not let him go. From this lump of city slime may be extracted valuable materials. In a few months the cowed, sullen face of the little vagabond is not very easy to recognise in the glow of the blacksmith's forge. Sparks fly merrily under vigorous blows which might descend with murderous effect from a Hooligan. The trades shops in Stepney Causeway under the National Waifs Association are Dr. Barnardo's factory for transforming young natives of No Man's Land into skilled artisans. Between 40,000 and 50,000 boys and girls, on the whole, have now been rescued, trained, and placed out in life by the Homes of which the trades shops form part. Some go to the Colonies, and 98 per cent. of the emigrants have succeeded in the struggle for independence. Miss Annie Macpherson was the pioneer who first took advantage of the discovery that Canada had an open door for London's crowded-out children. More than 7,000 have been helped by

Photo: London Stereoscopic Co., Ltd.

NATIONAL WAIFS' ASSOCIATION (STEPNEY): IN THE BLACKSMITHS' SHOP.

ALEXANDRA ORPHANAGE (HORNSEY RISE) : GOING TO BED.

Rise, where boys and girls enter from babyhood, and remain until nine years of age. For half a century Queen Victoria was a patron and friend.

Family life is the ideal set up by the managers of the Stockwell Orphanage, founded by the late Mr. C. H. Spurgeon for 500 boys and girls; in the Brixton Orphanage, founded by the late Mrs. Montague, for 300 girls; and in Miss Sharman's Home, Austral Street, Southwark, where a large family of 333, ranging in age from a few weeks to seventeen years, are under her care. To each elder girl within her gates is assigned a baby sister, and in the playroom every one has her own locker with her own pet toys and treasures. Ties of affection hold firm in spite of inevitable dispersion. The sewing class has a story to tell, with a pleasant flavour of romance, of unbroken attachment and of success in after life, for some of the garments, worthy of an exhibition of needlework, form part of the trousseau of a former inmate, now living in New York.

Not a few orphans, indeed, become the benefactors of their successors. The fine organ in the Memorial Hall of Stockwell Orphanage was presented by one of the ex-pupils who have used their training well, and the foundation-stones of the newest part cry out and tell with gladness of gifts of honest gratitude. For example, there is a record of how "Bray's bricks" were built in. Little Bray was dying in the Home, and he put all his savings, amounting to 4s. 6d., into the hands of the founder as a contribution towards the houses for girls which were added in 1882. Now, whilst 250 boys lead a sort of college life, 250 girls, under matrons in separate homes, practise

her, and she continues to receive them at the Home of Industry, 29, Bethnal Green Road, E., and to train and convey them to her Children's Home, Stratford, Ontario. Many sturdy farmers and farmers' wives are living witnesses of how well rescued waifs can be used to build up the Empire of Greater Britain.

If treasures are produced from unpromising materials, and worthy citizens from the flotsam and jetsam of humanity whose antecedents and early associations are generally sad, bad, or criminal, what may not be expected from those homes of innocence which abound for little children who are chiefly the legacies of deserving but unsuccessful parents?

When in 1758 a body of philanthropic gentlemen met at the George Inn, Ironmonger Lane, Cheapside, to open a home for twenty fatherless boys they set a snowball rolling. It grew into the Orphan Working School, which has educated more than 5,000 children, and has now 360 in its senior school at Maitland Park, and 124 in the Alexandra Orphanage, Hornsey

the domestic accomplishments intended to make them good servants or good house-wives. In the model laundry and in their kitchens and workshops they cultivate the art of self-dependence. This is a principle commended to the boys and girls alike.

What became of orphans and waifs of humanity before a modern St. Christopher attempted to lift them above the waves of this troublesome world? Of those who grew up the gallows greedily seized upon thousands, gaol fever devoured even more, and shiploads were carried abroad to transform an earthly paradise like Botany Bay into a hell. Even yet the great Reaper is more active than any philanthropist in carrying away infants from soul-destroying conditions. From such closely-packed quarters as the parish of St. George-the-Martyr He claims 189 in every 1,000. Those who contend with Death and Crime for the crowded-out children whom nobody cares to own generally take them into open fields and meadows, where the pure air is as the very breath of life to the feeble little frames. One institution after another moves farther and farther from the centre of life's hurly-burly. If the scope of this work allowed mention of the benevolent besoms that sweep the street tribes out of town, the Babies' Castle, Hawkhurst, founded by Dr. Barnardo when his old Tinies' House, Bow Church, over-flowed, the Princess Mary's Village Homes at Addlestone, and the Church of England Association for Befriending Waifs and Strays would have a prominent place. But the modern crusade to deliver childhood from distress is so extensive that even an attempt to produce snapshots of sample institutions, fostered by voluntary charity, actually in London must be of necessity imperfect. It is impossible to follow the great flock of Mother Carey's chickens that wing their flight from the *Warspite*, the training ship of the Marine Society, and from the *Arethusa* and the *Chichester*, under the National Refuges for Homeless and Destitute Children. To supply our ships with smart sailors made out of poor boys of good character is patriotic as well as benevolent.

What is the use of this expenditure of time, money, and labour? When a utilitarian community thus inquired what was the use of Franklin's discovery of the identity of lightning with electricity, the philosopher retorted, "Of what use is a child? He may become a man." All the possibilities of manhood are bound up in the little bundles that contain a spark of human life. They must not be lost; for the present generation is bound to hand on the heritage of its fore-fathers to posterity, not only as complete as when it received it, but with interest added to principal.

STOCKWELL ORPHANAGE : THE LAUNDRY.

A QUIET ROW : CHEAPSIDE.

KERBSTONE LONDON.

By GEORGE R SIMS.

GROUNDSEL.

NOT to be confused in any way with Costerland is Kerbstone London. The line of demarcation is broad. The coster-monger wheels his barrow or sets his stall down to the kerb in certain districts on certain nights, but the kerbstone merchant earns his living just where the pavement joins the roadway all the six days of the week, and may in certain localities be found there even on the seventh.

You want no guide to show you where to find this characteristic feature of London life. You have but to take your walks abroad through the great Metropolis, north or south or east or west, and there you will find the kerbstone merchant. You will need no introduction. The London "Camelot" will introduce himself. He will offer you his goods with the *aplomb* of the auctioneer or the whine of the mendicant, he will sell you the latest Parisian clockwork toy for eighteen-pence, or a boot-lace for a halfpenny. The newspaper hawker is not so common a kerbstone tradesman as he used to be, for he has taken of late years to advantageous corners and to places against which he can lean his back; but still in many thorough-fares he plants one foot on the kerb and displays his contents bill after the manner of an apron, or lays it down in the gutter and puts stones upon it, or nails it to the wood-paving, renewing it from time to time as the 'bus and cab wheels stain and obliterate the battles, the murders, and the sudden deaths.

But kerbstone character varies largely, not only according to the locality, but according to the day. On Satur-day night the kerb is a great market. In be-tween the coster-mongers' stalls allowed in certain thoroughfares on poor man's mar-ket day, men, women, and children post themselves, and cry their wares aloud.

There is an element

CLOCKWORK TOYS.

of the fair in the east and in the south of London, for the weighing chair, the shooting gallery, and the try-your-strength machine are to be found by the pavement's edge. These things are, of course, only possible where the space in front of the shops is broad, and the traffic principally pedestrian. But there are kerbstone merchants who take their stand wherever a street market is established. Among them you will generally find the man or woman with a tray of shirt-studs, two a penny; the comic song vendor; the man with cheap purses and brooches; the man who has a preparation for the erasure of grease stains and experiments on the caps of the company; the man with the toy microscopes — "all the wonders of Nature for a penny"; the doll seller; the man with egg-pipes—contrivances looking like pipes from which, when blown through, a paper rooster appears; the girl with bunches of flowers; the man with fresh roses which he has just washed at a neighbouring tap; the woman with boot-laces or camphor; the seller of needles; the blind musician; the groundsel seller; and the man with walking sticks.

And there are specialities of certain neighbourhoods. In one you find barrows of old books; in another barrows of old boots. In High Street, Marylebone, there is a small boy who sells home-made crumpets on the kerb. In Islington there was until lately an old gentleman who appeared regularly at the edge of the kerb on Saturday nights, with

" PAPER ! "

an elaborate church lighted inside by two tallow candles which throw the stained-glass windows into elegant relief. In the Whitechapel Road there is a kerbstone trade in hot peas. In the neighbourhood of Charing Cross you can buy gauffres at the kerb cooked "while you wait;" and in Hoxton and Whitechapel a kerbstone delicacy largely patronised is " eel jelly."

The Saturday night kerbstone trade in " market " neighbourhoods is a sharp contrast to the ordinary kerbstone trade in the West-End thoroughfares and in the City. Mingle for a moment with the jostling crowd, mostly on marketing intent. There is a good deal of pushing, but it is generally civil and good humoured. The coster barrows and stalls are doing a lively trade. The costers look fairly well off, and are business-like and jovial. At one of the bigger fruit stalls the proprietor is smoking a cigar and watching his assistants. The butcher's stall has a placard which informs you that it has stood in the same spot for thirty years. The proprietor has a gold pin in his scarf. The stout matronly woman in an old apron and a young hat, who is doing a roaring trade in fish, has a big gold ring in addition to the wedding-ring and the keeper.

TRYING HIS SKILL.

But these people are the aristocracy of the kerb, the people who do a steady business and make money. Some of them have stalls in half a dozen neighbourhoods on the Saturday night. The people to watch if you want to dive beneath the crust of the kerb commerce are the men and women who have no stalls, who simply stand with a small stock-in-trade on a tray or in a basket— sometimes in their hand —and endeavour to earn a few pence. Very poor and miserable they look as a rule ; their faces are anxious, their voices are weak. You may watch

REFRESHING ROSES.

in rags, and thinly-clad, emaciated women. Their attitude is statuesque. They do not even hold their goods out boldly to attract attention. There is a pitiful, appealing look

FRUIT.

some of them for hours and not see them take a farthing. But on their takings depends their bed that night. To many of the poorer kerbstone hawkers the night's receipts decide between the " 'appy doss" on a doorstep and the more comfortable bed of a common lodging-house.

Before quitting the Saturday night "market" kerb, note the contrast between the silent hawker and the patterer. Here and there stand melancholy figures, old men almost

BLIND MUSICIAN.

in their eyes, but their lips are dumb.

Close by them, sometimes on either side of them, are the patterers : men loud of voice who talk incessantly, who shout, make speeches, crack jokes and bang barrows or stands, until the crowd collects round them. Many of them have not only the gift of the gab, but a rough wit of their own. As a rule, the wittiest kerbstone merchants are the Jews. They vary their dialogue, and suit it to the occasion and the customer. In the White-chapel Road there are kerbstone auctioneers, knockers-down of old clothes and patched-up umbrellas, who will patter the whole night long and always keep their audience laughing. Their business formula is, however, always the same. They ask far more than they intend to take, and reduce the price rapidly, say, from half-a-crown to sixpence. You always know the final, because the auctioneer slaps the article and exclaims, "I ask no more—I take no less." That is the ultimatum. If the article is not bought after that it is put aside, and another one is picked up and subjected to the same process.

Along the kerb in the weekday the trade is of quite a different character. In the west in the daytime it consists largely of toys for children. Some of these toys are of an elaborate character and move by clockwork. You may walk along Oxford Street and see a hansom cab on the pavement going round and round in a circle, a black poodle dog which hops like a frog and barks, a man mowing imaginary grass, a woman drawing water from a well, a couple of pugilists engaged in a lively boxing match, an elephant walking down an inclined plane, a pair of fluttering butterflies, or a small Blondin performing on the tight-rope.

These ingenious toys vary in price. You can pay eighteenpence for them or considerably less. You can buy toy musical instruments, bagpipes, bird calls, Jews' harps, etc., for a penny. The sellers are mostly well-dressed men, smart young fellows who know their business, and do it quickly and dexterously. When the toy is a novelty it attracts the grown-up passers-by, and amuses them quite as much as it does the children—probably more. At the West-End you meet the kerbstone dog-seller—the man leading a

dog as a specimen of the stock at home—the man with a couple of tiny puppies, which he keeps in his pocket and puts down occasionally when he sees a likely customer. Ladies frequently buy these dogs under the impression that they are full grown, and will always remain "tiny mites;" it is needless to say their anticipations are not realised. The favourite kerbstone dog is the poodle, and the vendor is generally a foreigner.

If you take a walk through the town, say, along Oxford Street and into the Strand, along the Strand to Ludgate Hill, from Ludgate Hill along Cheapside, and so into the City, you will be struck by the fact that quite a number of the kerbstone merchants sell the same article. The article

I. PATTERER.   II. OLD CLOTHES.

PURSES, BROOCHES, ETC.

that attracted your attention in Oxford Street you will find being sold along Cheapside; a cheap novelty—the latest "catchpenny" on the market—will be on sale on the same day in every thoroughfare of London. And all the hawkers will cry it in the same words. The leaden water squirts, which with "scratch-backs" were at one time allowed to be sold on the kerb during periods of popular festivity, were known for years in hawkerese as "Get your own back." Then suddenly, in a night, the name was changed. From end to end of the world's greatest capital the vendors yelled them as "All the jolly fun." These squirts are still, occasionally sold on the street in spite of the police prohibition, but

UMBRELLAS.

a gentler age has substituted for Bank Holidays and national rejoicings the confetti of the Continent. On big nights of popular rejoicing some of the principal thoroughfares of London are strewn from end to end with bits of coloured paper.

BAGPIPES.

On these nights the kerbstone merchant does a roaring trade in the tissue paper that you light and fling in the air, in memorial buttons, in rosettes and streamers, and, alas! also in the old-fashioned bladder attached to a stick, which enables the London larrikin to bang away on the hat and shoulders of the peaceable passer-by to his heart's content.

The kerb trade alters with the seasons. In winter, except at Christmas, particularly in the City, it is dull, and there is little variety ; it is during the summer and autumn that the great kerbstone trade is done. One might in a walk of a couple of miles collect enough kerbstone curiosities to fit up a parlour museum. You might buy a summer hat for twopence, a fan for a penny, a Japanese parasol for any price the dealer thinks he can palaver you into parting with, a penny map

of London, a penny guide to London, and a penny history of England from William the Conqueror to Edward VII. You can obtain iced drinks at a penny a glass, sherbet from a can over which is spread a rough towel with an ornamental border ; ices are offered to you by swarthy-skinned Swiss-Italians at every hundred yards, and the coster wheels his fruit barrow along the kerb from morn till night. For the kerb hawker with the barrow must by police regulations keep on the move. Fruit is his general stock-in-trade in the summer. Strawberries, cherries, and gooseberries take the place of the oranges, apples, and walnuts of the colder months. The banana stall is now as common as the pineapple stall is rare. There are very few barrows along the West-End and City kerbs that are not either fruit or flower laden in the summer. Occasionally a man will turn up with a weird barrow-load of small tortoises, and explain to the gaping provincials that they are good things for the garden, but this is a sensation of the kerb, and only to be seen at rare intervals.

WALNUTS.

In Cheapside there are few fruit sellers. Here the great public want seems to be boot-laces and collar-studs. The boot-lace merchant and the women who stand with the little cards of studs are only one remove from mendicants. Some of them are so

In the City proper, in the neighbourhood of the Bank and the Stock Exchange, the kerbstone merchant is of a different order. He is a business man appealing to business men. Therefore he has something to sell, and he knows how to sell it. The City men

STUDS, ETC.   BOOKS.   CAMPHOR.

wretched-looking that your hand instinctively goes into your pocket to give them a copper.

Some of the dilapidated objects standing on the kerbstone of the Metropolis have strange histories. Among them you find University men and members of the professions, men bearing names famous in the land. And among them also you find the broken-down merchant, the ruined tradesman, and the gentleman who has had reverses of fortune. It is to this they have drifted as the last stand against the workhouse. They are, of course, exceptions. The boot-lace and collar - stud hawker is, as a general rule, of the broken-down labouring class.

are good patrons of the kerb "curiosity" merchant. The young stockbroker buys an ingenious toy and takes it back to the office —to amuse himself with. The staid stockbroker and the grave merchant buy their toys and take them home for the amusement of their families. Several City men have preserved the penny toys hawked in the streets, and one well-known stockbroker has quite a remarkable collection of them.

The street performer rarely appears on the kerb—the middle of the roadway is more welcome for the " pitch." But the singer of ballads— mournful ballads as a rule—occasionally stands with one foot upon it and makes doleful melody. The

OLD BOOTS.

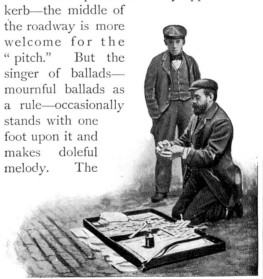

NEEDLES.

gentleman with the musical glasses—a rare performance nowadays—finds his way to the edge of the pavement occasionally in neighbourhoods where the factory hands spend half their dinner hour out of doors, and here the harpist, the blind fiddler, the boy with the penny whistle, and the long-haired man who sings hymns to his own accompaniment on the harmonium are also to be found—especially on Saturday afternoons when the work-girls are going home. For on Saturday the London work-girl has her wages with her, and it is rarely that she does not dedicate a copper or two to the relief of the kerbstone performers, halt, lame, and blind, who appeal to her charitable little heart.

On the London kerb, then, you will find all sorts and conditions of men, from the prosperous trader to the shivering, half-starved mendicant who disguises his mendicancy with a shirt-stud, a boot-lace, or the singing of a doleful ditty.

Every kerb has its characteristics. The kerb life of the Borough has nothing in common with the kerb life of Hoxton, and the kerb life of Notting Hill is as a foreign land compared with the kerb life of Islington. The City kerb dealer is brisk, alert, and business-like; the kerb hawker of Fleet Street and Ludgate Hill is, as a rule, cowed, depressed, and silent. But all make a living of one sort or another. They come day after day many of them to the same pitch, and stand through winter's cold and summer's heat, through drenching rain and biting blast, and at a certain hour they go. Like the Arabs they silently steal away. Whither? Some of them into the shadowland of the outcasts, others to the common lodging houses, where they cook their meal at the coke fire and discuss with their friends the condition of trade and the badness of the times just as the millionaire and the financier will discuss it at their West-End clubs. And on the morrow, however small the previous day's takings may have been, they will drop into their old places on the London kerbs again and wait patiently for the chance customers by whom they live. They have neither luncheon hour, dinner hour, nor time for tea. And they have no holidays. They are a human fringe to the pavements of London, a fringe that only completely disappears when the first hour of a new day has struck, and the last hope of a copper has departed. The police who guard the great City by night want neither boot-laces nor evening papers.

DOLLS.   BANANAS.   COMIC SONGS.   FLOWERS, ETC.   EGG-PIPES.

CASSELL AND COMPANY, LIMITED, LA BELLE SAUVAGE, LUDGATE HILL, LONDON, E.C.

LEAVING THE LONDON THEATRES.

By A. ST. JOHN ADCOCK.

TOWARDS ten o'clock at night a breath of the drowsy quietness that has already settled down in the heart of the City seems to blow out along the West-End thoroughfares, and lull them as with some passing thought of sleep. Office windows are dark; half the shops are closed, and others are closing; 'buses, no longer crowded, are no longer in a hurry, and the conductor is saving up his voice for an hour later, when it can be used to better purpose; traffic generally has dwindled on the pavement and in the road-way until you can walk the one without el-bowing your neighbours, and cross the other safely and at leisure.

LEAVING THE PAVILION THEATRE, WHITECHAPEL.

of white cloths, none of the tables are occupied. The waiters gather in idle knots to tell each other privately what they think of the manager, or they doze apart as if the business of their day was finished instead of being about to begin again; the young ladies at the confec-tioners' shops have time to look at their hair in the mirrors; and aproned men behind the oyster bars are yawning over the evening papers.

When half-past ten is turned, you feel the very air be-coming tense with expectancy of something that is to happen. Crush-hatted men in evening dress appear in the street, singly or in pairs, or with fair com-panions who trip beside them, bonnetless and in opera cloaks: the later items in the music hall programme were not attractive enough to keep them; the play bored them, and they have left before the end. Commissionaires or gor-geously-uniformed attendants are bolting back the outer doors of theatres in readi-ness for departing audiences; and the traffic in road and on pavement is momentarily thickening.

Glance into the refreshment-rooms and hotels, into the fashionable or Bohemian restaurants in the Strand and round by Leicester Square, and you will see only long rows of tables, their snowy cloths neatly set with knives and forks, silver-plated cruets, folded serviettes, and branchy, torch-shaped epergnes flaming atop into many-coloured flowers; and, except for some stray visitor, perhaps, who looks lonely amid the waste

Now, too, if you look up almost any byway of the Strand you will see that it is lined with hansoms and four-wheelers and hired and private carriages waiting to be called. Other cabmen, arriving too late to get front places in these waiting lines, sneak into the Strand by circuitous routes, and, failing to dodge past the policemen, hover as near as they dare to one or other of the theatres, keeping a wary look-out for the playgoers to emerge and a signalling umbrella to be hoisted.

With the advent of broughams and private carriages in the byways, dapper footmen go on sentry duty outside the principal entrances to the theatres, or stand patiently amongst the ferns and huge palms that adorn box-office vestibules. Here they pose, almost as imperturbable as a row of statuary, until the strains of the National Anthem filter out to them from within, then they come to life, and peer eagerly into the passages and up thick-carpeted stairs that converge on the vestibule.

Suddenly, one of them catches a glimpse of the figures he is looking for, and is out in a twinkling, and beckoning in the lamplight at the nearest corner. A carriage detaches itself from the line, sweeps smartly into the Strand, and draws up opposite the theatre. My lady and her guest, in a splendour of diamonds and low-necked dresses half hidden under loose cloaks, trip lightly into it; my lord and his guest, plainer, but no less immaculately garbed, step in after them; the footman slams the door, mounts the box, and they are gone.

In like manner come and go other carriages, and cabs that have answered to the shrill whistling of the commissionaire or have been fetched by some perspiring tout, who will gallantly hold a ragged flap of his coat over the dirty wheel whilst his more finely-garmented patrons are getting in, and trot a few paces alongside to catch the largesse that will be flung to him.

Men and women and a sprinkling of children—aristocrats and plebeians mingling—are now pouring steadily out of the Gaiety, the Garrick, the Tivoli, Criterion, His Majesty's, and all the theatres and music halls in the Strand, the Haymarket, Charing Cross Road, and thereabouts, the swelling tide in the main thorough-fares being fed by narrower but more plenteous streams that gush into it out of side channels from pit and gallery doors, till the surge and rush of foot passengers everywhere, of cabs and carriages and 'buses, are denser and swifter than even at mid-day.

It is an orderly crowd, talking for the most part of how to get home, but inclined to a desultory more or less impersonal criticism of the plays and players it has seen. It is an orderly crowd, but in a hurry; it is being whisked up, and whirled off momentarily in cabs and carriages; it mobs the 'buses at the top of the Strand, and swarms on to them till they are crammed full; it billows both ways along Coventry Street, dodging and darting in and out under the noses of cab and carriage horses, and making lightning dashes across the tumultuous road. Everywhere among the well-dressed multitude go opera-cloaks, and shawls, or hooded heads; white cloaks and black cloaks, blues, pinks, scarlets, and shawls as varied in hue, and always beside them the formal black and plenteous white linen of masculine evening dress.

For the most of an hour this pandemonium reigns—but it is a very respectable pandemonium, and very good-tempered. Some of the opera-cloaked ladies, waiting for a 'bus, may grow irritable because it is tardy in coming, and so full when it does come that they have to charter a four-wheeler after all; or a policeman, struggling in the welter of congested traffic, may lose his temper with a cabman, and goad him to such impertinent responses as result in his number being taken and a summons threatened; but, on the whole, the prevailing characteristics of the multitude are careless good-humour and a yearning for supper.

The majority speed straightway home for it; but a large minority prefer to sup in town. Wherefore, in the oyster bars the aproned men yawn no longer over newspapers, but toil behind their counters briskly ministering to the needs of a shopful of appetites that are not easily satisfied. Hebe at the confectioner's has no more time for setting her hair straight, for customers have flocked in from pits and galleries, with a sprinkling from the dress-circles, and, impatient with fears of missing last trains,

LEAVING HIS MAJESTY'S THEATRE.

all want serving at once. Look into the hotels, and fashionable and Bohemian restaurants, and the waiters are all wide awake and running their legs off in attentive zeal ; for where half an hour ago scarcely a table was occupied now scarcely one remains vacant.

In some places you shall take your supper to a musical accompaniment played on a piano and stringed instruments, or on strings and brasses ; in all, there is a constant effervescence of laughter and cheery voices ; bewildering visions of beauty and beautiful hats and dresses ; young men fully enjoying the freshness and novelty of their surroundings ; testy old men trying hard not to be bored by them ; blithe old men enjoying themselves as heartily as any youngster of them all—staid men and women taking their pleasure with the typical British stolidity.

Here, in one of the most fashionable of such resorts, you come upon a famous actor, fresh from his evening's triumphs, sociably supping with a select circle of admirers ; or a famous actress similarly entertained, and the centre of furtive glances from every corner of the room. There are cosy, elegant parties of two or four monopolising small tables ; there are larger, merrier, and equally elegant parties feasting royally round larger tables, and over all are the brilliance of electric lights and an air of contented affluence, and amid all are the delicate fragrances of flowers and scents, the mingling babble and laughter, and dreamy cadences of the music.

Nor do the humbler public-houses near the theatres lack for patronage. Unfashionable men, average men, and men below the average, several with wives or sweathearts, flock to these hospitable bars for liquid refreshment, supplemented, maybe, by a sandwich or a pork pie. Thither repair straggling units of emancipated orchestras with their instruments in funereal cases ; and there, too, smart young City clerks and shop assistants drop in for a last drink, which, in some cases, is a preliminary to so many drinks after the last that, in the end, they come out to learn they have missed the last 'bus, and accept the alternative with boisterous cheerfulness. One faces southwards alone, and has facetious farewells shrieked after him ; the others, after much striking of matches and relighting of pipes and cigarettes, set out northwards, and will

SUPPER AT AN EAST-END FRIED FISH SHOP.

by and by be scandalising sober suburban streets with cock-crows and rousing choruses.

The emptying of suburban theatres is a comparatively small matter ; for the suburbs have their theatres singly, and not in clusters. There is the same rush and scattering of the audience, but on a reduced scale, and, generally, the proportion of evening dresses is very much smaller. In fact, in many of these theatres evening dress is not the fashion, and anyone wearing it is by way of being a rarity.

Come down East on Saturday night, and see how the people pass out of the Pavilion Theatre in Whitechapel.

Whitechapel Road has scarcely begun to think about sleep yet. Not only do all the provision shops remain wide open, but tailors' and drapers' and toy and furniture shops, with many others, are open as well ; costermongers' barrows stand thickly by the kerb ; in the middle of them a huge brass weighing machine towers up, flashing dazzlingly in the light of

IN COVENTRY STREET, 11.15 P.M.

naphtha lamps, and near beside it is a hooded whelk-stall similarly illuminated. A baked-potato merchant passes and repasses, sowing sparks from the big black can on his barrow. The public-houses are full ; the pavement is covered with men and women and children, well-dressed, shabby or disreputable, shopping, or leisurely promenading. The curtain has not fallen in the Pavilion yet, but there is as much life here as there is in the Strand when the theatres are emptying.

It is five minutes to eleven. Two ancient four-wheelers and a single hansom have driven up, and are standing, forlornly hopeful, opposite the theatre. An attendant bolts the doors back, and a moment later a dark mass surges up the long bare passage

from the pit, and a second less compact crowd simultaneously flows by the broader exit from the stalls and boxes.

As the earliest to emerge from the gallery door round the corner are batches of rampant, hooting boys, so the first hundred or so to burst into the open air from the front entrances are all men. One, a seedy, melancholy-looking man, breaks out, solitary, stares round as if he were dreaming, and, with his hands in his pockets, pushes through the promenaders, and makes for home, taking his dreams with him. The huge poster that leans against the lamp-post opposite, and represents a scene from the play, has a strange fascination for many; they cross straight to it, and stand regarding

SUPPER AT THE SAVOY HOTEL.

it critically. "We never see that!" objects a lady carrying a sleeping infant. "Yus, we did, silly!" declares her husband, carrying an elder child, who is also asleep. "Ain't that where 'e's a-savin' of 'er from that Russian chap?" "Oh, ah! But they didn't do it like this," she insists, and follows him still protesting.

The general inclination, especially among the fair sex, is to discuss the play as if it had been sheer reality, and to pour scorn and loathing on the villain, a tearful pity on the distressed heroine, and unlimited admiration on the hero, but a select few of the male sex, who are habitual attendants at

the theatre, concern themselves less with the play than with the merits of individual actors, old favourites, to whom they refer in familiar, even affectionate, terms.

So for some ten minutes the crowd streams out from the front and round from the gallery door, and the larger crowd moving up and down Whitechapel Road easily absorbs it. Passing trams or 'buses are besieged; a weedy young man is regaling his much be-feathered sweetheart at the baked-potato can; two men in tall hats and a miscellany of less imposing persons congregate around the whelk stall, and hand the pepper and vinegar about with gusto. There is an influx of trade to the public-houses; the boxes of an adjacent fried fish shop are full of hungry revellers, and faces of men and women peer in increasing numbers over its counter, demanding "middle pieces" well browned. You meet these customers strolling a little later eating fried plaice out of scraps of newspaper, or carrying it wrapped up to be eaten more comfortably at home. Nobody has hired any of the cabs, but the drivers linger still, on the chance of finding a fare among the actors and actresses.

The illuminated arch of coloured glass goes out suddenly over the main entrance to the theatre; lights within are dying out; here, as in the West-End, doors are being closed up with a clanging of bolts and bars; players are filing into the street from the stage exit; while, in the desolate interior, attendants potter about, covering up boxes and dress-circle, and the fireman, swinging his lantern, tramps over the darkened stage, taking a last look round.

RELEASED FROM WORK.

LONDON SWEETHEARTS.

By GEORGE R. SIMS.

WHEN the twilight shadows have veiled the face of the garish day, then London becomes one vast "Lovers' Walk." Lost in the rapture of "Love's Young Dream" are thousands of young couples released from the world of work-a-day. You can see them everywhere with the old sweet story writ large upon their happy faces, and at a glance you know them. In one class of life their arms are linked and their fingers are intertwined ; in another class their arms are round each other's necks ; in another, *her* hand rests lightly on *his* arm ; in still another, they walk demurely side by side ; but no one mistakes them for aught but what they are. Young husband and wife never walk together as lovers walk. There is a different step, a different clasp of the arm, and the *al fresco* embrace is no longer in the programme.

Discreetly, modestly, and with the tenderest consideration for the feelings of the inhabitants, let us take a stroll this quiet summer evening through Love-land in London.

The houses of business have just closed in the West, and the main thoroughfares are filled with the lads and lasses released from toil. The girls come out by themselves in light-bloused, straw-hatted groups, and the young fellows walk up the street in little knots for a time. But gradually the sexes mingle, and in a short time almost every laddie has his lassie, and happy pairs stroll quietly away together.

The custom of raising the hat, once considered Continental, has won its way to-day among all classes, and many a hat is raised by fellow clerks and shopmen as they pass the proud swain walking by the side of his "young lady." Between eight and nine o'clock the shopping streets of the West are filled with sweethearts. So far, there is no pronounced affection displayed. The linked hands and clasped waists are for the less aristocratic streets and for a lowlier class of lovers, the factory girl and the working lad, the young hawker and his "donah," the general servant and her "chap."

You can walk through the streets of London at the evening hour, and read the honest love of lad and lass in a never-ending panorama of happy faces. There is no false shame about these young couples. They are proud of each other, proud of their tender relationship, and if every now and then they give outward and visible signs of the warmth of their affection, it is but the natural reversion of Adam's sons and Eve's daughters to the happy Eden days of the first sweethearts.

In the parks and along the Embankment many a pair of lovers sit side by side and gaze into each other's eyes heedless of the passers-by, who are generally sympathetic, and show their sympathy in a practical manner. If only one couple is occupying the seat or bench made to accommodate four, the vacant space is rarely intruded upon by the single man or woman. It is left for the next pair of lovers that may come along. For lovers do not mind other lovers sharing the dreamy silence of the seat beneath the tree. But the presence of any person, male or female, not absorbed in the tender passion would be considered an unwarrantable trespass on Cupid's domain.

London lovers of the class who nestle to each other when the evening zephyrs murmur among the trees have few opportuni-

ties of quiet courtship in their homes. There are too many noisy children and rough neighbours about, and there is no romance in the surroundings. Many a love scene in the London parks is as idyllic, as tender, and as true as any that ever poet sang, and the wooing of the swain is often as loyal and as respectful as that of the young curate who whispers honied words in the ear of the vicar's daughter among the roses of her father's garden beneath the first pale stars of eve.

Love is of no rank and no degree, and so, because the hush of evening is the hour of the heart, we, the wayfarers in Love-land, may see the lordly lover also, as he bends down and speaks softly to the blue-blooded maiden of his choice. Out on to the balcony of the great house they come, and stand against a background of soft lights in the beautiful room that we see through the open windows. What a charming picture they make! His black coat and wide expanse of shirt front throw into relief the soft chiffon of the graceful, willowy girl by his side. The rising breeze tenderly touches her wealth of wavy hair, but it is not that which brings the faint flush to her cheek. The young earl has bent and spoken softly in her ear the trembling words of love. We are too far away to hear the answer that she makes, but we can see her smiling face, and, when the rules and regulations of Society and its marriageable daughters have been observed, we may be sure that there will be an announcement in the *Morning Post*, and all the world will be told the sequel of that little love story of which we have seen the beginning on the Park Lane balcony to-night.

The blinds are down in this dull-looking house in a London square, and we cannot see if love is beneath the roof, but the area gate is open, and on the top

ON THE EMBANKMENT.

step a pretty London housemaid is taking the air. She looks anxiously towards the corner, every now and then throwing a furtive glance at the drawn blinds. Presently a young man comes sauntering along. He saunters until he catches sight of the fluttering strings of a little white cap. Then he quickens his pace, and the young housemaid trips lightly to meet him. In the shadow of the house next door, out of the line of sight of any eyes that may peer from the house in which she is a handmaid, Mary lingers with her lover for a while. He holds her hand in his, and they talk earnestly together. The policeman passes with a nod and a smile. The young man knits his brow a little, but it is only a summer cloud. Presently the clock of a church close by strikes ten. Mary gives a little start. "I must go!" she exclaims. Then there is a long lingering pressure of hands, and then—we discreetly turn our backs, but a familiar sound strikes our ears, and a minute later Mary softly closes the gate, and disappears down the area steps. The young man waits at the corner for a moment, then lights his pipe and strolls past the house along the square. I fancy he is going to have another look at that policeman.

In the fierce glare of the sunny afternoon a familiar pair of sweethearts come holding each other's hands along the outer circle of Regent's Park. How proud the little girl is of the bronzed sailor lover by her side! He has come up from Portsmouth to see her, and she has got a day off from the factory and walks on air. There is a chivalry as well as a heartiness about the love-making of the young Jack Tar. He has not the all-conquering air of the Adonis in scarlet, and he does not occupy himself so much with the twirling of a moustache and the flicking of a cane. The sailor and his lass are on their way to the Zoo, and there with his sweetheart on his arm Jack will gaze at the strange animals, and tell her of the far-off lands to which he has sailed and seen the like, not in iron cages, but in their native lairs. And Jack will be free with his money and treat his sweetheart generously. When the afternoon is over, and she is tired, he will take a hansom for her, and after tea at a little café he will suggest a music hall, and

ON THE BALCONY.

there he will enjoy himself to his heart's content and hold his little girl's hand lovingly all the time, and press it sympathetically when the serio-comic lady sings of sweethearts who are true "though seas divide." And at night he will see her to her mother's door, and kiss her heartily and with a sounding smack that all her folk may hear, before

THE AREA
BELLE.

he rolls off on his way to the other end of the town where his old mother is sitting up waiting for him. And you may be sure that when he went into a shop that afternoon, and bought a little present for his sweetheart, Jack did not forget his mother. He has something in his pocket that he is going to gladden the old lady's eyes with, as he sits down to the bread and cheese and cucumber and the big jug of beer that have been waiting for him since eleven o'clock.

The boy and girl sweetheart of the London streets are in their glory on Bank Holiday. It is the day on which the lad with the first faint signs of a budding moustache arrays himself in a new light suit and pair of yellowish brown boots, and counting the silver or the coppers that remain to him after the outlay on his wardrobe, invites the girl of his heart to accompany him to Hampstead Heath. Hampstead is the general choice of the boy sweetheart, because there is no admission, and the side shows are a penny instead of sixpence. His sweetheart has not spent much on her wardrobe, but she is generally neat, and has made deft use of her

fingers in arranging fresh ribbon on an old hat, and she has probably altered and retrimmed an old dress to make it look like a new one. Boots, as a rule, are the weak point of the little girl sweetheart on a Bank Holiday. Boots are a terrible item to many of us, but when your wages are ten shillings a week you have to make one pair do duty for a very long time indeed.

But the boy sweetheart is not particular about the boots so long as his "gal" looks smart about the hat. He is a good boy to her in his way and as far as his means will allow, and affectionate and considerate as boys go. He thumps her in the way of play with a force which a gently-bred girl would consider a violent assault. But Sally takes it in excellent part, and thumps back again with much top-note exclamation. In the matter of refreshment Tom is as liberal as he can afford to be. He treats his "gal" to a pennyworth of sweets as they come along. On the Heath they share an ice, bite an apple between them, and "drink fair" out of a ginger-beer bottle.

There is not much sentiment about these boy and girl sweethearts. They are practically children, and they play and romp. Towards evening, as they go home to the little side street where they live, their arms may be about each other's necks, but it is more "show off" than anything else. They both want to ape their elders. He tries to let the passing boys see that the girl is not his sister but "his young woman," and she is anxious that all passing females should know that she has attained to the dignity of a young man.

At the front garden gate of the suburban villa, as the clock strikes the hour after which it is not considered correct for the daughters of the house to be abroad, a young couple linger lovingly. The evening stroll through the lane near at hand is over; the hour of parting has come. This young couple are engaged. But the young fellow knows that the brothers and sisters of his adored one do not like the too frequent presence of a "spoony couple," and, moreover, he has a long way to go to get to his own home, and he has to be off to the City at eight every morning. So ten o'clock sees the parting, as a rule, but the linger at the gate is always sweet, and difficult to bring to an end.

After she has gone inside the front garden she does not go up the little pathway to the door. She leans on the gate for a while, and they stand silently gazing into each other's eyes and enjoy the silence of love.

But at last she breaks the spell. "I *must* go, Frank," she says. Then she puts her pretty little face over the gate, and he stoops down and their lips meet. Then a light dress flutters up the pathway in the semi-darkness. He watches it till it disappears. Then he says "Darling!" aloud to himself, and steps out briskly for his mile and a half walk. And the memory of that parting kiss goes with him and makes the dusty road a path of roses.

The sound of military music crashes on the early morning air, and there is a great rush of womenfolk to the windows. It is too early for the families to be up and about in this aristocratic neighbourhood, so the servants gather at the dining-room window, and some run upstairs to their own bedrooms to get a better view.

The Life Guards are out for an early ride.

WITH JACK AT THE ZOO.

AT "'APPY 'AMPSTEAD."

and smiles and nods, and Jenny is in the seventh heaven of rapture.

She is engaged to Trooper Thompson and means to marry him. It will have to be a long courtship. But Jenny does not mind. She has good wages, and she makes her soldier lover pretty presents—pipes, and tobacco pouches, and cigars, and all that sort of thing—and Jenny has been to the ball at the barracks and lived in fairyland, for her handsome lover in scarlet danced every dance with her. And she counts the hours till it is her evening or her Sunday out when she can meet her gallant admirer, and walk about or sit in the park with him, or treat him to the music hall.

When, as they walk along, she sees the young women turn their heads and cast sidelong glances of admiration at her hero, she gives a shy little laugh, and grasps his arm a little more closely to signify absolute possession, and she thinks she is the happiest girl in the world. She is a good girl, and will

The band is with them. Probably it is some special occasion. There is a head from every upper window as they pass, and, as a rule, the head has a little white cap on it.

Most of the troopers glance upwards and smile. Mars is never insensible to the glance of beauty, and is given to nodding pleasantly to ladies to whom he has not been introduced.

At one upper window there is a pretty face wreathed in smiles. Jenny, the parlourmaid, knows that her lover, Trooper Thompson, is with his regiment, and will be looking out for her. And Trooper Thompson knows exactly where Jenny will be; she told him the previous evening when they parted in Wellington Road. Trooper Thompson is a handsome young fellow with a fair moustache that Jenny thinks is absolutely perfect. He is not perhaps quite so much in love with Jenny as she is with him, but he does not make her jealous by smiling and laughing at all the other housemaids in the terrace as some of his comrades do. He looks directly in front of him, heedless of the admiring glances cast at him, until he comes to Jenny's house. Then he raises his head

THE PRIDE OF THE PARK.

make a hard-working, devoted wife. Let us hope that Trooper Thompson will appreciate the affection he has won, and that Jenny may never regret the love that loved a scarlet coat.

It is a long walk through Love-land, for north and south, and east and west, at every turn we find the old, old story being told again. To the busy tea shop, where neat-handed Phyllises trip from table to table, the patient lover comes now and then, and they exchange a word or two of tender greeting as she hands him his scone or cup of coffee. And all the girls in the establishment know that the young fellow is Phyllis's sweetheart, and after he has gone they talk sympathetically to her about him, and congratulate her on his loyalty in coming to the shop so frequently. The barmaid's sweetheart cannot linger as long by his lady-love in business hours, for the landlord has a keen eye for the engaged barmaid's young man, and discourages the attention that, as a rule, is long and unprofitable, and, moreover, monopolises the fair Hebe's conversation and sometimes keeps her from giving proper attention to the other " paying guests " of mine host.

There are the sweethearts of fashion, who meet in the Row and canter side by side ; there are the sweethearts who talk small talk at Society gatherings, and whose courtship is a diary of fashionable events ; there are the sweethearts of humble life, the working man who woos and wins some honest hard-working lass, and is as proud of her the day they stand before the clergyman as the elderly duke who wins the beauty of the London season.

And there are the old couples whom we meet arm in arm, with happy, smiling faces beneath their crown of silvered hair—men and women who have shared each other's joys and sorrows from youth to old age, and who, in the evening of their well-spent days, are sweethearts still.

THE LINGER AT THE GATE.

SOME LONDON HOME TRADES.

By ARTHUR B. MOSS.

WE are all familiar with the large trades by which men and women earn their living. The work of the carpenter, the bricklayer, the engineer, the printer, the tailor, and the bootmaker, is brought constantly before us in our daily lives, and most of the trades in which girls and women are employed in factory and workshop are well known. There are, however, a large number of small obscure trades in which men and women are engaged, and which have to serve in many cases as the sole source of income. These trades are conducted in the workers' homes, and to see them we must pay a series of visits and enter the dwellings of the poor without ceremony.

Let us call first at the humble abode of the Hat Box Maker. We find it on the third floor of one of the model dwellings in a thickly populated district in South London. As we have entered uninvited an introduction is necessary. Mrs. P—— is a widow who has one child of her own, and takes care of another that belongs to a friend. She has for many years earned her living by making hat boxes at home for a firm that supplies some of the chief manufacturers of silk hats.

"I only do the stitching," says Mrs. P—— in answer to a question; "I generally get a young woman to do the pasting for me."

HAT BOX MAKING.

By this she means that the box is supplied with an outside covering of white glazed paper which is stuck together with paste, but the body and the bottom of the box are sewn together with thread. Mrs. P—— knows how to do the pasting as well as her companion, but she finds that it materially assists the speed of putting together a gross of such boxes to have this assistance. "I have to find the paste, and the needle and thread, and when I've finished a gross I get half-a-crown. I don't grumble at the pay, for when I can get the work I'm able to make a very decent living for a poor widow. It's only when we're slack I don't like it, for then I have to go out charing, and such work is a little beyond my strength."

Still sticking to the paste and paper, we enter another room in which we find a young man and a young woman working away industriously at the Paper Bag Making. Paper bags of all sizes are made by this energetic couple, who supply the shops at a very low figure per gross.

"It's like this," says Mr. S——; "we make thousands of these bags every week. First we have to cut them to the size we want, then we paste away all round the edges except the top, then fold them over, and when they're properly dry we have to

FIRE-STOVE ORNAMENTS.

tie 'em in packets. I finish the business by taking 'em round to the shops. 'Paper Bag Poets?' Oh, yus, there's some fellers that write poetry, as they calls it, to put on the bags, but the printers engage them, and I expect they're the same chaps as write verses for the rag merchants."

Let us now turn our steps towards Tabard Street (late Kent Street), Borough, for here we shall find many home industries of the kind that people take very little notice of except at the particular time of year at which they are forced upon public attention. Here we see a poor woman making Ornaments for the Fire-stove. The little kitchen table is covered with coloured paper, and here and there are long strips of gold shavings, as well as rosettes of various colours ; these are dexterously pieced together and form a very pretty ornament. A very precarious income is earned, however, by hawking them about the streets of London, and many of these women find it necessary to follow another calling in addition, most of them making artificial flowers for the winter months.

While in Tabard Street we find ourselves in the midst of the Brush Making industry. A great deal of it is done at home. Here we find men and women engaged in making scrubbing brushes, laundry brushes, shoe brushes, etc. It is an interesting sight to watch them at work. First we see them cut the bass, or fibre, with a sort of guillotine knife, or, when they do not possess one of these, with a large pair of shears. Then we see one of the boys preparing the glue. The hairs having been dexterously placed in holes specially made, are again dressed round by the shears until they are of uniform length, and then prepared for sale.

In one of the model dwellings in the Borough we find a young woman who does some of the best sort of work. She is in almost constant employment at home, and she likes the work because it is clean and light and free from danger. "This is real hair I am using," says Mrs. M——, "and this brush when finished will be used in the confectionery business. You see how light it is ; it is a real good article, and they call it an egg brush."

But now let us go in search of the Rag Merchant Poet. We find him in a common lodging-house. He is no doubt a man of fine poetic genius ; at all events he thinks so, and that should suffice. He lays claim to being the author of some of the most moral poems ever written for the rag trade, as well as for the quack medicine man. He gives us a few samples of his work, but we fail to appreciate them. So we make our way to a rag merchant's and take down a few specimens of verse by the poets who are looked upon as the laureates of the trade. Two examples will suffice.

PEACE AND PROSPERITY.

Let's hope that trade will soon revive;
And each and all begin to thrive.
I think that things are on the mend;
So have a little cash to spend
To buy your rags, books, or papers,
Kitchen stuff or cuttings from the draper's,
Old clothes, old books; all that you can find,
Old bottles too of every kind;
Jampots, jars (not family ones I hope),
Blankets, string, or any kind of rope.

From the heights of Parnassus the poet always descends to the plains of the every-day world.

GOOD ADVICE TO ALL.

So, Sally dear, you think it funny
That I should save my rags and turn them into money.
Now if you'd like to have a happy home,
Nor wish to see your husband roam,
Remember this, a *Golden Rule*,
And one I learned when young at school,
"A penny saved is a penny earned,"
Which could not be so if my rags I burned.
If you waste such things as these
You lose the bread and want the cheese,
But if you're frugal, think what a treasure you will be;
And you'll save rags and bones as well as me.

Another branch of the rag and bone business is carried on by an itinerant vendor of Farthing Windmills, who pushes a barrow through the streets, and, having a number of these windmills and paper flags displayed, soon gets a crowd of children around his vehicle, and tells them that if they can induce their parents to part with their bones and bottles he will supply them with a flag or a windmill gratis. Windmill making is a home industry in London, and in the season the vendors do a brisk trade. But the season is short, and the harvest must be reaped at the proper time.

Since the establishment of large sanitary laundries in almost every industrial community, the amount of washing and mangling done at "small laundries" has been considerably reduced. There are still, however, a large number of poor women, mostly widows, in crowded neighbourhoods, earning a living by washing and mangling for those families who, in the belief that it is better and less expensive, prefer their washing and mangling to be done in a small private house, however humble, rather than in a large factory. And so we may reasonably expect that for many a long day yet small Home Laundries will continue to exist, if not to flourish, among the poor.

At a lodging-house of the better class we find two interesting persons. One of them is a manufacturer of Fly Papers—"Catch 'em alive O!" He sells them at a halfpenny a sheet. The other is the manufacturer and vendor of Penny Opera Glasses.

Let us go into the basement where the first man makes his Fly Papers and see them in the process of manufacture. There is a big basin of size and ochre lying on the table, and on a row of lines hang dozens of papers—old newspapers cut into various sizes, and covered with a thin layer of this solution. When these are dry there is another basin of solution, composed of resin, oil and turpentine, in readiness to be plastered over them, and then, hey presto! the "Catch 'em alive O!" papers are complete. An old Irishman is the hawker of these, and in the warm weather he does a brisk business.

The Penny Opera Glass Manufacturer is a young man, and a skilful workman in his own line of business. With the aid of two small bone ornaments, such as are generally to be found in the tassels of a parasol or sunshade, and a small brass ring similar to those used for hanging up pictures, or in lieu of the ring a little brass wire, he produces something in the shape of miniature opera glasses. Then having covered the top of them with a thin layer of glue, which has the appearance of transparency, they look for all the world like the real article. A remarkable number of these small articles are sold in the market places of the Metropolis every Friday and Saturday evening, and this man carries on a prosperous business for several months during the year.

Having witnessed the manufacture of these interesting articles we turn our steps in the direction of the home of a poor Single-handed Tailor. Only a few yards from the rear of Guy's Hospital, on the first floor of buildings that look from the outside very like

TOY WINDMILLS.

ARTIFICIAL FLOWERS.

a huge warehouse, we find our tailor seated on a big wooden table with his legs crossed hard at work. He does all kinds of work, from making a suit right out to repairing trousers or vest. As a rule, he works for a large firm of tailors, but he does not disdain to do an odd job or two for a private customer.

In every poor neighbourhood one of the flourishing "Home Trades" is that of the Boot Repairer, or, as he used to be called, the "cobbler." At various seasons of the year the boot repairer is very busy, especially after a series of wet days. He does his work, for the most part, in the front parlour of his little house, in the window of which is the announcement—"Boots and Shoes Neatly Repaired" at such and such a price. Sometimes the wording is in verse thus :—

> " If you think your boots are ended,
> Bring 'em here and get 'em mended."

Except that Monday is generally a lazy day with him, the cobbler is an industrious man who, generally, works all hours of the day, and sometimes far into the night, to please his customers.

In another building we find the Cheap Shirt Maker, who stitches away hour after hour for a miserable pittance. Tom Hood's "Song of the Shirt" still exactly describes her condition. She works every day from early morning till late at night. Mrs. W—— is a widow with a family of four, and if she relied solely on shirt making for a living she and her children would be often on the verge of starvation. Fortunately for her she gets occasional small jobs in the sewing line from neighbours, and thus she manages to subsist.

Wooden and Tin Toys are for the most part made abroad. They come principally from Germany. There is, however, a man in the Borough who makes toy tables and chairs. He does not make these articles for shops, but sells them in the street at a penny each. Judging from his appearance this mode of earning a living is not a profitable one. There is also a young woman who makes tin weights and scales for street sale, and a man who makes wire puzzles. But all these occupations are so ill paid that they are only aids to a living. The "manufacturers" have generally another employment.

But now we come to a real home industry that affords a substantial living to those who are engaged in it, viz., Haddock Smoking. Fifteen years ago there were a large number of "Smoke Holes" in the Borough, in Orange Street, Green Street, and Friar Street, as well as some in Bermondsey. Now most of them are removed to some of the back streets in Camberwell, where they still flourish. There

BRUSH MAKING.

BEETROOT BOILING.

manufactures thousands of pipes out of white clay, with a small machine, and with a dexterous use of his fingers. He then bakes them in a kiln which he has in his back yard. When they are complete he sells them to publicans at about one and sixpence a gross. The second mixes up a quantity of flour and water in a pail, and ladles it into a tin with small circular apertures, puts it on a large tin over a fire, and when it is withdrawn behold muffins and crumpets ready for the Londoners' tea.

The Italian Bronze Figure Maker is found chiefly at Saffron Hill and Leather Lane, but there are a few of them in the Italian quarter in the Peckham Park Road. It is not, however, an extensive business that is carried on there. Italians prefer the Ice Cream trade in the summer and the Baked Chestnut trade in the winter. And neither of these industries requires much capital. On the other hand a fair amount of money is required to carry on the business of a Bronze Figure Maker. The workman has to manipulate his plaster with skill, quite apart from the work that is done with moulds. And English people have so little appreciation of his art: a bust of Lord Salisbury or Mr. Joseph Chamberlain might have a sale among Unionists, but who cares for an art figure that represents somebody whom nobody knows? The Italian boy calls at various houses and asks in bad broken English a high price for his figures. But when he is offered half the price he takes it with only a shrug of the shoulder.

are two or three of them, however, still left just behind the Blackfriars Road, and a large one in Rockingham Street, Newington Causeway, but the chief smoking is done in Camberwell. Jem B—— is an old-established smoker. If you watch him at work you will notice that he puts a lot of haddocks on a long iron skewer, which he places in the smoke hole; he then sets fire to a quantity of oak sawdust and allows this to smoulder for hours, and thus the haddocks get well smoked and browned. Jem's haddocks have an enormous sale among the poor.

Another good trade is that of Beetroot Boiling. Mr. M—— is a general dealer, and when at home lives in Chapel Court, Borough. He is a bit of a philosopher in his way. " I boil hundreds of beets in this boiler, sir, in the season," he says, " and if you come about 'opping time you shall see me doing it, as you used to in Peter Street. But it's no good buying beetroots yet—the ones you get ain't no class; a little later on it'll be all right. Nobody can't teach me my business. In the season I sell hundreds of beets, as you know, in the streets, and in the market place in the Walworth Road on Saturday nights."

Two very interesting small Home Trades we find carried on in Bermondsey. One is that of a Clay Pipe Maker; the other that of a Muffin and Crumpet Maker. The first

Artificial Flower Making is an industry in which hundreds of girls and women are engaged. But it is a trade that is divided into several branches. The highest branch is that in which girls are engaged in making the flowers that adorn ladies' bonnets. Some of these are made at home, as our illustration on p. 25 shows, by girls who are most dexterous in the use of their fingers, but the best of them are made in factories. The artificial flowers most patronised by the poor are made of coloured paper, and are manufactured in their homes by poor women who, as I have said, divide their time between these articles and ornaments for your fire-stove. There are also men who make artificial flowers—and very real they appear too—out of raw carrots and turnips, and these have a very fair sale among a certain class, who find them last longer, and serve their purpose better, than natural flowers.

The last trade to which we can refer here is one which is not strictly a Home Trade, though all arrangements for carrying it out have to be made from that centre. It is the gentleman who makes a living by calling workmen early in the morning at sixpence per week. At many common lodging-houses an early caller finds constant employment, but I do not purpose to write about persons who wake up the lodgers for a consideration. I refer now to a very different sort of individual—a gentleman who finds his chief source of income in calling at workmen's houses and waking them up very early in the morning, so that they can be at their employment while the bell is ringing or the clock is striking the hour. All over London such men are engaged. There is one who does a large business in North Camberwell.

In the window of his front parlour may be seen the accompanying announcement. When you enquire you find that the price for being "called"

is twopence a morning or sixpence a week. The caller finds a good many customers needing his services, though he comes in constant competition with the night policeman, who is as a rule open to accept engagements on the same terms. But the gentleman in blue is liable to be called away just at the time he is required to wake his customer. Remembering this fact, workmen trust themselves to the man who has no other engagements to distract his attention. And so the old gentleman who begs workmen to "enquire within" does a very fair business. The only other business he takes in hand is selling books and newspapers, but these principally occupy his attention on Sundays, when the workman does not ask to be called early, but prefers to remain in bed and dream on undisturbed.

TAILORING.

JEWISH BOY REPLYING TO A TOAST AFTER A " CONFIRMATION " DINNER.

JEWISH LONDON.

By S. GELBERG.

A HUNDRED thousand men, women, and children, some of them fugitives still suffering the punishment of Cain, others just sloughing the Ghetto skin, yet others in whose ears the "*hep, hep*" of the Continent is a long-forgotten cry. A great congregation, the majority still standing (in its faith) with the Law-giver at Sinai, while a few are marching in the vanguard of the sceptics. An eager, restless body, most devout of peoples, yet swiftest of foot in the commercial race; fascinating microcosm of the latter-day world, yet branded with the mark of antiquity; full of the hopefulness of youth, yet seamed and scarred with the martyrdom of ages. Such, in brief, are the Jews of London.

Let us turn aside into the Whitechapel Ghetto, where they most do congregate. Many of its narrow courts and mean slums have fallen before the fiat of the sanitary authority or the advance of the factory owner. Yet enough still remains of its original quaintness, its babel of tongues and chaos of races, to make it stand prominently out as a unique entity from the dull grey mass of the East-End population. Its denizens are a complicated piece of human patchwork, with the ringleted Pole at one point, the Dutch Jew at another, the English Hebrew in his own corner, and the Gentile coster running like a strange thin thread through the design. The whole is a reproduction in little of the stricken Jewish world. If you would understand the immortal agony of Jewry, go into the East-End colony. Its cosmopolitanism is symbolic of the vagabondage of the race. Its beshawled women with their pinched faces, its long-coated men with two thousand years of persecution stamped in their manner, its chaffering and huckstering, its hunger, its humour, the very Yiddish jargon itself which is scrawled on its walls and shop windows, are part of the grand passion of the chosen people.

But it is its utterly alien aspect which strikes you first and foremost. For the Ghetto is a fragment of Poland torn off from Central Europe and dropped haphazard into the heart of Britain—a re-banished

Jewry weeping beside the waters of "Modern Babylon."

On Sunday Middlesex Street (better known as the "Lane") and its adjoining tho-

KILLING AND PLUCK-
ING POULTRY.

SLAUGHTERHOUSE WHERE POULTRY ARE KILLED.

roughfares are a howling pandemonium of cosmopolitan costerism, a curious tangle of humanity, with the Englishman (Jew and Gentile) in possession and the alien in the background. In these congested streets you can be clothed like an aristocrat for a few shillings, fed *al fresco* like an epicure for sixpence, and cured of all your bodily ills for a copper coin—the chorus of the children in the Hebrew classes often answering the roar of the gutter merchant, like a new and grotesque Church antiphony. The "Lane" on Sunday is, indeed, the last home of the higher costerism. Round its stalls the coster humour reaches its finest fancies, the coster philosophy its profoundest depths, the coster oratory its highest flights. But the most abiding impression it leaves on your mind as you struggle out of its seething, shouting, gesticulating population is of infinite pic-turesqueness, and the life-stream tumbling like a swirling torrent along its course.

On the weekday, however, the scene is transformed. The noise and bustle are gone. The alien with his Yiddish holds the field. You are in a city of endless toil. All day

long and far into the night the fac-tories make dismal music in the Ghetto. From break of day till the going-down of the sun rings the song of the coster through its grimy streets. "Weiber, Weiber! heimische Beigel!"* sing out the women, with handkerchief drawn tightly over head. "Customeers, cus-tomeers! veer are you?" chime in the men. "Stockings feer poor (pairs) a shilling!" groans a hapless elder driven in his old age to tempt fortune in a strange land. Often, soon after dawn, the costers are quarrelling with one another for a suitable "pitch," with a sneer, perhaps, at a Gentile sleeping off a public-house debauch on the pavement; and long after the shadows have lengthened in the Ghetto they are still vouching by their own lives or the kind-ness of the Shem Yisboroch (God) to Israel for the quality of their wares. So spins the toiling Ghetto round its daily orbit.

Why do these Jews labour so? It is because of their passionate yearning for a "place in the sun." Unlike the Gentile, they are in the East-End, not of it—strangers and sojourners in its midst; alien Dick Whittingtons in side curls and "jupizes" (long coats), who have put down their bundles a while to peer into the promised land beyond, and thereafter rest not till they have retired beaten from the struggle or found social salvation in Maida Vale.

And yet this Ghetto is not all poor. It is really homespun lined with ermine, Dives cheek by jowl with Lazarus. These in-dustrious female costers, for instance, arguing volubly with reluctant customers, have left a husband—working in a factory—who is preparing to blossom into an employer, a son retailing jewellery in a second street, and a daughter selling hosiery in a third.

* "Ladies, ladies! rolls for sale just like those in our native land."

In a few years a vigorous pull and a pull all together will have hauled the family up to a plane of comparative affluence and the Ghetto have become a distant memory. Quite a crop of Jewish *nouveaux riches*, too, has ripened in the various shops and factories that stud the Ghetto.

And if the Ghetto is not wholly poor neither is it entirely famished. Kosher restaurants abound in it; kosher butcher shops are clustered in thick bunches in its most hopeless parts (seven of them at the junction of Middlesex Street and Wentworth Street), and if the expert handling of the fowls on the stalls by ill-clad Jewesses is not a revelation of epicureanism in humble life, then, most assuredly, things are not what they seem.

Only the superficial think this Jewish colony a mere vale of tears. In the groan of its machinery and the roar of its markets I can distinguish an unmistakable titter—the titter of the Hebrew at his would-be converters, the full-throated laughter of the Ghetto at the Yiddish play, the merriment of the buxom and placid-faced Jewess taking the air by her street-door, the fun of the youth in corduroys who finds a foretaste of Gan Eiden (Paradise) in a game of cricket on the broad spaces of Bell Lane or the green fields of Frying-Pan Alley. On Chometz Battel night* the Ghetto even gives itself over to wild carnival till the flaring naphtha jets on the stalls have died to a spluttering flicker and the Christian world is fast asleep. Nay! let no one call the Ghetto melancholy who has not looked in at its dancing clubs and watched an old crony of seventy at a Hebrew wedding foot the furious Kosatzki with a gay old dog of ten winters more.

And there is learning as well as piety in the Ghetto—piety in a dirty face, scholarship behind a mask of rags. How interesting is the spectacle of the bearded elders — peripatetic philosophers of the Ghetto—wending their way slowly from the synagogue, rapt in Talmudic discussion. The coster, too, has sometimes much Rabbinic lore. As he sits, spectacles on nose, behind

* The night before Passover Eve, on which all "leaven" is removed from Jewish houses.

his stall absorbed in the political columns of one or other of the new-born Yiddish Press (which, by the way, never prints racing news, and once even boasted a kind of Yiddish *Punch*), I often wonder whether his ill-clad person may not enshrine the brilliancy of a stunted Lassalle, the genius of a Disraeli *manqué*.

The Ghetto's piety is written on nearly every pinched face and across every brick wall. Was ever such a religious slum—a slum with a passion for scattering little synagogues (or chevras) up and down its dark courts—even, so it is said, in garrets and basements? It is artistically religious, this Ghetto, delighting in hymns rendered with the proper trills and anthems delivered in an operatic dress—actually not hesitating to pay £300 for a few services to a truly musical chazan (reader of the services). In its fervour it has brought with it from Poland the melammed (or poverty-stricken pedagogue), who has set up his bare and humble little schoolrooms all over the district, and hammers Hebrew instruction by the hour into the jaded heads of the children of the Ghetto. These little scholars scurrying Chederwards of an evening, clutching the remains of a hurried tea, are one of the most touching and instructive spectacles of this strange colony. Now and then something like a shiver of horror passes over the Ghetto when

A CHEDER (JEWISH SCHOOL) IN WHITECHAPEL.

A "KOSHER" WARNING.

it is discovered that a traitor has been palming off trifah* meat on his customers as kosher. Then the Board of Shecheta,† which attends to such matters, pastes a solemn warning on the walls to the faithful, and the offending stall is promptly forsaken. Altogether, indeed, a unique little cosmos, this East-End Hebrew colony—a poverty-stricken, wealthy, hungry, feasting, praying, bargaining fragment of a "nation of priests."

But the Ghetto is not the whole of London Jewry. On its borders stands the famous Houndsditch—one of the world's great toy-lands, whence the Hebrew merchant scatters his playthings and fancy wares over the world, and where our roaring gutter-commerce hunts out its penny wonders. Out in Soho has been planted another vigorous little settlement—mostly of tailors. Across the North of London — Dalston and Canonbury — stretches a third thick Hebrew belt. Here you are in presence of the Jewish bourgeois — the well-groomed, prosperous English Jew (as he loves to call himself), with the keenest of brains and a heart of gold. His ear always to the ground to catch the first distant murmurs of every trade movement, he has made himself prominent in every commercial walk he treads. Go into the Diamond Club in Hatton Garden. It is nothing but a Jewish rendezvous. Speak to the salesmen

in Covent Garden. They will tell you, with a merry twinkle in their eye, of the portion of the market once called "The Synagogue"; and it is almost the same with the fancy, fur, cheap clothing, boot, and furniture trades. But this easily won Hebrew gold circulates freely. For the bourgeois Jews are full of the *joie de vivre*. You see it in their dances, their card parties, their "confirmation" dinners (when the Jewish lad of thirteen, having been called to the reading of the Law in the Synagogue, replies to the toast of his health in a carefully learnt speech), their enthusiastic patronage of the theatre, their great summer migration—like a new Exodus—to the sea-side, and the resplendent finery of their hand-some women-folk, without whom the North of London would be infinitely duller and the great emporia of Islington poorer indeed. Their religion, however, is in a state of flux. Some of them, like many "upper-class" Jews, have outgrown the spiritual outfit of the East without acquiring a substitute; hence a state of religious nakedness. They are far indeed from Nazareth. But they are equally distant from Jerusalem. They wander on a half-heathenish middle track.

Further afield—in Maida Vale, Hampstead, and Bayswater—are the tents of upper-class Jewry. In them mingle the arts and the sciences, fashion and beauty, Jew and Gentile;

PERIPATETIC PHILOSOPHERS OF
THE GHETTO.

* Not killed according to the Jewish rites; meat eligible to be eaten is said to be "kosher." The illustrations on p. 30 show a shed in which fowls are killed by the shochetim (slaughterers) at a penny a-piece.

† Literally the Board which looks after the slaughtering of the cattle.

for those who own them are often wealthy, frequently polished, English to the core always. In business they are stock-brokers, merchants, art connoisseurs. As professional men they are giving their fatherland a clever band of authors, artists, and lawyers. Year by year their offspring are found in the ancient English seats of learning in greater numbers—the grandchildren of the Ghetto studying at Jesus' or graduating at Christ's with equal impartiality What's in a name? And everywhere they are, in conjunction with other Jews, endeavouring by a huge effort —by Jewish study circles, literary societies, and the like — to save their people from the Gehinnom of materialism.

Yet let no one think that the Jewry of the East and the Jewry of the West are separate worlds revolving in

BEFORE THE BETH-DIN (JEWISH COURT).

separate orbits. In essential characteristics they are really one. East-End or West-End, the Jew is still the family man among the nations, delighting keenly in the joys of domesticity. Out of this love of a home and married bliss has sprung that humorous rogue, the Shadchan, or professional matchmaker — a glib fellow of elastic conscience who worries Hebrew bachelors into matrimony in return for a five per cent. levy on the dowry received. Occasionally, when the marriage is a *fait accompli*, the parties snap their fingers at Mr. Shadchan. Upon which he summons them to the Chief Rabbi, who, with two other rabbis, constitute the Beth-Din — a Hebrew judicial bench beset by

pious men in religious doubt, jilted women, landlords and tenants, and other members of a regrettably contentious race. In many cases the word of the Beth-Din is law.

All these London Jews, too, whether East-End or West-End, are patriots to their finger-tips. This patriotism has impressed the physiognomy of the race on at least one East-End Volunteer regiment. It converts the naturalisation returns into catalogues of Biblical (and Polish) names. It has given birth to what a British officer with an unkindly sneer once called the "Houndsditch Highlander." It has resulted in the flower of many a Jewish family being left to die on the African veldt. And it has produced the Jewish Lads' Brigade —an organisation for evolving the Joab and the Judas Maccabæus who lie buried deep down under the Jewish stock-broker or hawker. You can often see the lads of this brigade marching smartly to the beat of the drum through the London streets, like a new Army of the Lord of Hosts —though a juvenile one, to be sure. But while with the upper-class Jew the cry is, "England my Zion, and London my Jerusalem," the aliens' patriotism co-exists with their Zionism. They tumble in their thousands after the music of Zionist oratory as resistlessly as the children of Hamelin city after the ravishing note of the Pied Piper.

London Jewry is a wonderful network of charity. With the aid of his middle-class brother, the West-End Jew has built up a system of philanthropy which follows the poor from cradle to grave—educating their young ones (at the Jews' Free School, the greatest elementary school on earth), rearing their orphans (at the Jews' Hospital and Orphan Asylum), apprenticing their lads to honest trades through the medium of the Jewish Board of Guardians (itself comprising remarkable charities, prophylactic and curative), dowering their brides, tending their sick (in special Jewish wards in the hospitals), nursing their convalescents, feeding their aged, and laying their dead decently in the grave.

But it is on its religious side that the fascination of London Jewry is greatest. The squalid darkness. Look into the room whence it proceeds. A snow-white cloth covers the table. Two candles are burning with a joyous brightness. Two chalos (or twists) rest pleasantly one on the other. It is the Jew-pedlar's home on a Sabbath eve! Presently the master of this little paradise returns. "May God make you as Ephraim and Manasseh," he says, laying his hands on the head of his stooping boy. "May God make you as Rachel and Leah," he prays, extending his palms gently over his daughter's head. Then, for the rest of that evening, Psalms and good cheer. On the morrow, the Sabbath peace.

LADS' BRIGADE, JEWS' HOSPITAL AND ORPHAN ASYLUM, WEST NORWOOD.

return of the Jew to earth is devoid of the floral pomp that marks the interment of the Gentile. A plain deal coffin in a sombre black cloth, a few notes of submission to Providence moaned into the echoing air, the cry of the minister, "May he come to his place in peace," the heavy thud of the clay as it is cast on the coffin by the nearest kindred of the dead (oh! bitterest of Jewish practices!), and the Hebrew is at rest with his fathers.

Yet, this natural exception apart, the religion of the observant Jew is a perpetual joy to him, dashing his drab existence with the vividest colouring and hanging like a brilliant rainbow across his sky. The Hebrew wedding, with its many-hued canopy, its crashing of a tumbler under foot, its conjugal pledges in "Babylonish dialect," is like a calculated variant on the monotony of life. Then, the Sabbath! High up in an East-End model dwelling a gleam of brightness pierces the

The Passover, with its unleavened cakes, subjects the Hebrew to a not unpleasant little dietary revolution. The festival of Pentecost, bathing his synagogue in flowers, puts sunshine and springtide into his blood. The Feast of Booths wafts him for nine days into a fruit-and-lamp-hung arcadia*; while the blast of the ram's horn on his New Year's Day transports him in spirit back to the land where the sound of the shofar† proclaimed rest to the soil and liberty to the slave. It is a time of reconciliation and brotherhood and peace; for are not the destinies of all being decided before the judgment seat of God? and so between Jew and Jew pass New Year cards bearing the familiar device in Yiddish, signifying: "May you be inscribed for a good year in the Book of Life." Then,

* That is to say, into the succah or tent in which the Jew is supposed to live during the whole of the festival—a memory of the booths in which Israel dwelt during its journeying in the desert.

† "Shofar" is the Hebrew name for the ram's horn.

that day of days, the great White Fast.* Go on that solemn fast day into the Cathedral Synagogue, down East. There, wealth in the person of Lord Rothschild rubs shoulders with poverty in the form of the alien refugee; and West in the shape of evening-dress meets East in the form of the long white gown (or kittel). The edifice is packed with a great penitent congregation—prominent among them the Yom Kippur Jew making his annual call on Providence. The Cohanim, or priests,† with outstretched palms and praying-shawls on their heads, bless the people, saying: "May the Lord bless thee and guard thee." Through the livelong day rise the plaintive prayers for pardon. Time and again the penitents beat their breast and prostrate themselves humbly in the dust. The morning slowly wears to afternoon, the afternoon fades into night. The air grows close and heavy. Yet not till the "day has turned" and the lights are lit is the atonement ended. Then the congregation draw their white praying-shawls over their heads and say after their Reader the prayer for the dying:

"Hear, O Israel, the Lord is our God, the

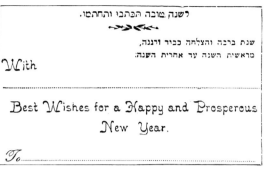

A JEWISH NEW YEAR CARD.

Lord is One." The congregation repeat the words with a shout like a thunder-crash.

"The Lord, He is God," sings the Reader.

"The Lord, He is God," repeat the people seven times, with a roar like the cry of a lost nation. Then, with a shrill note from the ram's horn, the congregation is dismissed—the merchant to his office, the clerk to his desk, and the penitent, perchance, to his crooked ways again.

Such is the London fragment of the Eternal race. It is a growing community, not unmarred by faults, yet not without its ideal side. And it is testing in its own person the combination in one body of the devoted Jew and the English patriot. If it fail, it adds yet another chapter to its people's martyrdom. If it succeed, it knells the end—however remote—of the great Jewish tragedy.

* So called by Gentiles on account of the many white praying-shawls, white caps, etc., in the synagogue on that day. The Hebrews call it Yom Kippur (Day of Atonement).

† Shown on the right of the full-page picture entitled "In the Cathedral Synagogue."

JEWESSES TAKING THE AIR BY THEIR STREET DOORS.

PAWNBROKING LONDON.

By C. A. CUTHBERT KEESON.

PAWN-TICKET.

LONG before the inhabitants of London were blessed with a County Council the at one time universal practice of attracting customers to a shop by means of a sign had fallen into almost complete disuse; but even in this twentieth century no enterprising pawnbroker would think of opening a shop without there hung over it, conspicuous from every point of view, "The Three Brass Balls," "The Swinging Dumplings," "The Sign of the Two to One."

It is the fashion in the trade to speak of these emblems as the insignia of the old Lombard Merchants, and the arms of the Medici. What, however, do those three bright globes mean to thousands of people who walk the streets of London? Some perhaps may pass them unnoticed, but to the poor—the working man who finds it difficult to properly apportion his weekly wage, the clerk out of a berth, the racing man who has had a spell of bad luck, to the small shopkeeper and the costermonger in want of ready money to replenish their stock, to the actor and actress not "in the bill"—they mean a great deal. They mean food for the wife and children when cupboard and pocket are empty—a little money to keep things going till next pay-day; they mean to thousands shelter, warmth, and something to eat; and although many may consider the pawnbroker's shop an encouragement to improvidence and unthriftiness, every philanthropist who would abolish it admits that he would have to substitute some municipal or charitable pawnshop in its place.

It has been asserted that "to one in every two persons in London the pawnbroker has been in some period of his or her life a stern and unavoidable reality." This estimate may appear to be somewhat exaggerated, but investigations into the amount of business done in the pawnshops of London show that the statement is not very wide of the mark. Within a radius of ten miles from the Royal Exchange are 692 pawnbrokers' shops. From figures obtained from a trustworthy source (the *Pawnbrokers' Gazette*) it appears that the average number of pledges taken in per month at each shop

ARRESTED WHILE PAWNING.

is 5,000, making an aggregate for all the shops of 3,460,000, or 41,520,000 pledges per year, or rather more than six to each head of the population. In these figures pledges of more than £10 in amount are not taken into account, and a very large proportion of the London pawnbrokers do a big business of this kind. Inquiries made at some seventeen shops in different parts of the Metropolis show that out of a million and a-quarter pledges extending over a period of twelve months 66,700 only were for amounts above ten shillings. In the trade these are known as "Auctions," having, if left unredeemed at the end of twelve months and seven days, to be disposed of at public auction. All pledges for sums under ten shillings at a like period become the absolute property of the pawnbroker. In the seventeen shops referred to the average amount lent upon each pledge worked out at four shillings—£250,000 in all. Taking the total number of pledges made annually in London upon the same basis,

within the shop of that mysterious "Uncle" of whom his companions have talked so glibly. What his business was is known only to that "Uncle" and himself, and as he walks triumphantly down the street, relieved in mind and circumstance, he asks himself why he made all that fuss about so simple a matter. Yet it takes a good many visits before he feels quite at his ease. The interview usually lasts less than a couple of minutes, and as a memorandum of it the obliging pawnbroker hands his customer a

STORING BUNDLES IN THE "WEEKLY PLEDGE" ROOM.

viz. 41,520,000 at four shillings each, it will be seen that the pawnbrokers supply the "hard-ups" of London annually with the very large sum of £8,304,000.

There are few things in the ordinary way of life more calculated to unnerve a man than a first visit to the pawnshop. Hence most pawnbrokers, to put their customers as much at ease as possible, have their shops divided into separate compartments known as "the boxes," with the entrance up a side street, or rendered as inconspicuous as the character of the house will permit. For the better class customers the modern pawnbroker provides a comfortable "private office."

The nervous pledger, dreading he knows not what, surveys for some minutes the contents of the window, and only after much hesitation and many false starts finds himself

neat little square-shaped envelope containing a piece of paste board bearing upon its face a description of the article deposited and on the back an abridged version of the Pawnbrokers' Act.

Very differently does it fare with the pawner of stolen property. Ask a pawnbroker in what way his suspicions are aroused. He will tell you that he does not know. "There is generally something," he says, "about the pawner's manner or in his replies to questions that sets the pawnbroker on his guard." He cannot define precisely what that "something" is, but he plies the would-be pledger with more pertinent queries, sets a junior hand to run over the "Police List," looks again at the article offered and at the offerer. Experience may not have made him infallible, but his daily dealings have made him wary. If the man

SATURDAY NIGHT AT A PAWNBROKER'S.

is a "wrong 'un" the long delay makes him fidgety, and then " Uncle," confirmed in his suspicions, secretly sends for the man in blue. Sometimes a thief will stay and try to brazen the matter out, at others he makes a dash for liberty, frequently only to run into the arms of an officer waiting at the shop door. If the article be not in the " Police List," or if the pawnbroker be not satisfied in his own mind that the goods have been dishonestly come by, he may decline the goods and let the man depart, for it is a dangerous thing to be too hasty in delivering any one into custody.

Pawnbrokers know that if they take in a stolen article they will have to restore it to the owner, lose the money lent upon it, and attend the courts. That knowledge makes them cautious. Many magistrates and public officials contend that a considerable portion of the property stolen in the Metropolis finds its way into the hands of the pawnbrokers. Every day reports appear in the papers in which stolen goods have been pawned, and there are a still larger number of cases which are not reported. Unquestionably quantities of stolen articles find their way to the pawnbroker, and it is generally a good thing for their owners when they do, for by means of that "automatic detective," the pawn-ticket, they are generally traced and restored. A pawnbroker has to keep a pledge by him for twelve months and give a ticket, which many thieves seem to have a peculiar fondness for preserving. Stolen articles, however, form but an infinitesimal item in the forty-one millions of pledges made yearly. Statistics prepared for the House of Commons show that they fall far short of one per month for each of the 692 pawnbrokers in London.

To redeem a watch or an article of jewellery is an easy matter, and for even the nervous man it has usually no terrors. There are times, however, when the act of redemption is not so easy. Come with me to a busy working neighbourhood like Walworth, where pawnbrokers' shops abound and thousands of homes are dependent upon them. It is Saturday night, and the shop and stall keepers are doing a roaring trade. We turn down a side street, where the lamps do not burn so brightly, and meet a continuous procession of women hurrying away with bundles of all

sorts and sizes. Some carry but one, others, assisted by children, have as many as half-a-dozen. They all come from that little door by the side of a pawnbroker's. Standing in the background of the shop, we are confronted by a row of faces peering over the counter. The shop is one that, possibly for the convenience of so large a throng, dispenses with the boxes, and the customers all mingle together. It is a strangely animated scene, with nearly all the characters played by women. It is a rarity to see a man among them, though children are too many for our liking. Girls and even boys are there, all ready with their money, for they may redeem pledges, though the law forbids the pawnbroker to receive a pledge from anyone under the age of sixteen. The women are mostly bare-armed, and look as though they had just come from the wash-tub. They betray no sense of shame if they feel it. They talk and gossip while waiting for their bundles, and are wonderfully polite to the perspiring assistants behind the counter. Though everybody is in a hurry there is little noise or unseemly jostling. An assistant seizes a battered tin bowl, and the front rank of pledgers toss their tickets therein. He then rapidly sorts them out, and gives some to a boy, who darts away to the far end of the counter. The remainder he places in a canvas bag which we have noticed dangling at the end of a string at the back of the shop; he shakes the rope, and immediately the bag is whisked out of sight up the well of the lift used for conveying pledges from the shop to the warehouse above. In a minute it begins to rain bundles until the floor is thickly strewn with them.

In a conspicuous spot on the wall is a notice that no furniture or heavy goods will be delivered after 4 p.m. From that time the rapid delivery of bundles has been proceeding; and so it goes on, hour after hour, Saturday after Saturday, year after year; every pledge produced systematically; no disputes, no haggling about change; unexamined bundles exchanged for money; money swept into a huge till; the whole accompanied with a running fire of bundles from the unseen regions above, hurled down what the pawnbroker calls the " well," but what is more familiarly known as the "spout"

FURNITURE ROOM IN A PAWNBROKER'S WAREHOUSE.

Pawnbrokers' Act, the police, so far as London is concerned, have stamped these latter pests out of existence.

The nature of a pawnbroker's business can, perhaps, be best estimated by a visit to his warehouse and an inspection of the heterogeneous collection of pledged articles. This differs, however, with the character of the shop. There are the chief pawnbrokers of London, who lend only on plate, jewellery, and property of the highest description. By the courtesy of Mr. Henry Arthur Attenborough, we were permitted to inspect the well-known premises of Messrs. George Atten-

—that spout up which so many things have mysteriously disappeared.

The year round there is an average of 2,000 bundles delivered each Saturday night from this shop, and if we chance that way on the following Monday and Tuesday we shall meet that same procession of women, though this time trooping towards that little side door. Occasionally a man comes on the same errand, shamefacedly trying to conceal his bundle beneath his coat. It is undoubtedly a sad scene for the moralist, but these people know no other way of living, have no place where their Sunday clothes will be safe, have no one but the pawnbroker to apply to when they feel the pinch of hunger. He is their banker and their safe-deposit, and although they know they pay dearly for it in the long run, they are thankful that they have him to turn to in their need. They might easily be worse off, might have no other resource but to sell their sticks and clothes, or, what is as bad, take them to a "Dolly" or "Leaving" shop, so named after the "Black Doll," the conventional sign of the small brokers and rag shops, where articles that a pawnbroker will not receive may be "left" for a short term at high interest. Thanks to the provisions of the

borough and Son, at the junction of Chancery Lane with Fleet Street. As in most pawnbrokers', there are the boxes for the general pledger, and in addition there are two or three small offices for the reception of persons who wish to transact their business privately. All sorts and descriptions of men, and women too, come to Messrs. Attenborough. They have lent £7,000 upon a diamond necklet, a present from a royal personage to a celebrated member of the demi-monde, the said necklet being redeemed and deposited again time after time. The coronet of an Austrian nobleman remained in their custody for several years with a loan of £15,000 upon it. A savant pawned the fore-arm and hand of a mummy wearing a fine turquoise scarabæus ring on one of the fingers. Upon the day of our visit we saw that an advance of 1s. 6d. had been made on a ring, and we were shown an application for a loan of £40,000 upon jewellery.

The seamy side of the picture is presented by the warehouse of the pawnbroker, whose chief business consists of pledges of "soft" goods. The whole house from basement to roof is built up in skeleton frames or "stacks," in which the pledges, each carefully done up in a wrapper, are neatly packed, the tickets to the front. On the first floor the weekly pledges are usually stored, that they may be ready at hand for Saturday night. There is one room devoted to the storage of furniture, in another are rows and rows of pictures, looking-glasses and over-mantels. There are shelves for china and glass, ornaments and clocks; tools of every kind, sufficient to start many workshops. In odd corners we come across odd sights—sea boots and the huge boots of a sewerman; a bundle of sweeps' brooms, apparently not very long retired from active employment, picks, spades, fire-irons, musical instru-ments, cabmens' whips, um-brellas — yes, even a tiny pair of child's shoes— everything.

Of the thousands of pledges stored in a pawn-broker's warehouse the majority are redeemed, but there are many, variously estimated at from 20 to 33 per cent. of the whole, which remain unredeemed at the expiration of the twelve months and seven days' grace. These are known in the trade as "forfeits," and

HER CHILD'S SHOES.

WITH STEALTHY TREAD.

are disposed of in divers ways. Forfeited pledges, upon which sums of less than 10s. have been ad-vanced, become, as already stated, the pawnbroker's property. Some are placed in the sale stock; occasionally the whole bulk of two or three months' forfeits are sold to a dealer at a discount of 15 or 20 per cent. off the price marked upon the tickets, the pawnbroker being anxious to get rid of them at almost any price. The remainder are sent to public auction.

Of the auctioneers who make a speciality of this business the rooms of Messrs. Deben-ham, Storr and Sons, King Street, Covent Garden, are, perhaps, best known to the public. On the first floor a sale of "fashionable jewellery," silver plate, watches, plated ware, etc., is proceeding. Suspended upon hooks at the far end of the room near the auctioneer's rostrum are watches too numerous to count. You may buy a bundle of them for little more than a sovereign. An irregular horseshoe of glass-topped cases, in which the more important lots are stored,

AN UNWELCOME PLEDGE.

form the boundary of an inner ring, into which the privileged and well-known buyers are alone allowed to enter; wooden desks or tables form the outer boundary for the smaller dealers and that peculiar class of people who haunt the auction-rooms—people who display an interest in every lot, yet have never been known to buy.

Simultaneously a miscellaneous sale of "sporting goods" is taking place on the ground floor. People of quite a different type attend this sale: men of sporting tendencies and horsey appearance take the place of the Jews, who form a large proportion of the buyers at the jewellery sales. Here are sportsmen's knives and bicycles, guns by the score, walking sticks, shooting boots, billiard cues and fishing rods, boxes of cigars, and bottles of champagne or burgundy; all things which no true sportsman should be without.

Incredible as it may seem to the uninitiated, there are thousands of persons in London alone who are making a comfortable living out of "Uncle" by buying or manufacturing and pledging goods. There are regular manufactories where clothing can be purchased

at a price which the unwary pawnbroker will advance upon, and several pledges in the course of a day will bring a handsome profit. Plate and jewellery are manufactured for the same purpose. Now it is a gold charm for the watch chain; again it is a silver cigarette box, the weight of which has been considerably increased by the insertion of a piece of base metal between the cedar wood lining and the silver exterior. Everything that the pawnbroker will lend money upon—that is to say everything that has any market value whatever—is manufactured for the sole purpose of deceiving him, while sometimes even the natural beauties of goods are artificially enhanced by the aid of scientific knowledge.

To please his clients, to be careful without giving offence, to prevent fraud, and to detain the guilty while trying to make a little for himself, is no light task. If "Uncle" does not give satisfaction all round it is scarcely to be wondered at. He does his best under difficult and often disagreeable circumstances, and those who are too prone to blame him for a mistake are generally quite ignorant of the nature and extent of his business.

A SALE OF UNREDEEMED GOODS (DEBENHAM, STORR AND SONS).

LONDON SCOTTISH : THE ORDERLY ROOM.

VOLUNTEER LONDON.

By CAPTAIN J. E. COOPER.

THE Londoner born and bred is probably no less attracted than his country cousin by the sight of a regiment of Volunteers. The most casual observer could not fail to notice how greatly Volunteering has become an integral part of the life of the Metropolis. Every evening signs of it are to be noticed, and the occasion of a Church Parade on a Sunday morning is a popular event in many suburbs. The regiment will assemble most probably at its headquarters, all the men as smart in appearance as careful attention to uniform and accoutrements can ensure. For this muster the full-dress head dress is worn, and the men carry side-arms. Preceded by the band, as they march to church, they are sure to be keenly watched by the residents. The service will most likely be conducted by the chaplain of the corps, and there are few preachers who cannot so fit the words of their sermon as to make a definite impression on their hearers. In accordance with military usage the service concludes with "God save the King," and, filing out of their seats, the men form up outside. Once more they march through the

streets, where doubtless a throng of persons await their return, and on arrival at head-quarters they will be dismissed.

But Saturday afternoon is, of course, the grand opportunity for an interested spectator. At the Armoury House, Finsbury, he may see the historic Honourable Artillery Company, a lineal descendant of such a train-band as that in which John Gilpin was a captain. The Honourable Artillery Company takes precedence of all Yeomanry and Volunteers, and is amongst the very few corps which have the right to march through the City of London with fixed bayonets. It will be observed that it has two batteries of Horse Artillery, the men of which are clothed in a somewhat similar manner to the Royal Horse Artillery, and an Infantry Battalion, turned out in scarlet and bear-skins, very much like the familiar uniform of the Foot Guards. As a spectacle of pomp and circumstance, let the observer, if possible, be present when the colour is "trooped" by the H.A.C.; and fortunate indeed will he be if he can procure an invitation to one of their dinners, and listen to the traditional cry of "Zaye, Zaye, Zaye!"

As one passes through the Metropolis many men will be seen, in various uniforms, all wending their way to the rendezvous of their several corps. A goodly number of those in dark green will possibly belong to the 2nd London.

In whatever direction a journey be taken Volunteers will be conspicuous. Passing

collective exactitude displayed by the young athletes would form a convincing proof of how erroneous it is for pessimists to declare that the nation's manhood is degenerating.

Let us now go out into the crowded streets again. Surely that sound we hear is the wail of the pipes? Yes; in a few minutes a kilted battalion marches by in grand style, the 7th Middlesex, the famous London Scottish. "Certainly," remarks a critical

Photo: Gregory & Co., Strand, W.C.

THE H.A.C. : A MARCH PAST.

Somerset House may be heard the strains of "God Bless the Prince of Wales," for the 12th Middlesex (Civil Service Rifles), the Prince of Wales's Own, are on parade in the square. We pass on to the School of Arms, a truly fascinating spot for the lover of all kinds of physical exercises. Here take place bouts of fencing—best of training for quickness of hand and eye in combination— and rounds of boxing, an equally exacting test of pluck and good temper. The gymnastic apparatus — parallel bars, horizontal bars, trapeze, rings, vaulting horses, ladders— speak for themselves. The keen activity and

bystander, "the physique of the men from over the Border is not to be surpassed." We enter the orderly room of the regiment to find the colonel seated at the table, and the adjutant giving instructions to staff-sergeants. The adjutant is here responsible for the accuracy of no mean amount of correspondence and "Returns," as on the parade ground he is answerable for the instruction of all ranks, and the correctness of drill.

Turn aside for a moment from the purely official side, and look at another aspect of Volunteer life in London. Near Charing

LONDON IRISH : THE CANTEEN.

the 1st Middlesex Royal Engineers. Here a detachment is busily at work building a bridge. Without Engineers the best army in the world is likely to be useless. The Engineers render points of vantage accessible, roads passable, woods clear, rivers no hindrance. They extinguish, as it were, time and space by means of the field telegraph. Hard would it be to fix a limit to the extent of their functions of utility.

We next betake ourselves to Hyde Park. On the way let us call at the Guildhall, where a company of the Royal Army Medical Corps (Volunteers) is drilling. The name suggests the province of the corps, as the particular duties pertaining to military ambulance receive most attention.

On reaching Hyde Park a large mass of troops are to be seen taking up position. On the right of the line are over a hundred mounted men, the Mounted Infantry Company of the 13th Middlesex, Queen's Westminster. The corps, in neat grey uniform and the still very general slouch

Cross are the headquarters of the 16th Middlesex, the London Irish. The Emerald Isle has furnished many gallant soldiers for the Empire, and its Volunteer representatives on this side of the water are generally "as smart as paint." We see some of them here pleasantly occupied in the canteen.

Imagine the interested observer to be shod in a pair of the legendary seven-league boots. He takes one short stride and stands in the headquarters of

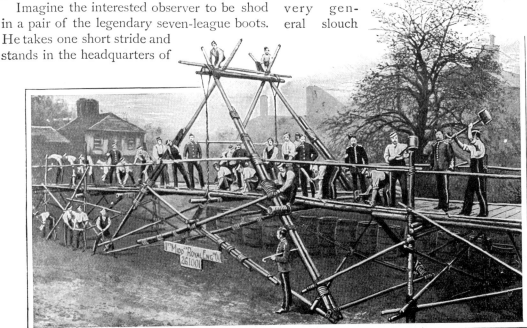

1ST MIDDLESEX ROYAL ENGINEERS : BRIDGE BUILDING.

hat, is deservedly popular. We go to their headquarters, Buckingham Gate, where we see a line of men awaiting their turn to take the oath of allegiance to the Sovereign and to be duly enrolled. Who will wonder that the line is so long? Yet not a few who wished to be numbered in that line have been rejected. The height standard, the chest-measuring tape, the heart and lungs examination, the sight test, all contribute to their exclusion.

Once more returning to Hyde Park, a strong battalion clothed in a serviceable light grey uniform is encountered. An expert explains that they are the 20th Middlesex, widely known as the Artists'; and before the Park is left behind a party of signallers attracts attention. The men are engaged in "flag-wagging"—the slang term for this method of signalling. Any message can be communicated by means of the Morse alphabet, as far as the movement of the flag can be discerned. A powerful telescope enables flag signals to be read at a considerable distance. By night the same effect, the Morse combination of long and short signs — technically "dashes" and "dots"—can be obtained by the use of a flash-lamp. And great results have been exhibited by the heliograph, which, as its name implies, avails itself of the sun's aid to produce the necessary succession of long and short gleams on a reflector, on the same principle that the naughty boy on a sunny day creates flashes of light on the ceiling of the schoolroom by means of the polished blade of his new pocket-knife. Messages have been directly conveyed a distance of eighty miles by the employment of the heliograph. Ponder these facts and view the signalling party with added respect.

Proceeding to Regent's Park, below the sheen of bayonets a glimpse is caught of scarlet and busbies. A hoarse voice is heard shouting the order "Advance in Column," followed by the voice of a captain giving the command "No. 1, By the Right, Quick March," and the band strikes up "The British Grenadiers." "A Volunteer battalion of the Royal Fusiliers," announces one who knows. In the distance yet another assemblage of citizen soldiers looms in sight. On nearer approach a critic, closely scrutinising, remarks, "All very young — boys in fact."

Quite true. They are the 1st Cadet Battalion of the King's Royal Rifle Corps, but as thorough in drill, and as well equipped with signallers, Maxim gun, and ambulance as the most severe, old-fashioned martinet on the one hand, or the most up-to-date theorist on the other, could desire. Think of what a boy learns in a cadet battalion; and, ye educationalists, forget it not that he *likes* to learn it. He is taught how to stand, how to turn, how to march. He is taught the intricacies of squad drill, and, later, of company and battalion movements. Then he is given his carbine, in lieu of the longer rifle, and is instructed in the manual and firing exercises, physical drill with arms, and the bayonet exercise. Judicious attention is paid to aiming drill, and even in the heart of London he can procure a species of target practice and become an accurate marksman by the use of that excellent invention the Morris tube. All the training tends to cause the cadet to acquire habits of discipline, punctuality, and exactitude, which can but stand him in good stead in his journey through life.

Pride of place has been given in this article to the H.A.C.; but the Londoner must not think that he has seen all the Artillery. Let him come to City Road, and watch the members of the 2nd Middlesex Artillery Royal Garrison (Volunteers) engaged in gun-drill. Truly in these days a gunner has much to learn, but then gunnery and its kindred subjects are most absorbing studies. See, in the hall, the concentrated attention of a batch of recruits while a patient lecturer is giving theoretical instruction. Outside a detachment is seen, all the men with their coats off, evidently prepared for "Repository exercise." They are about to lift and move a heavy gun, and then to mount it on a carriage.

Again we go down into the heart of London and pass within the charming precincts of Lincoln's Inn. On one side of Stone Buildings is the orderly room of the 14th Middlesex Volunteer Rifle Corps. The 14th Middlesex are the Inns of Court Rifles, and, owing to the legal profession of the members, are known to the humorist as the "Devil's Own."

It is meet and right now to journey

CIVIL SERVICE RIFLES : SCHOOL OF ARMS.

ROYAL ARMY MEDICAL CORPS (VOLUNTEERS) : AT DRILL.

QUEEN'S WESTMINSTERS : ENROLLING RECRUITS.

VICTORIA AND ST. GEORGE'S M.I. :
RIDING DRILL.

regiments afford. As a gradual step from grave to gay, attend a parade of a very "crack" corps in the Volunteer Force, the London Rifle Brigade, on an occasion when a leading feature is the presentation of "The Volunteer Long Service Medal" to those veterans who have completed twenty years' service. In London the recipients are not unlikely to receive it from the hands of the general commanding the Home District ; and the proceedings naturally arouse enthusiasm and the spirit of emulation in the breasts of the younger Volunteers present in the ranks. Another somewhat similar *fête* will be the annual distribution of prizes. The greater number of prizes are, of course, generally awarded for success in shooting ; but knowledge of and smartness in drill, attendance at parade, and skill in almost any gymnastic exercise or fencing are not often left unrewarded.

On another evening we attend a smoking concert of some Volunteer regiment, nearly always an agreeable *réunion*. Every corps as a general rule possesses a sufficiency of musical talent, and the songs are usually well-chosen and popular. The good-feeling existing between officers and men is also apparent.

In this article little or nothing has been said about the relative positions of the different ranks. In London especially, it may often happen that home or civilian relationships are completely reversed on donning the King's uniform. Yet a combination of tact, common-sense, and soldierly instincts has rendered unpleasantness from this cause practically unknown. Still, at the military quarters of the corps, rooms and general accommodation are necessarily

to Westminster, to 45A, Horseferry Road, the home of the Cyclist Corps. The members of the 26th Middlesex are all cyclists, and are drilled and exercised as such, hence the official title. At present the Corps is attached to the 2nd (South) Middlesex Volunteer Rifle Corps ; but it is not unlikely that eventually, on adding to the strength, it will have a separate identity. Particularly worthy of attention is the Maxim gun, most ingeniously mounted on cycles, a weapon with which the special detachment has several times given a striking display. The sight of this mobile corps suggests Infantry differently mounted. The above illustration affords a characteristic scene of some members of the Mounted Infantry Company of the Victoria and St. George's Rifles qualifying themselves in military equitation at the Riding School in the barracks, St. John's Wood.

A view has now been granted of various corps representing all branches of the service, and nearly always occupied in learning or practising in some form their professional duties as soldiers of the King. But many, nay most, of our London Volunteers become more closely knit together, and their *esprit de corps* thereby increased, through the opportunities for social intercourse their

separate for the officers, sergeants, and men. Particularly well-arranged and commodious are the headquarters of the 17th (North) Middlesex V.R.C., situated in High Street, Camden Town. Entering through an arched gateway, we first get a peep at a good-sized drill hall. Turning to the left we pass the orderly room, and proceed up a number of stone steps distinctly suggestive of barrack life. After having noticed the sergeants' mess we go further down the passage and reach the spacious mess-room of the officers. Here, if we cannot be present on a guest night and drink the health in response to the formula " Mr. Vice, the King," "Gentlemen, the King," we are at least sure to be hospitably entertained.

Acquaintance with the social side of Volunteering in London is not complete without attending a Volunteer ball. Soldiers are proverbially the best of hosts, and as now on the parade ground the Volunteers are in very close touch with the Regulars, so in the ball-room they perform their duties in an equally soldierly manner. How attractive is the scene! The extensive room, the brilliant lights shining on an artistic arrange-

ment of weapons and the regimental crest, the gay uniforms, all contribute to produce a picturesque effect. And how excellently is the music performed by the regimental band!

Do not, however, imagine that Volunteer life in London is all " beer and skittles." Many of the duties that sound quite fascinating when mentioned are wearisome and tedious when the novelty has worn off. It is hard for a man, after a long and harassing day's work, to turn out and drill attentively, perhaps having to journey far from his home to do so. Then those who desire promotion must contrive to study no small amount of technical matter, and will have to face searching examinations. It would be easy to multiply drawbacks. But, all said and done, the days spent in Volunteering generally stand out in a man's memory as amongst those he would wish to live again. We have been accused of being " a nation of shopkeepers." But our thousands of citizen soldiers—" the boys who mind the shop," as *Punch* once so happily put it—prove that the military instinct is far from being dead within us.

26TH MIDDLESEX CYCLIST CORPS : A GUN TEAM.

AT PICCADILLY CIRCUS.

LONDON'S FLOWER GIRLS.

By P. F. WILLIAM RYAN.

PICCADILLY CIRCUS is a brilliant whirl! Vehicles of every size and colour roll hither and thither. Pedestrians, obviously much concerned for the safety of their bones, step briskly from the circumference to the centre, or *vice versâ*, sometimes sacrificing dignity to a comical little trot. The air quivers with a thousand blended sounds, in which nothing is clear but the frequent tinkle of the 'bus conductor's bell. In the centre of the changeful scene, the bevy of flower girls, seated on the steps of the Shaftesbury Fountain, are models of industrious and stolid indifference.

They are fashioning buttonholes. In a small way they are rivals of the great florists in Regent Street or Piccadilly. How artistically their stock is disposed! Delicate roses are perched coquettishly on stakes a foot high, which stand in baskets of dark-green moss. And what colour combinations! Every vagary of taste is anticipated. Business is brisk. Between attending to customers and preparing for them they seem to have scarcely an idle minute. But as the sun goes down you may sometimes see a flower girl absorbed in her evening paper, while gilded London throbs around her.

The Shaftesbury Fountain is a luxurious position for the flower-sellers compared with some others. At the junction of Charing Cross Road with Oxford Street they have to stand at the kerb hour after hour, their baskets suspended from their necks by a strap. Their busiest time is Saturday night; and on a fine Sunday they do a roaring trade with pedestrians making their way to Hyde Park. The flower girls at Ludgate Hill are in much the same line of business. They too, stand at the kerb. But the fever of the' City has touched them, and they push their wares much more vigorously.

For the flower hawker, Ludgate Hill is one of the best thoroughfares. Profit is light, but the turnover is rapid. During the middle of the day people making their way to and from luncheon or dinner throng the footpaths. Working girls form a large proportion of the crowds; they are frequent purchasers.

A well-defined economic law decides whether a flower girl shall sell bouquets or loose flowers, or both. Where women are the chief purchasers loose flowers or large bunches predominate. Oxford Circus is the headquarters of this trade. But Westbourne Grove, the great shopping centre of the Bayswater district, runs it very close as a mart for loose flowers. On a smaller scale, one sees the same thing in Euston Road, and in Southampton Row, the favourite resort of the Bloomsbury flower girl.

The buttonhole is a speciality of the Royal Exchange flower girls. Amongst their patrons there are no ladies. The well-to-do City man is a dapper fellow, who feels that his coat fits all the better for being decorated with a smart flower. The women who sit in the shadow of the Duke of Wellington's monument sometimes make seven or eight shillings in a day out of this little foible of his. Outside some railway stations seasonable buttonholes are generally on sale. This is so at Ludgate Hill Station, Cannon Street, King's Cross, and Victoria. But railway stations do not seem to be favourite stands for flower sellers. You seldom see one at such important places as Euston, the Great Central, Paddington, or Waterloo.

One branch of the trade is plied mainly at night. See its representative in an oldish draggled woman, framed in a panel of white light, cast on the pavement by a flaming shop-front. She sells in public-houses It is a precarious mode of obtaining a livelihood, for the publican often gives the hawker an inhospitable reception, lest she should annoy his customers. Nevertheless, it is a form of the industry that flourishes in almost every quarter of London. The best locality for it is the neighbourhood of Leicester Square. If the public-house hawker carries a basket it is a sign of prosperity. Many flower sellers who visit the public bars at night make a tour of the residential streets by day, calling at likely houses to show their gladiolas and asters, and perhaps huge bunches of sunflowers, or whatever else happen to be the flowers of the season. The coster frequently hawks not only cut flowers but potted plants and stunted shrubs for house decorations. A neat hand-cart, laden with flower-pots ar- tistically decorated, may regularly be

seen passing through the streets, in charge of a prosperous-looking couple—the woman perhaps carrying a gaily-dressed flower-pot. The restaurants are their best customers.

Amongst the army of flower girls are skirmishers who "advance to the attack." St. Paul's Churchyard is the skirmishers' paradise. Sir Robert Peel's statue at the western end of Cheapside is their base of operations. They leave their stock around the pedestal while they move about, lynx- eyed, eager, prompt. It requires boundless energy to bring their wares under the eyes of the sprinkling of people in that jostling crowd who are potential purchasers, and need but to be tactfully tempted. There are often as many as nine girls at the statue ; but that is only for a minute or two, to replenish their stock from the reserve. They are quickly off again to the kerbstone. The skirmisher in the Strand or Fleet Street has an easier time. But there, trade is far from being so lively. For flower girls of this class Primrose Day is a golden anniversary. Many volunteers, however, divert much of the profit from the pockets of the regular members of the craft. Such interlopers are not welcome. There is also a sort of militia who join the ranks of flower sellers every Saturday night, especially in summer, having bought their rather faded stock for a trifle from the ordinary hawkers.

Covent Garden market in the morning is the place to see the various types. You notice that the prosperous flower "girl" is more often a woman than a girl, and that in the

SHOWY AND CHEAP.

dress of all there is a remarkable similarity. A trio are bargaining over a box of China asters, that look like the face of a finely wrought marble slab. They wear large black knitted shawls, hanging loosely from their shoulders, and wide white aprons with mitred hems. A trifle lends them a slightly un-English air. It is their large earrings. A melancholy-looking woman of middle age bends over a box of sweet pea. Her dark hair is parted in the middle. A rusty bonnet is set far back upon her head. Her apron is also mitred, and her shawl is home-knitted, but its ends are fastened by the

services at their mission hall in Clerkenwell —the headquarters, by the way, of the Flower Girls' Christian Mission, an institution which from its birth attracted many earnest and generous friends, amongst the number the Baroness Burdett-Coutts. On such occasions the girls avail themselves of the resources of their wardrobe with becoming pride. But it is

ROUND SIR ROBERT PEEL'S STATUE (CHEAPSIDE).

OUTSIDE LUDGATE HILL STATION.

at a wedding that a flower girl's delight in warmth of colouring is most palpable. Flowers are not obtrusive; but her hat, her frock, her jewellery are tropical in their contempt for sedate tones.

belt of her apron. Not far away is a girl whose hair is drawn tightly into little knobs with curling-pins. A fat slattern with twinkling eyes is considering the saleable prospects of a box of apple blossom. A beautiful species of speckled lily engages the attention of a young woman with much jet embroidery on her tightly-fitting black silk bodice. She is of the aristocracy; and so too is a scrupulously tidy old lady, with a self-centred air that suggests a snug bank account. A great number of flower girls attend the weekly

Tea and bread and butter at Covent Garden are often the flower girl's breakfast. More usually she has her meal before leaving her home, especially if she is well off. Her husband, if in the trade, sometimes fetches her midday meal. After buying her flowers, she generally proceeds at once to her stand, which may be a couple of miles away. Nowhere is competition keener than in the East-End. On Saturdays particularly, baskets and barrows of flowers make many bright

" VIOLETS."

splashes in High Street, Whitechapel. In Aldgate, principally near the Metropolitan Railway Station, there is a large trade done in buttonholes and loose flowers. The passers-by are mostly Jews. Yet, strangely enough, one rarely, if ever, sees a Jewish flower girl. Working men returning home buy large bunches of loose flowers in White-chapel to brighten their humble tenements on Sunday. The weary-looking factory girls cannot resist the temptation to take half a dozen roses for a penny. Jewesses dressed in their best for the Hebrew Sabbath are also good customers.

The flower girl tries to avoid bringing home any of her stock save on Saturday night, which must of course be an exception if she purposes to work next day. At Piccadilly and Oxford Circus, and all the principal stands, business goes on much as usual on Sundays. The very prosperous, how-ever, begin the week by taking a rest, while women with families often remain at home a day in mid-week to do their house-work. For the well-to-do a summer holiday out of town is not uncommon. On Sundays many flower girls, with admirable shrewdness, flock to the leading hospitals to dispose

of their stock to visitors at somewhat reduced prices. In some quarters the hawkers make Sunday rather depressing with a display of funeral wreaths of doubtful freshness.

Now and then the flower girl stands out vividly from the crowded canvas of the streets. Perhaps she is little more than a child, and holds out a solitary bunch of violets. Observe, too, a mother and daughter —at least you guess that to be the relation-ship—standing at the kerb opposite a big tobacconist's in Oxford Street. Just for a moment their pose is matchless, as for some reason they search each other's eyes, seriously, questioningly. The girl is a lovely dark-eyed creature, with raven hair brushed back from her forehead, and tied with a ragged crimson ribbon. One bare, earth-stained toe peeps through a worn, misshapen boot. A small basket hangs from her neck by a piece of cord ; and cord to match fastens her boots !

Here is a pretty incident of the pavement. A young exquisite, whose business in life might be the spending of a handsome allowance, pauses to take a lovely flesh-coloured rose nestling in maidenhair from a girl-woman ; a young mother, you feel sure, as you note the melting tenderness in the depths of her eyes and the waxen hue of her fingers. A piece of silver passes between them, and he turns on his heel. He is above small change.

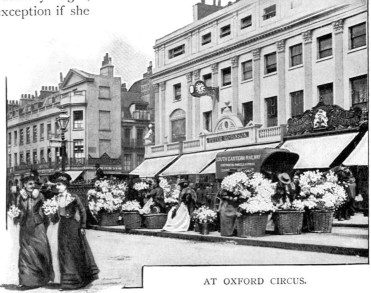

AT OXFORD CIRCUS.

There are flower girls the poorest of the poor. To them winter is pitiless. You have only just turned your back on the glitter of a theatre perhaps. The north-east wind and December sleet sting your face. As you hurry forward, a bloodless hand at the street corner is outstretched with dripping blossoms. From beneath the drenched shawl comes a faint cry—a baby's tiny voice. That is one of the haunting, heart-breaking spectres of the great city!

The flower girl's funeral! It must come. Sometimes it is the last act in a sombre drama. But happily not always. There was one that fell in the opening days of this century. Its memory will live long. She was a white-haired woman of seventy when the Reaper beckoned her away. But even so, her heart was young at the end. For her life was lived in the midst of life where, year in year out, the pace never slackens and one loses count of time. Her sisters of the craft came from far and near to say good-bye. Around the sleeper they strewed lily-of-the-valley, and violets, and snowdrops, and rare blooms their pockets could ill afford, for it was winter, when choice flowers were scarce.

The last journey to Kensal Green was taken with a funeral car and four horses; two mourning coaches, and six cabs! The number will never be forgotten, will not at all events ever grow less. They ranged themselves round the graveside, silent, puzzled, solemn, their eyes fixed curiously on the gaping bed. Sharp contrasts they presented: some quite young, some more than middle-aged. One worn and haggard, another bronzed and vigorous. Here a flabby matron, there a refined-looking girl. None prim—a few rakish. Not a tear was shed. They had no tears. From infancy they had been out in the storm, hardening in the stern school! But over all was the glamour of simplicity, the poetry of rugged truth. When the first horrid rattle of earth on timber changed to the muffled thud of earth on earth the spell was broken, their tongues were loosened. It sounded strange to hear the young ones, mere slips of girl-hood, speaking of her glibly by name as though she was the flower girl still. . . .

The men rested upon the handles of their shovels while lovely wreaths and crosses were heaped on the freshly-turned clay. It was her last stock, left there to yield up all their sweetness for her—just as though she were a fine lady for whom flowers were grown, only to die at her breast!

A FLOWER GIRL'S GRAVE.

MUSEUM-LAND IN LONDON.

By JAMES BARR.

IN the heart of London there is a land where speech is hushed and the soul of silence reigns; a land where dwell the people of sibilant tongue, and to which doors are closed and when night spreads its black mantle over grinning idol and dried human head, the silence is denser indeed, but only a little denser than it has been all

BRITISH MUSEUM : THE READING ROOM.

hasten those of the soft tread; a region of silence and of drift — Museum-land. Thrown up by the waves of time and caught in shelves and cases, as flotsam caught in the crannies of the cliffs, is the quaint drift-wood of the world; and to view this come the people, who stare and pass on. And those that dwell in the land, they hear nothing of the roar that fills the outside world, but their ears catch the sounds of silting feet and the sibilant whisper. All day long the people drift, drift, drift, through the highways and byways of the dim land; but even when

day. The policeman's foot sets up a more hollow sound, but a not much louder din than it did during the hours when Museum-land was a land for the people.

To the English-speaking world "The Museum" means one Museum, and that is the British. Secure a permit and slip into the Reading Room! At once the similarity to a mighty hive is evident: the lofty dome, the busy workers, the hum and buzz, the little hole-like door at the far point where in and out crawl the bee-like workers, as it were, bringing in the honey in the shape of books, to be consumed by the human bees inside, who grow big through much eating. Every visitor sees this startling likeness to a hive. But how few know that the likeness is carried even farther? Round this hive, behind unseen doors, are miles and miles of honeycomb cells, narrow, dim passages, one on top of the other, divided by gratings through which an uncertain amount of light from the glass

BRITISH MUSEUM : A LECTURE IN THE ASSYRIAN GALLERY.

roof slides down; and against the walls of each passage is stored the honey of ages, the books of all lands and all times; and here are many workers in semi-gloom and still air. These store back the particles when those in the hive have finished, or produce fresh sweets as they are called for. This honeycomb in itself is one of the most wonderful curiosities of the Museum, and to be ushered in and led through a section will give one a better idea of the enormous resources of the Museum than any amount of listless gazing at the show cases.

Directly opposite the door by which one enters the great Reading Room is the passage which leads to the home of all the most precious books the library contains. Before one can gain permission to visit this—the Holy of Holies—one must first have secured entrance to the Reading Room, and there obtained specific permission to be shown into the inner room.

But this British Museum is a region of many unseen or seldom seen nooks, to enter which one must either get written leave or at least ring a bell. The jangle of a bell usually betokens the waking up of an expert in some out-of-the-way path in knowledge, old coins and medals, china, flint finds, ancient prints and paintings from India, and such-like curiosities. From every quarter of the world come strangers with things precious and things they think precious carefully hugged to their heart, and no matter what its class, or where it comes from, there is a cool-brained, cold-eyed expert who takes the thing, turns it one critical turn, and tells the anxious owner exactly what it is, where it came from, and what it is worth.

However, the majority of people shun bells and stick to the "open road," and this road leads quickly through strange lands and distant ages. If you are so favoured by fortune as to come upon a lecturer surrounded by his little knot of listeners industriously going through, we'll say, the Assyrian Gallery, attach yourself to the party and listen to the strange things he tells. For a few minutes it will strike you as almost unholy to hear a man speaking loudly in a museum, more especially among those mammoth personifications of silence the stone bulls; but this feeling will wear away, and you will enjoy an experience typical of the educational side of this many-sided institution.

In museums everyone employed, whatever

his position, is in a way a detective. This is a necessity. Museum treasures are in danger from almost every description of the un-regenerate, ranging from the maniac who smashes into smithereens the Portland Vase to the cowardly sneak who surreptitiously tears a rare engraving out of a book. Not one visitor in a thousand is able to recognise the Museum detectives. For instance, if you slip in to see the Portland Vase, you are sure to find a gentleman gazing with mighty admiration at the treasure. He looks for all the world like an ordinary spectator; but drop in again next day or next month, and you will still find him there. His eggs are all in one basket, and he watches that basket. The thief who steals for mercenary profit, although he is found at museums, is nothing like so dangerous a character as the dishonest man with a mania for collecting, or the savage who loves destruction for its own sake. Thus to their ordinary duties is added that of keeping a sharp eye on all who enter the place, and especially those who have in their possession for a time precious books and specimens. Therefore it is that in the British Museum there are many bells to ring and doors to be knocked at before a glance at the choicest treasures can be had.

Staring across Lincoln's Inn Fields at each other are two

BRITISH MUSEUM: LOOKING AT THE PORTLAND VASE.

museums so totally dissimilar that their juxtaposition is one of the grim humours of London. Facing towards the south is that sleepy little Soane Museum, so like an ordinary solicitor's office of the usual Inn type that the unknowing hundreds who daily pass, if they learn the nature of the building at all, learn only by chance. A century ago this dwelling-house belonged to Sir John Soane, an architect famous in his generation, and when he died he left the house with all its treasures—the collection of a busy life-time—to the public. Few Londoners consult a guide-book dealing with London, therefore few know of this Museum, the names on its visitors' book being mostly foreign and provincial. To enter the place is to step into a section of the sleepy mediæval. Somewhere in the loft of the building one knows there is a curator,

VICTORIA AND ALBERT MUSEUM: "PUFFING BILLY."

INDIAN MUSEUM : FAÇADE OF A NATIVE SHOP.

UNITED SERVICE INSTITUTION MUSEUM : MODEL OF TRAFALGAR.

and a silent-voiced man shows one through the rooms full of strange inanimate things, but empty of all animate. Of all the denizens of Museum-land not one is so lonely, so sleepy, so empty of human life: the din and stress of Hogarth's "Election" and his "Rake's Progress" almost seem out of place on its walls. Soane's Museum, too, hibernates during the winter, going to sleep at the end of August and waking again in March.

Across the "Fields" and facing the north is the other museum, wide awake and full of horrors. The entrance to the Museum of the Royal College of Surgeons is as noble as the Soane is unpretentious, and those who flock to its doors are of the bustling, breezy stamp of character, for few except surgeons and medical students care to visit this place of skulls and bones, and of bottles filled with "specimens" in spirits. Inside, the light falls strong and glaring on the exhibits, and before cases sit the medical students, book in hand, alternately reading a paragraph and gazing upon the bottled object to which the paragraph refers. In this section of Museum-land no children wander, and few womenkind visit it. Indeed, it is not a place for those that do not care for ghastly sights and the glint of steel lances and cruelly-shaped instruments.

It is strange that people should hate the surgeon's knife, yet love the bayonet and the sabre. The change from the Surgeons' Museum to that of the Sailors and Soldiers—the United Service Institution Museum—is a striking one. Our country's defenders were fortunate in obtaining possession of the historic Banquetting Hall in Whitehall, from one of the windows of which King Charles stepped to the place of his execution. In this ancient and majestic room the Services have stored their curiosities, relics of many a fierce fight and fruitful adventure, and among these sailors and soldiers stride in numbers, for all who wear the uniform of his Majesty are made welcome without price. The blue jacket and the red or khaki coat are the predominating garb to be seen, and the comments heard smack of the salt sea and the tented field. The centre of popularity in this place is the mighty model of the Battle of Trafalgar, little white battered motionless ships, friends and enemies apparently in a hopeless mix, upon an equally motionless sea of glass. The attendants—some of whom are shown in our photographic illustration on the opposite page, and who are all retired sailors and soldiers—are taught to explain the fight to visitors. There is a breezy air of jollity abroad in this Museum, for even the civilians who pay their sixpences at the door are for the most part of the healthy, lusty sort, as should be when strife and struggle are the themes brought to mind by the objects all about.

South Kensington, the home of museums, has not one so popular as that of the alive-seeming dead, the Natural History Museum. All people love contrasts, and those who take care of this Museum and guard its treasures live in an atmosphere of contrasts. Exhibit contrasts strongly with exhibit, visitor with visitor. Here flock the little children; hither hobble the aged. Like takes to like. The daintily-caparisoned children cluster round the glass cases of exquisitely-plumaged birds and soft-furred animals; the aged and dried, spectacles on forehead, peer searchingly at the bones of beasts that disappeared as living things from this earth ages ago. Each of the staff that guards over the alive-seeming dead is deeply learned in Nature's lore, and, as part of their recompense, they see treasures which the drifting public are not privileged to behold. For the exhibits that so proudly display plumage and fur to the casual sightseer are by no means the best specimens of their time and tribe in this bit of Museum-land.

The truth is that light kills colour; brightness of plumage is dimmed, blackness of fur is blurred, by the light that floods in through museum windows. So it comes to pass that not in the public halls, but in dark basements, are the true treasures of this Museum, and there they may be seen by those who can gain entrance. Down in the gloom student and custodian turn over and study the skins of birds and beasts in all their pristine glory, for those pelts and hides and skins that are the choicest specimens of their kind are all hidden away from the garish light, so that only the people who have a serious interest in the exhibits are allowed to handle and hold them. Under this roof in South Kensington the staff is small, but the real roof of the Natural History Museum is the blue sky, and under it, in all impossible places of the world, scurry men, gun or net or trap or hook in hand, surprising the unwary, circumventing the cunning of Nature to add to the shelves or dark rooms of this building, which, like the Nature it represents, has an appetite that is insatiable. The " Living " Natural History Museum, therefore, is not to be found at South Kensington, but is scattered over the face of the globe, wherever insect crawls, beast runs, or bird flies.

Near to the home of Natural History stands that amorphous bit of Museum-land now known to the public as the " Victoria and Albert." This Museum sprawls over a vast extent of ground, and its exact shape is not easily grasped, while, as to its moods and its personalities, they are many, ranging from the dreamy, Eastern, mystic show of gaudy things in the Indian Section to the harsh practical pulsations of the Western machinist's constructive genius. And with the visitors who stream in at its many doors the practical is easily the most enthralling of its moods. Stand and glance at the great vista of working models of engines. The wheels turn silently, the little pistons dodge forward and back, everything working mysteriously silent. But clustered about each indolently industrious

NATURAL HISTORY MUSEUM : PREPARING SPECIMENS
FOR EXHIBITION.

machine see the big-eyed, excited knot of boys, watching every motion, skipping about and straining for a better view of the polished model. And then the joy of actually feasting eyes and surreptitiously laying fingers on " Puffing Billy " ! The unattached urchin raises a " whoop " when he first sights the ancient locomotive, and the schoolboy shepherded by his master, although less demonstrative, is quite as gleeful. To see a crowd

of schoolboys examining this old engine makes one wonder what boys admired before engines were invented. This section of the " Victoria and Albert " is the happy hunting ground of the lads of London ; lads by themselves, school lads with a master trying his best to keep some sort of order among his bevy, and to tear the atoms of his class away from the mechanical toys. In this portion of the Museum is certainly to be seen one of the heart-warming sights of Living London.

Contrast makes London what she is, a city of more lights and shadows than any other place in the world. And here in South Kensington the contrast is great. From the Engineering Section of the Museum one should skip across to the Indian Museum, which nestles by the impressive Imperial Institute. Once inside, the visitor finds himself transported to the Orient. All the indolence of the East is in the air, the atmosphere is heavy and the light subdued, and the attendants who stand among the cases filled with things barbaric in the splendour of colour, seem to dream the hours away. There is no bustle, no sense of unrest, and the visitors are few. In at the door occasionally drift groups of picturesque natives of the great empire of India, and these loitering through, looking at things familiar to their eyes, seem part of the Museum itself.

Altogether Museum-land can scarcely be called a part of Living London ; it would be nearer the truth to name it dreaming London, sleeping London. Living seems to infer bustle and noise and strife, but in Museum-land all these are far away ; are swallowed up in an all-encompassing silence and subdued lights.

"MONKEY BOATS" WAITING AT ENTRANCE TO ISLINGTON TUNNEL.

ON LONDON'S CANALS.

By DESMOND YOUNG.

A STAGNANT waterway, on which slides a narrow, slender "monkey boat" drawn by a horse that occasionally gets his head down at so much collar work. In front of the animal a budding bargee (he ranks as fourth mate—or fifth, or sixth), with a fine display of shirt sleeve and a gift of repartee never allowed to lie dormant when the tow line gets crossed. Now and again he makes a flick at a fly on the horse's "near" ear, thereby hurting his charge considerably more than the insect. In the stern of the boat, behind the entrance to the cabin, on top of which a caged throstle pours out a ceaseless song, and partly hidden from view by the dog kennel—perhaps a soap box or an old caustic soda tin—a buxom female whose russet face is framed in a print sun-bonnet of the "truly rural" pattern, her hand on the tiller, her eyes generally looking ahead, as a good steerswoman's should.

The picture is familiar to bridge loungers in many parts of London, though it is much more frequently to be seen north of the Thames than south. Not very often is it to be witnessed on the Surrey Canal, because

that "cut" leads nowhere, running as it does only from Rotherhithe to Camberwell Road and on the way throwing out an arm to Peckham. But on the Grand Junction and the Regent's it is common. While the craft that frequent the one are mostly wide, mastless boats for local traffic and brown-winged barges which bring chalk, flints, and the like from Kentish and Essex ports and take away in exchange coke and other products, the majority of the tiny argosies on the northern canals carry everything and go everywhere. They are "monkey boats," or, as they are called in the country, "fly boats." The origin of that term is plain. "Fly boats" are the greyhounds of inland waterways. Given anything like "good luck," they can reel off on an average about four miles an hour.

Flat barges (never to be classed with "monkey boats," any more than you can lump together dirty ocean "tramps" and crack liners) there are, of course, on the Grand Junction and the Regent's also; but it is on them only that you see many "monkey boats." Life on these arteries, indeed, is really canal life ; and a trip along the Regent's, moreover, is an epitome of canal navigation in general.

Leaving Paddington on the right, a boat bound for the City Road Basin or Limehouse is drawn as far as Maida Vale. There the towing path ends at a tunnel, which has to be passed through by "legging." Meanwhile, the captain, having come on in advance, has hunted up a man, or, if he is not in the humour for much exertion—

the two men pushing their feet against the wall—which is worn away from end to end by contact with hob-nails—till the day dawns again.

After leaving this bore the horse takes up his burden anew, and there is a stretch of sylvan scenery, succeeded by miles of houses relieved by an occasional wharf. Presently another arch, on the left of which is fixed a signal that seems to have strayed from the iron road, stretches over the

READY TO START " LEGGING."

and " legging " *is* work—two men. The canal company allows for only one assistant, and if the skipper engages an extra help the shilling he has to give him comes out of his own pocket. By the time the boat reaches the tunnel nearly everything is in readiness for the subterranean journey. Two " wings " are fixed to the sides of the boat so that they project at right angles to the keel, on these the men throw themselves at full length, having previously tucked up a coat, or anything else that is handy, for a pillow, and then away into the pitchy darkness—absolute darkness, save for the light from a single lamp. Under villas and roads and gardens the little craft goes, propelled by

waterway. This is Caledonian Bridge— the western entrance to the longest tunnel on the canal.

Again does the little "flyer" glide under London, this time drawn, in the wake of other boats and barges which have been waiting, by an engine suggesting an impossible compromise between a locomotive and a raft : under thousands of toiling citizens, under busy Chapel Street, under the Agricultural Hall, under the New River, the presence of which is unpleasantly manifested by water dropping from the roof, to emerge at last at Colebrooke Row, three-quarters of a mile, by tunnel, from Caledonian Bridge.

The rest of the journey is easy. To drop down to the City Road Basin or to Limehouse is plain sailing, everyday work, the work which the idler sees and which seems neither hard nor disagreeable.

Ah! that picture! The eye, taking in merely the broad details, does not see that the principal figure—the woman at the helm —is often steering, suckling her last born, watching her older children on the cabin floor, lest they come to harm, and paying attention to the pot on the top bar simultaneously. And the little inhabitants of the floating home need to be carefully watched. Be sure of that. You will have to take a long walk on the towing path before you find a boy or girl of fifteen who has not had at least one narrow escape from drowning. In fact, your journey would extend from London to Liverpool, if not farther. To understand canal life aright, moreover, other pictures need to be viewed. You want to be in Mark Lane sometimes, and see the good wife, when her boat is tethered to a wharf, and when she is supposed to be resting, turn up, alert and businesslike, ready to receive orders for the return journey to Birmingham, Nottingham, Stoke, Wolverhampton, Derby, or elsewhere. Not that the titular skipper always, or even generally, casts this burden on the broad shoulders of his spouse. She does his work a great deal oftener than she should—that is all.

A HALT FOR REFRESHMENT.

"My dear woman," said a staid City merchant, looking hard over his spectacles at a buxom figure in petticoats who had come straight from the canal bank, "where—*where* is your husband?" "My man?" quoth the feminine skipper. "Oh, I can't trust he!" In that remark there is a whole volume. The "cut," too, should be seen at early morn and late at night. Long before London is awake—at half-past four or five o'clock— the boat-woman is astir, and it is asleep when she lies down to rest.

And that cosy-looking little cabin, is that what it seems? Drop into it, and you find yourself in a home with rather less elbow room than a railway compartment—to be exact, about 250 cubic feet. On your right is a locker forming a seat, on your left a small stove, or, if the boat is new, perhaps a range, polished a beautiful glossy black and the brass rods above it, as well as the ornaments at the side nearest the bow, glistening like burnished gold, for the women, as a rule, keep their domiciles spotless. Beyond the fireplace knobs of cupboards and more lockers, and that is all, with the exception of a clock and a few household articles here and there. The eye has completed its survey of a narrow boat cabin.

You wonder how people live in such a miniature

AT TEA IN A "MONKEY BOAT" CABIN.

domicile. They don't; they live outside it, at all events in the summer. Take a walk along the canal, and you get endless glimpses of boat folk's domestic life. Here a meal is in progress on the cabin top, there the family wash is likewise being done in public, and presently you hap on youngsters engaged in the delicate operations of the toilet in full view of all the world that cares to look. Canal people are veritable children of the open air.

other youngsters would be on the cabin floor, underneath their parents' bed.

This is home as canal folk know it, the only home in very many cases. Sometimes a family works a pair of boats tied side by side, and in that case the older children have the cabin of one to themselves; but this arrangement does not alter matters very much, for, although there is more room, the environment is the same always. Here the typical boatman is born. Here he spends

MORNING TOILET.

Beds there are none visible in the cabin, though in some cases one can be seen at the end. And yet this dwelling, small as are its dimensions, is registered for four people—a man and his wife and two children. Where, then, shall we discover the beds? If we could take an Asmodeus glimpse of the cabin, we could see them—and, possibly, the lack of them. The captain and his helpmeet would be revealed asleep at the far end of the cabin, resting on a cupboard door (kept closed during the day-time) let down and extending from side to side, and the children would be curled up on a locker near the door—some of them, at all events. If the boat should carry more than her regulation complement, the

his boyhood and early manhood. Here, or just above, he does most of his courting. Here he brings his bride, having used the address of a friendly ratepaying bargee or of a shopkeeper for the publication of the banns. Here he rears and brings up his family with all the worries incidental thereto, only accentuated enormously. Imagine, for instance, washing-day on board a canal boat in mid-winter, with the little home reeking of soapsuds and the air laden with steam from the drying clothes suspended on lines from the roof. Ugh! Not even use can make that aught but a misery. Here he lies in his last illness. And here, amid the old familiar surroundings, he probably closes his eyes on the world for ever, though only very rarely does his body remain afloat to the last.

Many a mournful procession has actually started from a boat lying at a wharf, but the funeral has been that of an infant, not of an adult. When the long, weary struggle is at an end, and the tired spirit has fled, the corpse is taken ashore and deposited either in the home of a charitable canal-side dweller or in a towing-path public-house, where it lies till it is committed to the dust. Thus it happens that even in London, of all places under the sun, a

cause it's in a book," chimed in the youngest, a bright-eyed urchin of fourteen.

As for the ability to read, that is a rare accomplishment among canal children. Nothing else can be expected considering their upbringing. Few boatmen are in the position of a well-known "character" of the Surrey Canal, who is wont to declare that he has never seen all his olive branches together. Able to dispense with their services in navigating his boat, he has

WASHING-DAY.

man often rests longer under a roof in death than ever he did in life.

The children of the canal, again : what is their lot? As a class, they are as wild as gipsies, and as ignorant. Of this the energetic and earnest agents of the London City Mission could give many proofs. Not long since a gentleman attached to that organisation discovered three boys seated in a cabin. As a means of introduction, he asked one of the lads, aged about fifteen, his name. "Jonah," promptly replied the youth, adding, "Jonah and the fish." The oldest of the trio— he was about seventeen—then remarked, "It is strange that they always talk about the fish when they talk about Jonah." "It's be-

scattered them among his relations, who are attending to their education. In general a man has to carry his children with him, and, as he is nearly always on the move, he can only send them to school for a day or two occasionally. If he choose to set the law at defiance—and sometimes he does, partly because he is indifferent to the future, and partly because his offspring, when they grow big, complain tearfully of being put among the "babies" in a Board school and of being laughed at as dunces—it is very difficult to prevent him. To track one of his youngsters a "kidcatcher" has to display the tireless persistence of a bailiff laying siege to the domicile of a suburban debt dodger and the agility and fleet-footedness of a 120 yards' runner.

OUTSIDE MAIDA VALE TUNNEL.

Out at Brentford, where the long-distance boats stop, a highly praiseworthy attempt is being made to teach the little ones to read and write at least without any of the usual restrictions. Here a school was opened specially for them by the daughter of Mr. R. Bamber, of the West London Canal Boat Mission (London City Mission). And a curious little school it is. Over its well worn desks on most mornings are bent a number of children, most of them engaged in laboriously forming pothooks and hangers. Some of the older girls are accompanied by the youngest born of the family, and they can learn nothing till, after infinite sh—sh—sh—ing, they get their charges to sleep. The boys are, with few exceptions, without collars, and some, bargee-like, have neither coat nor waistcoat. One or two, moreover, want a wash—want it badly. These an ordinary teacher would punish or send home ; but the tutor here adopts neither course, because if she did the youngsters would not come again. No ; when a scholar is shockingly begrimed he is gently taken out and introduced to soap and water.

It is equally impossible, of course, to insist upon punctuality, and its twin sister, regular attendance, is beyond hope of realisation.

You might visit the school at ten o'clock—when work should be in full swing—and find it empty, and yet at eleven there might be a dozen scholars present, and at three in the afternoon as many as fifteen or twenty. Everything depends on the number of boats which arrive. Never, too, are the same faces seen on more than two or three days in succession. Children depart into the country, and do not return for weeks. Of the 500 on the register only about a score are present at any one time.

That they make much progress in these circumstances is not claimed ; but for all that some of the little wanderers fill their parents with boundless wonder and pride. They can read, they know a little geography, and occasionally they have mastered the intricacies of long division. Great achievements are these to people who cannot themselves read the name on their own boat and who use words in a sense which would surprise even Mrs. Malaprop herself. One woman, in describing the death of a poor fellow who had been killed in an accident, assured her friend that they "held a portmanteau on him," and another said that a certain child had "happy collection fits."

No less admirable than the school, let

me say in passing, is another department recently added to the Boatmen's Mission—a maternity room. Such a provision for the needs of our canal population had long been wanted, and there can be no question that it will be the means of saving many valuable lives. A minor, but still important, consideration is that it will tend to lessen the number of irregularities in connection with births. A case in point—one out of many —that came to light may be mentioned. For certain reasons the exact age of a child about three years old was wanted. When the mother was appealed to she could give no definite information. She had neglected to register the birth of the child, and she could not remember where it took place. All that she knew was that the weather was cold at the time. On her suggestion, recourse was had to a medical man at Birmingham, but without success, and to this day the mystery remains unsolved.

Apart from education, however, the little ones of the towing path will bear comparison with any class of youth. They lack nothing physically. Fed on plenty of good plain food, kept of necessity in the open air, initiated into work as soon as possible by being taught to look after the horse and run ahead and open locks, they grow up strong, robust, and self-reliant, able to fight their way in their own world.

On the whole, canal life is not exactly what it seems to the chance observer. But if it is not idyllic, neither is it so vile as some have delighted to paint it. They have seen only the drunkenness, the fighting, the immorality —which, after all, are dying out, or, at least, are not nearly so common as they were only twenty years ago — among boat people. They have shut their eyes to the noble charity, the sturdy independence, the self-sacrifice, the toil and stress—in a word, the poetry of canal life.

LOVE'S YOUNG DREAM.

DISSENTING LONDON.

By HOWARD ANGUS KENNEDY.

DO you remember Mr. Stiggins? Does not a vivid portrait appear in your mind's eye when you hear the name of Chadband? They were among the unloveliest of Dickens' creations, scarcely less repulsive than Bill Sikes or the monster Quilp. Yet in the novelist's pages, and in the minds of a multitude who knew no better, the hypocritical "Shepherd" and the oily expounder of "terewth" appeared as types of the Nonconforming ministry.

There are some keen-eyed folk who profess that they can always tell a Nonconforming from a Conforming parson by the cut of his clothes, and even, by some miraculous insight, distinguish a Wesleyan from a Congregationalist. But these clever people are often mistaken, especially when they are most positive. As a rule we do not pay our ministers very well, so they cannot indulge in much elegance of apparel—to which, indeed, they are somewhat indifferent; but then there are many of their Anglican brethren who are no better paid, and scarcely more punctilious about the cut of their clerical uniform. On the other hand, some of our preachers habitually appear in the clerical collar which more than any other week-day sign is believed to betoken the minister of the Established Church.

On Sundays—well, even then you might go into one of our places of worship and imagine you were in an Anglican Church. For instance, at the magnificent edifice in the Westminster Bridge Road, notable for the ministries of Dr. Newman Hall and the Rev. F. B. Meyer, the liturgy is used every Sunday morning. So it is in a number of Wesleyan Methodist churches, at least at the morning service. Indeed, there are other points in which the public worship of the Wesleyans resembles that of the Established Church. If you are in the neighbourhood of the City Road on the first Sunday evening of the month, drop into the chapel where John Wesley himself used to hold forth. You will find the congregation joining in the communion service very largely in the words and forms prescribed by the Prayer Book. "The table at the communion time"—so opens the form of service prescribed by the Wesleyan governing Conference —"having a fair white linen cloth upon it, shall stand in some convenient place"; that is, generally, on the platform in front of the pulpit, at the edge of which the people come and kneel, several at a time, in order to receive the bread and wine. In at least one church of this denomination you will see the choir, of men and boys, all clad in black gowns; but it is only, so far as I can discover, at the church of the Countess of Huntingdon's Connexion in Spa Fields that you can see a choir in full-blown surplices, and there the minister himself wears a surplice till sermon time comes, when he puts on the black gown. In most of our Nonconformist places of worship the people take the communion sitting in their pews, the bread and wine—almost always unfermented wine, by the way—being carried round by those who have been ordained as elders, deacons, or stewards. A recent innovation, inspired by modern sanitary ideas about the spread of infection, is the provision of a separate cup for each communicant. The Presbyterians prepare for the sacred ordinance by spreading white cloths over the book-boards in front of each pew.

Practically the whole Nonconformist community—that is, the people who call themselves Christians but do not belong to the Roman or Anglican communion—are comprised in the Congregational, Baptist, Presbyterian, and Wesleyan churches, with two or three minor branches of the Methodist stock, and the Salvation Army—which is so much more and also so much less than a church or denomination that it can hardly be dealt with in this article. Even

A COMMUNION SERVICE (WESLEY'S CHAPEL, CITY ROAD).

A BAPTISM (METROPOLITAN TABERNACLE).

A NIGHT SERVICE (GREAT ASSEMBLY HALL TENT, MILE END ROAD).

bow, as the County Councils bow to the national Legislature, yet they have in the last few years become federated in a Free Church Council, at which the plans are laid for all sorts of united campaigns against the common enemy—the forces of evil. The union of all Nonconformists, and even of Dissenters with Church folk, for certain forms of philanthropic and religious work is, happily, no new thing; and at many a society's May meeting in Exeter Hall you may see rectors and vicars and Free Church pastors co-operating in the most brotherly and effective fashion.

Londoners like to go where there is a crowd. Where for one reason or another a congregation has begun to decrease—by the migration of the old members to a more pleasant locality in the suburbs, or through the displacement of dwellings by warehouses and factories—it is very hard to get new people to come in; the vacant places they might fill only frighten them away. So in the older and more central parts of the town you will find great buildings which once were crowded by hundreds of eager worshippers now frequented by a few score. But even in these central regions there are churches to which congregations flock. There is the City Temple, on Holborn Viaduct — identified with the names of Dr. Joseph Parker and the Rev. R. J. Campbell—crowded twice every Sunday by worshippers from every part of London, and even by country cousins, as well as the young men who live in the City's wholesale drapery stores, all singing triumphantly to the accompaniment of trumpets and organ. There, too, amid the whirling life of "The Elephant," in South London, stands the Metropolitan Tabernacle, equally identified with a great name—the name of

the few churches I have named are united in so many points and divided in so few that you might worship with them all, going from one to another, Sunday after Sunday, without finding out the difference. To tell the truth, the only important difference is in the way they govern themselves; and methods of church government are of too little importance to be often mentioned when the people have come together in public to worship God. Just as Kent and Essex have their County Councils for local administration, without one being a jot more or less English than the other, so the Methodists have their Conferences, the Presbyterians their Synods, the Baptists and Congregationalists their Unions and Church Meetings, without one being a jot more or less Christian than the other. Though it would not be quite correct to say that the Dissenting churches have a supreme church parliament to which they all

Spurgeon. The original "Charles H." has departed, but the Tabernacle is still a shrine to which thousands of pilgrims weekly wend their way. Another Baptist chapel which has been made famous by the name of a great preacher, the name of Clifford, is situate at Westbourne Park. On certain occasions if you happen to be at the Tabernacle—or, indeed, at any Baptist chapel—you will see a chasm open in front of the platform, into which the candidates for church membership descend one by one to be baptised by immersion at the hands of the minister. You will see no musical instrument at the Tabernacle, by the way: the only organ you will hear is

are Scots and the children of Scots, but they no longer insist on the ways of their Caledonian kirks, nor grumble at the minister for giving them short measure if he preaches for twenty-five minutes instead of an hour.

When you have joined in the hymns—generally the same hymns, wherever you go; when you have bowed in prayer and heard the Bible read; when you have listened

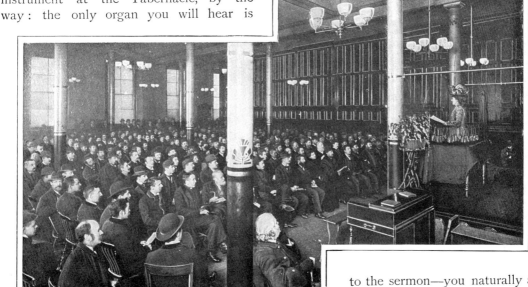

A DINNER-HOUR CONCERT (CITY TEMPLE HALL).

to the sermon—you naturally ask yourself the question, "Who *are* these people in the pews around me?"

They are just your neighbours; ordinary men and women like yourself, and of almost every class. Happy is the church where the rich and the poor meet together, remembering that the Lord is the Maker of them all; and happier still the church where the minister can be at the same time simple and profound, so that he "breaks the Bread of Life" in a manner that suits every kind of mental digestion. In the dumb hearts of the common men and women you meet in business or in the street there is more self-examination and striving after the highest life than you would imagine. And the minister, as a rule, tries hard to help them with preaching of the most practical kind.

that which God has built in every human throat.

This is very exceptional. Even the Presbyterians have outgrown their prejudice against the "kist o' whistles"—the Presbyterians in London, that is. Yes, and they sing hymns, three or four of them to perhaps one of those "metrical psalms of David" which used to afford the congregation its only vocal exercise during the "diet of worship." Only the minister's gown and bands remain, and perhaps his northern accent, to remind you that you are "sitting under" a successor of John Knox. To a large extent these London Presbyterians

A MAY MEETING (EXETER HALL).

Even in the highly respectable suburban congregations there is always a sprinkling of "working men," though they are disguised in black coats and sometimes in high hats. Nearer the centre of the town you will find churches practically made up and controlled by members of the industrial classes. They certainly prefer services of their own, and the "Pleasant Sunday Afternoon" gatherings contain hundreds of artisans, labourers, and other frankly plebeian persons of the male persuasion, singing with stentorian lungs to the accompaniment of a cornet or even a full brass band, and echoing the strong points of a colloquial address with cheers instead of "amens" and "hallelujahs." And it must be further confessed that in the present stage of their religious experience the ordinary working man and woman feel a certain shyness about entering a "regular church." They will flock in their thousands to Mr. Charrington's Great Assembly Hall and Tent in the Mile End Road, or the "Edinburgh Castle" taken over from the liquor trade by Dr. Barnardo at Lime-

house, or the Great Central Hall managed by Wesleyans in Bermondsey, or the Whitefield "institutional church" of the Congregationalists in Tottenham Court Road.

Anyone who listens to the long string of "notices" given out from the pulpit or platform on a Sunday must get the idea that the whole of the Dissenters' week is crowded with church activities; and that is the fact. There is always an evening service in the middle of the week; there are prayer meetings, and mothers' meetings, and Christian Endeavour or Guild meetings, and social gatherings — even entertainments, concerts, and lectures. The mid-day concerts held in the hall underneath the City Temple cater particularly for men and women at a distance from home who have no pleasant place to spend the dinner-hour in. There is the Boys' Brigade drill, too—one of the most effective antidotes to Hooliganism yet discovered. And in connection with some churches, if there is room to spare, there are club rooms where the working men can chat or read the papers, and even engage in a friendly game of billiards without the stimulus of either alcohol or betting.

Among the Methodists there are two regular events which you will find rather out of the ordinary, if you have never been to them before. One of these is the "class meeting." The rule is that every member of the church must come regularly to one or other of the weekly "classes" unless unavoidably prevented; and in a large church there may be as many as twenty classes, held at different times, to suit the working hours of all sorts of people. In the old days the class leader, who is generally a layman, used to ask every member in turn to give his or her "experience"; but this is not generally insisted on nowadays. And then there is the "love-feast," generally held after a Sunday service, when the stewards hand round plates of biscuits and mugs or glasses of water, and anyone whom the Spirit moves to relate some striking passage of individual heart-history does so.

The operations of these Christian brotherhoods that we call churches are by no means confined to their own premises. It is not often that you see them marching through the streets with banner and drum, after the fashion of the Salvation Army; yet this does sometimes happen, and open-air preaching is carried on at many points of the Metropolis Sunday by Sunday. There is, for instance, the Wesleyan West London Mission, established by the late Rev. Hugh Price Hughes, which thrice every summer Sunday holds services in Hyde Park. But if you want to see the churches at work in unchurchy surroundings, go with a little band of devoted workers into the wards of our workhouses; or, better still, dive with them into the kitchen of a common lodging-house, where the gospel is preached and sung while the inmates cook their suppers and dry their clothes at the common fire.

I have given you scarcely a glimpse of many of the ways in which the army of Christian workers forming the backbone of Nonconformity are toiling from week's end to week's end to lighten the spiritual and moral darkness of the modern Babylon. I have not even mentioned the Sunday Schools, in which every church without exception is supplementing and filling out the religious instruction given in the day schools, though rarely, if ever, teaching any doctrine that could be called sectarian. Nor have I touched on the numberless charities by which the churches collectively and church members individually are constantly trying to relieve the physical necessities of the poor. But I have said, perhaps, enough to make it plain that in the best way they know the "Dissenters" are taking an active and important part in the great fight against evil, and are contributing largely and unselfishly to the sum of those influences which will one day lift the life of London to a level of health and purity it has never yet reached.

LEAVING WESTBOURNE PARK CHAPEL AFTER A SERVICE.

COSTER TYPES.

COSTER-LAND IN LONDON.

By C. DUNCAN LUCAS.

HE may like his pot of ale, and in times of stress his language may be a trifle lurid, but there is not much that is harmful in the London costermonger. When Big Ben tolls the hour of four in the morning sixty thousand costers are getting out of their beds and wondering where the next meal is to come from. Men whose fathers and grandfathers have been barrow-pushers before them, raw recruits, ex-shopkeepers, solicitors who have been struck off the rolls, artists, actors : young and old, female as well as male, nearly every class is represented.

The annual turnover of these people is several million pounds sterling, yet a very large number of them cannot afford to rent more than a single room. For all that the coster's home is his castle. It is the only place in the whole world where he rests his feet ; and let us not forget that he is on them for sixteen hours a day. Besides, he is a family man, and proud of the fact. With his missis and the baby he shares his bed ; in each corner, buried in a mound of miscellaneous wrappings, is another offspring ; before the grate stands the inevitable orange-box on which his clothes are spread out to dry ; a table, a couple of chairs, and washing utensils complete the outfit.

To maintain this home, the London coster labours incessantly. Watch him as he starts out of a morning to fetch his barrow, the stabling of which costs him a shilling a week. He may be fat, he may be lean, but the tired eyes and the tightly-drawn cheeks show that there is not much joy in his life. He has had, perhaps, three hours' sleep. It was wet the night before, and you can wring the water from his clothes. Even his billycock hat and

SELLING A PONY AND BARROW (ISLINGTON CATTLE MARKET).

the faded neckerchief that does duty as a collar are soaking. No matter; he has but one suit, and the terrors of rheumatism are nothing to him as long as he can bring "somefink 'ome for the kids," and put a lump of beef on the Sunday dinner table. To provide that lump of beef with regularity is the one ambition of his weary life. And so he goes to market.

He is a cautious man, this coster. On him the flowery and persuasive eloquence of the auctioneer of fruit is lost. He gazes at the sample boxes behind the rostrum and reflects.

markets, the biggest of which is in Lloyd's Row, Clerkenwell.

The coster is now ready to earn his Sunday beef. If he is a Hoxtonian he may sally forth to Hoxton Street or Pitfield Street; if a South Londoner he may go to Walworth Road, the New Cut, or Lambeth Walk; or he may make for Farringdon Road, or Goodge Street, or Whitechapel. He may go on the tramp. Ten to one he is a "little punter" with few friends—one who has only enough capital to buy a day's stock. No man fights more fiercely for bread

GROOMING COSTERS' DONKEYS.

He wonders whether the contents of those boxes are not a good deal better than the stuff that is to be sold.

"Blessed if I don't go down into the slaughter-house!" he exclaims; and making his way forthwith to the "slaughter-house," which is the warehouse basement, he rummages the stock. If he is satisfied, he returns and buys; and, his purchases over, he proceeds to dress his barrow, a task requiring no little ingenuity. For not only must the coster so arrange his fruit that it will appeal to the eye, but he must balance his barrow. A tyro will often so load his barrow that he cannot move it; the bred-and-born coster, on the other hand, distributes his wares so cunningly that he can push a load of twelve hundred-weight with comparative ease. The barrows can be hired from one of the various barrow

than the "little punter," for if trade is slack and his goods perish he has no money to replenish his barrow. With the old and respected coster it is otherwise. He may be "down on the knuckle" once a month, yet he need never be hungry. Such is the loyalty of these men to a comrade in distress, they will literally strip their barrows, one here giving a bushel of apples, one there a box of grapes, to save him from standing idle.

The tragedy of the coster's existence is best realised on a wet Saturday night, but to understand it one must have been behind the scenes. The line of barrows stretches for perhaps half a mile. Butchers, bakers, fruiterers, fishmongers, booksellers, sweetstuff vendors, dealers in winkles and mussels, crockery merchants; sellers of plants, bulbs, and seeds of all descriptions: half a thousand

I. BASKET RACE (COSTERMONGERS' SPORTS).   II. MID-DAY IN COSTER-
LAND (HOXTON STREET).   III. A COSTER'S FRUIT STALL.

are engaged in one continuous roar for custom. Apparently there is not much sadness here. But study the faces of these toilers by the light of the flaring lamps. There is not one that is not careworn. For the truth is that a wet Saturday brings ruin to the coster. The poor decline to come out and buy, and this means in many cases that the stock, a perishable commodity, will have become uneatable by Monday. A succession of wet Saturdays drives hundreds to bankruptcy. There are few more melancholy spectacles than that of a coster running up his pony on the stones at the Islington Cattle Market. Barrow as well as pony he must sell, for the weather has hit him hard. Saturday after Saturday it has poured, and he has not the heart to begin life over again. We laugh at the "pearlies," but there is little laughter in the coster's life. Nor are there any "pearlies," for the true London coster never dreams of sporting such buttons.

What stories one could tell of the patient heroism of these men! Once upon a time a little "punter" lost his all, and his barrow stood empty. On a Wednesday he met his sister, who took him home and lent him her husband's Sunday clothes to pawn. He was to return them on the Saturday, so that the husband should not know to what use his suit had been put. With the money he received from the pawnbroker the "punter" bought some fruit, but it rained on the Thursday, and the weather was even worse on the Friday, and there was no money to redeem the garments. On the Saturday this man tramped for sixteen hours, first north, then south, then east, then west, trying to get enough to buy back the suit. It was a battle against time. The pawnbroker closed at midnight, and if the money was not forthcoming by then the owner would have no Sunday clothes to wear, and there would be strife between husband and wife. At eleven o'clock he was still half-a-crown short, and it was raining, and trade was slackening fast. Five minutes before twelve he was still in want of sixpence. He wondered if he should put an end to his life. Providence decided for him. As the clock of Marylebone Church was striking midnight the "punter" sold six-pennyworth of grapes. Leaving his barrow

to the mercy of any passing thief, he ran to the sign of the three brass balls as he had never run before. The shutters were going up; a moment later and the brave little "punter" would have been too late. During the night the suit was smuggled into the house of the owner, and all was well.

This is no exceptional instance of the perseverance of the coster. At four o'clock one Saturday morning a coster left Edgware Road with a barrow on which was heaped ten hundredweight of fruit. He pushed that barrow to Woolwich, and stood by the gates of the dockyard till ten at night. And he pushed it back again.

What of the coster's love story? It is a very brief and unromantic one. The coster does all his courting in the gutter, with one eye on his "filly" and the other on his stall. The wedding is generally a "walking" one, the principal parties proceeding to the church by different routes and meeting at the door. When the clergyman has done his work, the bridegroom returns to his barrow, and his wife celebrates the occasion with her friends as best she can.

There is a certain costermonger whom we will call George. He is one of the leaders of the fraternity. George's description of his nuptial day applies to the average coster wedding. Says George: "When I got married I come out of church and give my ole woman two shillin's, and went to work and didn't see her till 12.30 at night. I hadn't a pound in the world."

But there is high society in Coster-land as there is elsewhere. If the bride's parents possess a few shillings, and if the bridegroom has a sovereign in his pocket, the usual thing when the weather is propitious is to have an outing. The friends bring their donkey chariots, and, the ceremony over, off the party goes — it doesn't much matter where, provided there are a few refreshment-houses on the road. On wet days the parents of the bride invite the company to partake of a chunk of beef, potatoes, and greens, and a bucket of beer. A peculiarity of these feasts is that they last all day.

The best points of the coster are seen

BARROWS FOR HIRE.

when the days of a comrade are numbered. Peep reverentially into the chamber of death. Day is breaking, and the grey old fellow on the bed has but a few hours to live. By the ragged bedside are two men, rough-looking perhaps, yet each is as gentle as the gentlest lady in the land. Listen! The dying coster's mind is taking him back to Covent Garden. He asks the price of grapes, whether oranges will sell. The watchers humour him and wipe his brow. These costers were pushing their barrows at one o'clock in the morning, and they have been here since two. They will work for another sixteen hours before they sleep. Presently there is a tap at the door, and another coster enters. He will sit with the patient through the day. He may not have a penny to bless himself with, and there may be naught in the larder for the children. What of that? A neighbour will tend and feed the youngsters, "and the missis will look arter the barrer." These men are heroes. When a coster lies sick, there is not a barrow-pusher in London who will not help him.

But to return to our little punter. He

has drawn his last breath, and his comrades have arranged a "brick" or "friendly lead" in his behalf. The "brick" is held in the parlour of a public-house. On a table near the door is a plate into which every visitor drops a coin. The most valuable coin is usually contributed by the man who was the deceased's greatest enemy, for on these occasions it is the custom for those who have not been on speaking terms with the departed to do their best for him. At the far end of the room are seated the chairman and the vice-chairman. Pots of beer figure somewhat conspicuously; the ladies criticise each other's feathers rather loudly; and the young bucks relieve the tedium of the wait with a little hat-bashing. Regarded as a whole, the "brick," got up though it is to bury a dead man, is remarkably free from any trace of melancholy. Not that the chairman is forgetful of his responsibilities. If you remain long enough you will hear a great hammering.

"If you don't shut up I'll sling you down!" roars the president, fixing a fierce eye on a young and frolicsome lady coster. "I will, straight. Now then, Mary, 'The 'At my Farver Wore.' Quiet!"

Another bang with the hammer, and up rises Mary. The artistes follow each other in quick succession, and the "sing-song" is kept up till near closing time.

A big affair is the funeral. No London coster goes to his grave without twenty or thirty vehicles "behind him," and no widow leaves the graveside without receiving many pressing invitations to drown her sorrows at the nearest hostelry. The poorer

"ALL A-GROWIN'."

a coster is, the greater is the attempt made to provide him with a brilliant send-off to the other world. Some months ago a young coster was fighting with death in a London infirmary. He had neither father nor mother, and his brother was in prison. Two comrades were sitting by his side, and to them he observed as his life was fast ebbing away : " I'd like to see my brother come 'ome afore I kick, but it's no good a-wishin'. Get me a bit of paper. I want to nominate my old pal George to receive anyfink as may be due to me."

they contribute to their society—the Costermongers' Federation—has to be spent in upholding their rights in the courts of law.

With the exception of a few hours snatched for the annual parade of donkeys, the London costers enjoy but one holiday in the year, and this they devote to attending what is called " The Costers' Derby," but which is in reality the Costermongers' Athletic Sports, one of the most amusing events in the programme of which is a basket-carrying contest. To Kensal Rise, where the events are decided, they go in their thousands,

A COSTER'S FUNERAL
'WALWORTH).

PART OF THE PROCESSION.

Only a shilling or two was due, but George saw that the man had four horses to draw him to the grave, five pounds' worth of flowers on his coffin, and a band costing fifty shillings to play him to his last resting-place.

These, then, are the men who are buffeted about from pillar to post—men who help their fellows as no other class does, and who, although they labour for sixteen hours out of the twenty-four, live literally from hand to mouth. Perpetually at war with the local authorities, who are determined to clear them notwithstanding that they are indispensable to the poor, the word peace is not contained in their vocabulary. Nearly every man's hand, save that of the policeman, is against them, and almost every penny which

and every man who boasts a " moke " drives his missis up in style. Not one coster in a hundred, by-the-bye, possesses a donkey. If a barrow-pusher wants a four-legged assistant he goes to a stable where these animals are kept for hire, and on presenting the owner with half-a-crown gets a " moke " and a barrow for a week. The photographic illustration on p. 75 shows a stable yard at Notting Hill where three donkeys are being groomed preparatory to a day's work.

The costers have their foibles like other men. When they find themselves with a spare sovereign they worry themselves until they get rid of it; but let us always remember that the coster never thinks he can go too far in serving a friend.

MAIL VAN LEAVING MOUNT PLEASANT.

THE GENERAL POST OFFICE.

By BECKLES WILLSON.

TELEGRAPH MESSENGER.

IF you were to tramp through all broad London, and penetrate its most occult official recesses, you would probably not find a nearer human similitude to a bee-hive than those three great stone buildings which comprise St. Martin's-le-Grand.

We cannot enter the General Post Office at the front—the old public corridor has been utilised for official purposes. Let us, then, ascend a flight of stairs at the back, and, presenting our order of admittance to the Circulation Office (as this department is officially styled), be conducted at once to a gallery overlooking the appropriated entrance corridor.

Standing here, from our position in the gallery we are able to command a bird's-eye view of the central room in the Circulation Office—that is to say, the Receiving and Stamping Room—with the two great Sorting Rooms to our right and left. The middle room, which was formerly the public entrance-hall, until, as I have said, the exigencies of the service demanded its utility, is crammed with some two hundred employés, who, seated at long, plain tables, are engaged in what one of them described to me (professionally, no doubt) as "breaking the back" of the correspondence. For this great room lies just behind the letter-boxes, through whose apertures descends an unceasing and heterogeneous rain of letters, packets, newspapers, and post-cards destined for London—its heart and suburbs—and for each of the four quarters of the whole earth besides. London and the Universe—these are served here—the United Kingdom is another matter. A regulation provides that that class of matter known as "Country" correspondence must be sent to and dealt with at Mount Pleasant, another large establishment half a mile away. To this we will revert later. London and the Universe ought, surely, to suffice to fix our present attention upon St. Martin's-le Grand.

In a narrow cubicle just behind the letter-boxes are two employés, attired in grey blouses, busily heaping the letters into baskets. As fast as they are filled they are seized by the waiting carrier boys and borne to the long, flat "facing table," as it is called, where newspapers, circulars, pamphlets, and letters proper are severally disengaged with quick fingers, after which they are hurried to the stampers, whose brief, brisk, official thud at one blow defaces the stamp, and indicates the time and place of posting. To illustrate how everything in the Post Office is regulated, how every act can be traced to the individual cog or wheel in the great instrument, we may mention that when each of these stampers arrives for his day's work he is obliged to enter his name under the particular stamp or postmark he intends using that day, so that the device on any letter out of a million can, if necessary, be brought home to its perpetrator.

A row of desks, marked off into compartments three feet wide, occupies the entire space of the south room, that is, the room looking towards Cheapside. It is at these desks that all the City or East-Central letters are sorted, and by the ingenious moveable index strips, upon whose surface are inscribed all sorts of Metropolitan localities, the desk is made to serve for as wide an area as the necessity of the occasion demands. Thus, at one moment the strips at the desk would seem to indicate a series of pigeon-holes—as Fenchurch Street, Minories, Eastcheap, Ludgate Hill, Mile End, and Moorgate, while, if a paucity of correspondence for these localities occurs, a twist of the sorter's thumb and forefinger and the index strip presents an entirely new set of names to guide him in the process of sorting. As a matter of fact, an expert operator often manages to dispense with the pigeon-hole indexes altogether, and, much to the perplexity of the visitor, goes arbitrarily piling up epistles addressed to places in the neighbourhood of St. Paul's in a compartment distinctly labelled "Bethnal Green."

As he works, the carriers are piling up unsorted correspondence at his left hand, while postmen are striding the length of the tables, pausing at every sorter's com-

LETTER SORTING (ST. MARTIN'S-LE-GRAND).

partment to snatch up bundles of letters concerned with their own itinerary. In the case of packets and newspapers, large baskets are substituted for the pigeon-holes on the sorters' desks. And while we speak of newspapers, we must by no means overlook the newspaper "detective," whose peculiar function it is to lay hold of newspapers at hazard on the supposition that they may contain letters, money, or articles which should, if sent in another class, render his Majesty a greater pecuniary profit on their transmission. Yet, absurd as the hypothesis appears, it is sad to have to state that this particular official is astonished several times a day by the discovery of this illicit device for cheating the Post Office.

At this building in St. Martin's-le-Grand alone there are nearly two thousand employés engaged on inside and outside service. Of course, prior to the removal of the Country Mails Department to Mount Pleasant in 1901, the strain was tremendous, and the exciting scene known as the "Six o'clock Rush" was one of the features of the establishment. The pressure having thus been lightened, matters assume, as evening draws on, a less nervous tension; but there is yet throughout the building and without it greater life and animation than in any other department under the Government.

We have glanced at the sorting, which is the same in the two great halls at either end of the building. Before noting other and, though minor, yet more curious departments on the ground floor, the eye of the visitor will have fallen on the legend "Blind"

I. WIRE REPAIRERS AT WORK. II. A REEL OF WIRE.

at regular intervals throughout the desks. This is a technical expression for letters whose address is either illegible or insufficient, or perhaps is absent altogether. If the former, the "blind" correspondence is carried in bundles to the "Blind" Department, where it passes into the hands of several clerks whose function it is to ascertain by means of directories, gazetteers, and other aids to knowledge, the more precise whereabouts of the addressee. "Mr. Wite, J., Lead Gate, Senpoll's, V.C.," is, it will be admitted, a superscription not remarkable for its perspicuity; but it took an official of the "Blind" Department just two minutes to discover its signification to be, "Mr. J. White, Ludgate House, St. Paul's Churchyard, E.C." Similarly mystifying were those familiar examples: "Santling's, Hilewita," and "Obanvidock," for "St. Helen's, Isle of Wight," and "Holborn Viaduct," which are inscribed amongst the archives of St. Martin's-le-Grand.

"That is the hospital yonder," murmurs our guide, as we thread our way between the tables. We peer through the intervening space, while visions of maimed and crippled postmen and van-drivers, martyrs to duty, flash across our senses. But we may spare our sympathy: the hospital is for maimed letters, packages, and newspapers, whose outer vestments have so suffered in their journeyings as no longer to hide their nakedness or preserve them from fatal loss. Such are "Found Open and Officially Sealed," either by gummed paper or by twine. Senders of wedding cake, fragments of which are strewn over the desk, are the chief offenders, and it is a standing joke amongst the other officials that the surgeons of this letter hospital largely subsist upon "blind" wedding cakes, an insinuation which, being indignantly resented, has, of course, no foundation.

The presence of one or two registered

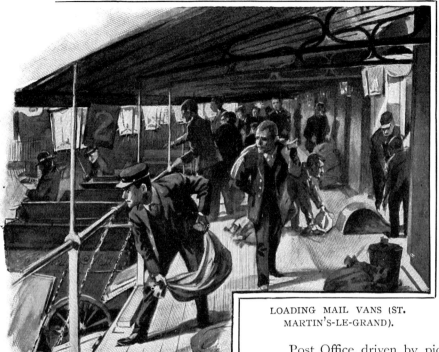

LOADING MAIL VANS (ST. MARTIN'S-LE-GRAND).

Again descending the stairs, we came across several openings to the street through which bags are being flung — bags in all stages of rotundity hailing from, or destined for, all parts of the globe, *viâ* Waterloo, Paddington, or Charing Cross and other railway stations. Several fully-loaded crimson mail coaches are now leaving the Post Office, driven by picturesque drivers in picturesque costumes, a species of apparel descended to them from the days of the stage-coach, when it drew up in spanking style, after a hundred miles' journey, at these very portals seventy or eighty years ago. The royal van-drivers, notwithstanding their uniforms and gold lace, are not employés of the Government, inasmuch as all cartage of the mails is performed nowadays by private individuals under contract.

letter packets in the hospital reminds us that these are, as they should be, the aristocrats of the mails; that practically, unless they happen to be damaged, they pass through only two men's hands from the time they arrive until they are sent away from the building. As a registered letter is taken out of bag or basket it is handed to a separate clerk who gives a voucher for it and does not part with it unless and until he receives a similar receipt from another clerk.

The department in which letters from and for abroad are received, sorted, and despatched is on the upper floor. · The process, although the same, demands a different degree of ability, for it must be borne in mind that the superscriptions are executed in every known language (and occasionally a dead one), and therefore actually involve somewhat greater knowledge and possibly more alert faculties. "Examination in Foreign and Colonial Sorting" is the title of a placard I noticed as we passed into the room, and hints at a special kind of ability and special remuneration.

A G.P.O. INTERPRETER.

As to the volume of the business done here, statistics give little idea when they tell us that a billion letters and postcards and four hundred millions of newspapers are annually handled at the General Post Office. A City firm has posted 132,000 letters at one time; while as many as 167,000 postcards have been received in a single batch. Parcels are taken in here, but are immediately despatched to Mount Pleasant, where the Returned (or Dead) Letter Office is.

The chief Money Order Office of the kingdom is situated a few streets away in Fore Street. Here the business of posting up and checking off the vast aggregate sum (nearly £100,000,000) which millions of people send annually through the post is attended to by a numerous staff. Again, although the Government has acquired a huge telephone business—worked in connection with the Post Office—it is carried on at some little distance from St. Martin's-le-Grand, which has nothing to do with telephones. "Telephone London" is treated separately in another part of this work; and the Post Office Savings Bank is referred to under the heading of "Thrift London."

Mount Pleasant is not, as its name would lead a stranger to suppose, a vernal eminence crowned by an Ionic fane. Its name suggests less the Ionic than the ironic, inasmuch as it was formerly the Coldbath Fields Prison, now converted into a Government building and christened with the title of an adjacent street or lane. It is in Farringdon Road, and now vies with St. Martin's-le-Grand in importance as a receiving and distributing centre. Our illustration on p. 80 shows one of the mail vans, laden with parcels, about to start from there on a night journey to the country.

For a more important and fascinating department under the control of the Postmaster General we need not travel so far as Farringdon Road. Immediately opposite the leading Post Office of the kingdom is the headquarters of the telegraph system of these islands, and by far the greatest telegraph office in the world. A reminder of its vast ramifications is furnished to us in the small pictures on p. 82, showing, first, a couple of men repairing a wire just below a street pavement; and,

next, several lusty employés rolling along a huge reel of wire, eight feet in diameter, for use by the department.

To those who have never before visited a telegraph headquarters the sight of these vast galleries packed with their hundreds of operators, male and female, together with their throbbing instruments, at first suggests a factory. But the simile in the mind's eye is gone in a moment. The machines click-click eternally, but there is no fabric woven. There is a restrained intensity about the place; it is reflected in the keen eyes of the operators; a vivid intelligence seems to float in the very atmosphere; there is no running to and fro, no movement of bodies as at the Post Office; there is nothing needed to simulate excitement; you feel as if you were in the presence of a mighty brain. And it is so: you are not deceived. In each of these four or five huge rooms, each with its two hundred or so operators, are the concentrated intelligence, the action, the movement, the aspirations of the world. Everything is passing here—from the death of a nation's ruler to the result of a horse-race. Three hundred thousand messages a day pass through these galleries.

Living London—what could be more alive, more vital than this? These operators are a nervous race—ever busy with their instruments—even when there is no necessity for being so. Meanwhile let us glance very briefly at some of the features of this great department, whose very existence would have been an incomparable puzzle to our grandfathers.

First in our itinerary is the room or, as the authorities prefer to denominate it, "Instrument Gallery," from which and through which messages are sent to the Press of these islands. By means of a wonderful invention (*not* of transatlantic origin) known as the Hughes' Perforator, a long telegram is instantly duplicated on eight narrow ribbons of paper, each of which is put into a separate instrument and its purport automatically delivered to eight provincial cities. So that a description of a tragedy, a boat-race, or a new drama, while speeding into the office, perforates eight strips of paper in such a fashion as to make each equivalent in verbal value to the

THE PNEUMATIC TUBE ROOM (ST. MARTIN'S-LE-GRAND).

THE SUBMARINE CABLE ROOM (ST. MARTIN'S-LE-GRAND).

cylinder of a phonograph, and these being immediately transmitted in turn, Liverpool, Glasgow, Manchester, and Birmingham almost simultaneously receive the account, not in perforated paper, but in dots and dashes.

In another gallery is the headquarters of the London telegraph system, in another the Provinces, in another the Foreign. The last-named is the Submarine Cable Room, the wires of whose specially - constructed instruments are laid beneath the English Channel. All the Atlantic cables are, of course, worked by private companies.

A feature of the galleries soon after half-past four in the afternoon is the appearance of tea-cups and bread-and-butter. It was figured out by a former Postmaster-General that if the two thousand employés were to be granted a short interval for tea outside the establishment it would cost, in round figures, £8,000 a year. It would also cost the employés themselves about £8,000. By serving them tea *gratis* at their desks, therefore, a saving of £4,000 to the Department would be effected, to say nothing of the economy to the purses of the operators. Tea in the Telegraphs costs the Government just £4,000 per annum. Indeed, the Government may be said to look after the physical welfare of its assistants with some benevolence.

It contributed to the acquisition of the enclosure popularly known as the "Postmen's Park," close to St. Martin's-le-Grand, and it has even constructed a spacious tennis-court on the roof of the great new building known as G.P.O. North.

There is another department which has not been mentioned. It is in connection with the Pneumatic Tube system—by means of which cylinders propelled by air travel with the speed of lightning underground to and from some of the principal branch offices in London, as far west as the Strand. The tubes are served by boys ; and our picture on p. 85 shows the room in which their contents are dealt with. The engines in the basement, which primarily accomplish the work, are four in number, of 50-horse power each.

But the greater engines—the real engines, after all—are the brains that devised and that now maintain the whole system which I have attempted to describe : the marvellous accuracy, the amazing promptitude, the ease and quietness with which the whole correspondence, posted or telegraphed, of over forty millions of Britons at home and many millions abroad is conducted, and which must, in spite of occasional disparagement, ever remain one of the proudest monuments of Living London.

IN THE POSTMEN'S PARK.

KING'S CROSS CORNER.

LONDON STREET CORNERS.

By GEORGE R. SIMS.

IF you would watch the great panoramas of London life unfold themselves, there is no better standpoint than a busy street corner. There you may study the ever-changing crowd. There you may watch the wondrous traffic converging from the four points of the compass, mix itself together for a moment, then separate and widen out into broad distinct streams, each stream flowing towards a different quarter of the Metropolis. Stand, for instance, at the Elephant and Castle on a sunny afternoon. You see on one side the trees and green gardens of St. George's Road, on the other the crowded pavements of Newington Causeway. You gaze in one direction and Walworth Road, with its typical scenes of South London bustle, lies before you; you turn your head and the New Kent Road gives you a totally different picture. Another turn of the head and the London Road opens up to your wondering eyes. In every direction heavily-laden trams and 'buses are passing each other. By you on the pavement is a line of 'bus and tram timekeepers, every one of them busily making notes in a bulgy pocket-book with a stumpy lead pencil.

The folk who pass you are of all sorts, but mostly of the humbler class. The shopping ladies who come from Newington Causeway are some of them smartly dressed and suggest villadom, but the female note of the district is the useful little basket in one hand, and the purse and latch-key in the other. The brown paper parcel that is carried past you is generally loosely tied. It suggests home manufacture. The factory girl and the coster girl mingle with the crowd, the male loafer leans against corner posts, the Irish lady with a faded shawl and a top-knot order of *coiffure* comes and goes at intervals, and the halfpenny evening papers are eagerly purchased by horsey-looking men and youths who turn instantly to the racing results. Just across the road in a little shop there is a picture of the Elephant a hundred years ago. Let us look at it, for it is in-

ELEPHANT AND CASTLE CORNER.

the patients of St. George's can see Buckingham Palace and the broad avenue up which many a time and oft come the glittering Life Guards escorting Royalty. This is the most picturesque, the most inspiriting, corner of London. Past it roll daily the equipages of the noblest and the wealthiest of the King's subjects. Everywhere the eye rests on splendid architecture and vast expanses of turf and tree. But the Hospital is always there. In the great building facing the Park of Pleasure and the Palace of the King the maimed and suffering lie in agony.

Ludgate Circus. What a change of scene! Here all is crowded and noisy, and men and women hustle each other without apology. Trains rattle and scream across the bridge that spans Ludgate Hill, heavy waggons clatter along Farringdon Street, 'buses and vans and cabs are mixed up in apparently hopeless confusion in Bridge Street. Country folk coming from St. Paul's stand nervously on the kerb waiting to cross the road. At the office of Messrs. Cook & Sons intending tourists are studying the attractive window bills, and forgetting in their admiration of the Italian lakes that they are blocking the footway in one of London's narrowest busy thoroughfares. One young fellow, who is evidently off for a Continental holiday for the first time, calmly reads a book until he is run into by a newspaper boy rushing off towards the City with the four o'clock edition of an evening paper on his shoulders. The young fellow drops his book. It is " French Conversation for Travellers."

Down Fleet Street and round the corner from Bride Street the newspaper carts are dashing. Journalists and Fleet Street celebrities, printers and press messengers, pass you at every moment. Down Ludgate Hill come carriers' carts from the Old Bailey. The name of the places they serve are painted on many of them. They bring a breath of country air into the fumes of the tar—for, of course, the wood pavement of Fleet Street is " up."

King's Cross. Stand at the corner opposite the Great Northern Railway side

teresting. In the vast open space now filled with trams and 'buses, and carts and cabs, there are four-horse coaches, horsemen, and porters carrying heavy packs. There is a postchaise with a young gentleman and a young lady in it. It looks like an elopement. A pretty girlish face is pressed to the window while we are looking, and a man's voice exclaims, " Look, 'Lizer, that's the old Elephant a 'underd years ago ! " We turn and see the bride of to-day leaning on her young husband's arm. She is in bright blue satin, and wears a big white hat and feathers. The newly-wedded couple attract little attention. Brides and bridegrooms threading the crowd arm in arm are by no means novelties at the Elephant, where the honeymoon is the afternoon walk and an evening at the music hall, and both parties to the contract go to their work the next morning.

Hyde Park Corner! On one side the great Hospital abutting on the street ; opposite it the stately archway through which the tide of fashion flows into the famous Park. This is surely the corner of pleasure and of pain. Through the windows of the wards

entrance, and if the proper study of mankind is man, you will have a great opportunity of pursuing a profitable course of education. Down Gray's Inn Road, Pentonville, Euston Road, and York Road flow endless streams of humanity, and the noise of the traffic is deafening, for here three great railway centres contribute their carrying trade to the general confusion. Travellers, especially provincial travellers, abound on the pavements, and the dialects and accents of all the counties of the United Kingdom mingle with the cockney hubbub. It is here that the provincial newly arrived by rail is first faced with the problem of London's vastness. He wants to take a 'bus, but he doesn't know which 'bus to take. The policemen at the corner are directing provincial inquirers in the matter of 'buses for the better part of their time. I should say that the policemen on duty at King's Cross are the best authorities on 'bus routes to be found in the whole of the Metropolis. The cabs that pass you here are mostly luggage-laden. The people that pass you carry hand luggage oftener than not. The brown paper parcel fastened with a leather strap is a common feature of the corner, so is the hot, perplexed, buxom young woman with several parcels, a handbag, a baby, and an umbrella. Family parties are frequent.

From dawn to midnight you will see a knot of loafers hanging about the King's Cross corner. If you are poetical and blessed with a strong imagination you may picture them as men who have been waiting year after year for friends from the provinces —friends who have never come. If you are matter-of-fact you will guess that the loafer loafs here because there are many opportunities of an odd copper, or a proffered drink. Outside the public-house there is frequently a four-footed traveller waiting for a friend. It is the drover's dog from Islington Cattle Market. His master is inside. The dog waits patiently, apparently unobservant. Sometimes he stretches himself close to the wall and slumbers. But the moment the drover comes out wiping his mouth with the back of his hand the dog springs up, and, close at his master's heels, disappears in the traffic.

Right in the full tide of East-End life is the corner of Leman Street. Standing there one can see the ever-changing multitudes that throng Whitechapel High Street, the Commercial Road East, and Commercial Street. Type is writ large in the crowds that eddy round you, and the alien Jew is the most pronounced of all. The joyless,

ST. GEORGE'S HOSPITAL CORNER (HYDE PARK).

pensive features of a persecuted race contrast strongly with the careless good-humour of the native population. The work for which the district has a reputation "jumps to your eyes," as the French say, in the barrow-loads of slop clothing that are pushed past you by stunted youths. The rapid rise of many of these aliens from serfdom to comparative

melancholy-eyed men are conversing. Presently you catch sight of a poster or two, and a theatrical announcement printed in cabalistic characters, and then you understand that the conversation around you is being carried on largely in Yiddish and Lettish. But there is plenty of English "as she is spoke" at this corner, for sailors and

FLEET STREET CORNER (LUDGATE CIRCUS).

comfort is shown in the gay dresses and showy hats with which young Russian, Polish, and Roumanian Jewesses of the second generation brighten the thoroughfares on the Jewish Sabbath. Even the babies make strong splashes of colour among the dark-coated men: for baby's hat is often a deep orange or a flaming red, and his little coat of plush is of a brilliant hue. There are not any perambulators at this corner. Most of the babies on the Saturday afternoon are carried by father, for the reason, probably, that mother is engaged at home.

You have not been standing long at the corner of Leman Street before you wonder what language it is in which the dark-haired,

ships' hands, and carmen, and English working folk abound. Here there is no quiet hour for the 'buses and the trams that pass continually; they are generally full. But you notice that the hansom cab, which in the West is such a feature of the traffic, is very little in evidence here. After you have passed Aldgate Station the hansom becomes rarer and rarer. A little way beyond Leman Street it is practically extinct.

It is in Leman Street that the first note of Oriental London is struck. The Asiatics who make their temporary home in West India Dock Road and in Limehouse stray occasionally as far as this in little parties. But they rarely loiter. Timidly, almost apologetically, they thread their way through the crowd and disappear in the light mist that has wandered from the Thames and apparently lost its way in the Commercial Road.

Liverpool Street! Here it. is no question of flowing tides of humanity. If we are to remain faithful to the simile of the sea, whirlpool is the only word to use. Take your place—you will have some trouble to keep it—any Saturday afternoon about three o'clock on the kerb opposite the Great Eastern and North London termini. There it is a perpetual swirl and eddy of human beings amid a vehicular traffic that appears chaos—that is, in fact, chaos constantly being reduced to order by the most matchless traffic manager in the world, the London policeman. Across the road you see never-ending processions of people mounting the steps to Broad Street, and in another direction a broad stream of human and vehicular traffic pouring into the Great Eastern Company's station. Between the two great termini lies the Goods Station of the London and North Western Railway, so that the two streams of passenger traffic are perpetually divided by a line of heavily-laden railway vans.

The great crowd that throngs the pavements is sharply divided. From Broad Street, the Stock Exchange, the banks and insurance offices, and the great City warehouses, comes a high-hatted, well groomed and tailored mob of business men. From the other direction comes a surging mass of men in billycocks and caps. Mixed up with both streams are the hansoms, and the excursionists arriving from or departing to the provincial towns and the seaside resorts served by the Great Eastern Railway.

The transfer of luggage from Broad Street to Liverpool Street is a feature of this "corner." Porters come and go with luggage-laden barrows. They wheel these dexterously among the cabs and omnibuses, and are followed with much anxiety by the owners. Nervous females grasping a country nosegay in one hand and a bundle of wraps in the other vainly endeavour to keep one eye on their luggage and the other on the cab that is bearing down upon them and is already in perilous proximity. The hardiest cyclists dismount at this corner and carry their machines instead of allowing their machines to carry them. And every minute, if you have an amiable countenance and look like a Londoner, anxious inquirers will test your knowledge of the 'bus and railway system. You have no sooner informed a stout, square-built gentleman with a small portmanteau which is the way to Rotterdam than two young ladies carrying a little box between them will ask you which is the station for Yarmouth. You are fortunate if you are not expected to point out in rapid succession the 'bus that goes to Clapham, the nearest way to Waterloo, the staircase one must mount to find a train for Ball's Pond Road, and the point at which the trams start for the Nag's Head, Holloway. And even after you have answered these questions satisfactorily your knowledge

LIVERPOOL STREET CORNER.

TOTTENHAM COURT ROAD CORNER.

of London may be further tested by an inquiry as to the nearest pier at which a steamboat may be boarded for Blackwall.

In direct contrast to the Liverpool Street corner is the corner where the Holborn district and Oxford Street meet Tottenham Court Road and Charing Cross Road. Busy the scene always is, but the seethe and swirl are absent. There are no train catchers, and the loitering, shop-seeing element leavens the work-a-day portion of the movement. The stage, the music hall, and the British Museum contribute their special features to the crowd. Business men will come up from Holborn at the swing, but the ladies of the suburbs loiter from shop window to shop window, and when they have finished, and wait for the 'bus that is to take them to their homes in Camden or Kentish Town or distant Hampstead, they betray no undue anxiety or haste. The pretty, neatly-dressed chorus or small-part lady may be seen at this corner constantly, for there is a theatrical colony in the streets that run from Tottenham Court Road to Gower Street, and in those around Bloomsbury Square. The sportsman—or rather sporting man—is not unknown here, for near to this corner was for many years a spot where the odds could be obtained in ready money in spite of the law, and the corner has never quite lost its sporting character. The Twopenny Tube station just across the road receives a rivulet of passengers all day long, and ejects a stream at frequent intervals. The foreign element from Fitzroy Square comes by Tottenham Court Road, and lends dark hair and flashing eyes and comic opera hats to the corner occasionally. But it rarely loiters. It crosses the road and works its way towards the maze of streets that make up Soho.

But the main characteristic of this corner is the " domestic English." The shopping lady, the tradesman, the commercial traveller, the occupiers of furnished apartments, and the inhabitants of North London villadom are more largely represented than any other element ; for the nursemaid and the perambulator, and the working population that make High Street, Camden Town, and Hampstead

Road impassable on Saturday night, stop short about Euston Road, and rarely come as far as this corner, where the roadway runs direct into the City in one direction and direct to the West-End in another. The carriages that pass are more of the family vehicle than the smart order, and their presence is mainly due to the fact that in Tottenham Court Road are half a dozen of the most celebrated house furnishers and drapers in the Metropolis.

I have enumerated but a few out of the famous street corners of London, but they are fairly typical ones. The Angel at Islington, the Nag's Head at Holloway, the corner of Piccadilly Circus, the corner by Camberwell Green, the Royal Exchange, and certain corners in the Borough, Hoxton, Kennington, Shoreditch, and Charing Cross have each a special feature, but in general character they fall into line with those dealt with in this article.

I have taken the London Street Corners from the point of view of their characteristic crowds, but they afford plenty of opportunities for the student of manners from the individual point of view also. The street corner character is an interesting personality. The loafer is to be found there in all his glory night and day. For the lovers of London it is at once a meeting and a parting place. The provincial sightseer is never absent from certain corners—notably the Baker Street corner near Madame Tussaud's—and there are some corners which are at night time meeting places for the local youth, and occasionally for the local rough. The street corner is a favourite pitch of the pickpocket and the confidence dodger, and the policeman lingers longer there than at any other part of his beat. The corner of the street is a place for good-byes, not only for lovers, but for friends and relations who live at opposite ends of the town. " I will walk as far as the corner with you " is a phrase that is on the lips of thousands of Londoners every night in the year. And "just round the corner" is a meeting place hallowed by centuries of poetry and song. To many an Englishman and Englishwoman there are " corners " in London streets which are fraught with hallowed memories — and they are not the *busiest* corners either.

LEMAN STREET CORNER (WHITECHAPEL).

TRAM, 'BUS, AND CAB LONDON.

By HENRY CHARLES MOORE.

CABMAN WITH
ROSETTE (ROTHS-
CHILD COLOURS).

DURING the hours which elapse between the arrival of the first tram at Aldgate, crowded with working men, and the departure suburbwards of the last 'bus, loaded with cheerful folk fresh from an after-theatre supper, cabs, 'buses, and trams carry between them all classes of his Majesty's subjects, from the peer and the millionaire to the coster and the workhouse woman.

Let us begin by seeing the trams at work. It is eight a.m., and at the entrance to a big North London tramyard stand some eight or nine smartly-uniformed

for them in a big many-columned book. A car comes slowly from the back of the yard, and the men at the gate stand aside to let it pass. A conductor jumps on it, dons his bell-punch, and prepares for work. In less than a minute the car is at the starting-point, where clerks, shop assistants, office boys, and tea-shop girls have been anxiously awaiting its arrival. Several youths and one girl jump on the car before it stops; the others wait until it is at a standstill. Then ten of them attempt to step on the platform at the same time, and not a little pushing ensues, followed probably by some hot words. In a few moments all the seats are occupied; the conductor rings his bell, and the car starts.

At the Finsbury Pavement terminus of the North Metropolitan Tramways we find cars, nearly all carrying their maximum number of passengers, arriving in rapid suc-

WASHING L.C.C. TRAMCARS.

conductors and leather-aproned drivers discussing the latest news. Close by, in the yard inspector's office, are three conductors receiving their boxes of tickets, and signing

cession from various northern suburbs. At the Hampstead Road and other termini north of the Thames they are arriving and departing every minute. Passing to South

OMNIBUS DRIVER.

agree with his way bill, he enters the little yard-office and hands it in, together with his unused tickets, to the night inspector.

When the last tram has entered the yard, which is now crowded with cars, the gates are shut, and the washers and stablemen are left to themselves. The washers vigorously sweep the dirt and the "dead" tickets from the roofs and insides of the cars, and not until this task is ended is the washing begun. It is nearly five o'clock before the last car is washed, but the washers' work is not yet finished—the windows have to be cleaned, the brass work polished, and the panels rubbed with chamois leather.

Now let us watch the 'buses. It is a quarter past seven, and the driver of the first 'bus to leave one of the London General Omnibus Company's many extensive yards is already up, standing with his legs astride the brake pedal, and wrapping his rug around his body. A stout, grey-whiskered, red-faced old man, with his rug already strapped around him, is climbing laboriously to the box seat of the second 'bus. He is a conservative old fellow, and wears a tall hat, in spite of the fact that such headgear is going out of fashion among 'busmen. Drivers, ranging in age from twenty-one to seventy, and conductors, mostly under forty, hurry into the yard, greeting and

London we see proof of the great popularity of electric trams. The London County Council's cars, filled with almost every type of the great city's male and female workers, are following each other closely on their way to the termini at Southwark, Blackfriars, Waterloo, and Westminster Bridges.

During the afternoon the trams, in all parts, are less crowded, but at six p.m. they begin to fill up rapidly at every town-end terminus, including those of the electric cars at Hammersmith and Shepherd's Bush, and struggles to get on them are fierce and frequent. At ten o'clock the trams begin to pass into the yards; at long intervals at first, but after eleven o'clock every two or three minutes. Here is a horse-drawn tram, its last journey for the day ended, entering a yard. A stableman is there awaiting it, and the moment it stops he promptly takes out the horses, and leads them upstairs to unharness, feed, and make them secure for the night. As the horses are being led away, the driver and the conductor put their shoulders to the car and push it along the lines until it is close against the one in front of it. The driver then marches off home, with his rug on his arm and his whip in his hand. The conductor, however, is not quite ready to depart; for two or three minutes he sits inside the car checking his last journey's takings. Having made his money

OMNIBUS CONDUCTOR.

LONDON BRIDGE STATION YARD.

chaffing each other in vigorous language. The only man who appears at all depressed is an "odd" driver who has been three days without a job; but soon his spirits revive, for a bustling little woman enters the yard, and informs the foreman that her husband is "that bad with rheumatism he can't raise a hand, let alone drive a pair of young horses like he had third journey yesterday." The "odd" driver takes out the sick man's 'bus, and the "odd" conductors regard his luck as a good omen.

By half-past eight 'buses of almost every colour, except black, are arriving in rapid succession from all quarters of the Metropolis, and, setting down the last of their passengers at the Bank, rumble onwards to join the queue outside Broad Street Station, or to add to the busy scene in London Bridge Station yard. An hour later the London General's Kilburn express, "sixpence any distance," is rattling Citywards along Maida Vale; and at Oxford Circus 'buses are passing north, south, east,

and west. Here, too, are the large motor omnibuses—yearly increasing in number—of the London General Omnibus Company, the Road Car Company, the Atlas and Waterloo Association, and Tilling, Limited, as well as others which came into existence with the introduction of the modern horseless 'bus. Before mounting to the top of one of these motor omnibuses we notice, crossing the Circus, a "Royal Blue"—a name which has been familiar to Londoners for more than half a century—and during our ride down Regent Street towards Piccadilly we meet Balls Brothers' "Brixtons" and the very old-fashioned blue "Favorites" of the London General Omnibus Company.

Near by, crossing Trafalgar Square, we see the yellow 'buses (dubbed by 'busmen

A "FRIENDLY LEAD" TICKET.

express, "sixpence any distance," is rattling Citywards along Maida Vale; and at Oxford Circus 'buses are passing north, south, east,

"mustard-pots") of the Camden Town Association, the oldest omnibus body in London. To this and other associations belong the

majority of the leading proprietors, including several
very old-established firms
and such comparatively
youthful limited liability
companies as the Star
Omnibus Company and
the Associated Omnibus
Company. Proceeding to
Victoria, we find 'bus after
'bus starting from the railway station yard, including
the well-lighted red "Kil-
burns" of the Victoria
Station Association.

Now it is early in the
afternoon—a slack time
for 'busmen. Here comes
a Road Car with every
seat vacant, but the
silk - hatted driver is

MOTOR OMNIBUS.

keeping a sharp look-out, and soon picks
up three ladies bound for Westbourne
Grove. Not far away an empty London
General is standing at a "point." Here is
a "pirate." Two ladies enter this 'bus, be-
lieving it to belong to the London General
Omnibus Company. It is painted and
lettered to give the public that impression,
but the company's name is not on the
panels, and the horses, instead of being
strong, well-fed animals, are lean "cabbers."

Later on, an almost empty 'bus, which
belongs to one of
the great companies,
is coming along Fleet

Street from Ludgate Circus. The driver
glances up at the Law Courts clock, and
calculates that by driving somewhat slowly
he will arrive at the earliest closing theatre
just as the people are coming out. But the
Strand policemen's duty clashes with his, and
they hurry him on, with the result that, instead of leaving Charing Cross with a full
complement of passengers, he has only five.

The day cabmen, their hansoms and four-
wheelers clean and bright from the washers'
hands, begin to appear in numbers about
nine a.m., some hurry-
ing Citywards with
fares, and others

IN A CAB YARD.

proceeding slowly to various stands, where they find a few unfortunate and somewhat despondent night cabmen waiting in the hope of obtaining at least one good job before taking their cabs back to the yard.

Soon we find cabs everywhere, for there are 7,500 hansoms and 4,000

HANSOM.

FOUR-WHEELER.

four-wheelers licensed to ply in the streets. A long line of cabs, each with luggage on its roof, is just quitting Euston Station. Several of the fares have arrived *via* Liverpool from distant parts of the world, and can scarcely conceal the pleasure they feel at finding themselves, after many years of exile, once more in a London cab. Down Grosvenor Place hansoms and four-wheelers are hastening to Victoria Station. On a summer day Middlesex and Surrey are perhaps playing at Lord's, and outside the ground the line of empty hansoms, patiently awaiting the close of the day's play, extends more than half way to Maida Vale. Now the theatres have closed, and hansoms and four-wheelers are following close upon each other in all directions. Some are bound for the suburbs; others, the majority, are hurrying to the various railway termini. Even Gower Street, peaceful from morning until night, is noisy with the tinkling of cab bells and the clattering of hoofs.

Here is a smart young cabman ready to mount his dickey. He is, perhaps, the lucky

recipient of one of the Rothschild Christmas-boxes—a brace of pheasants—which are given annually to the majority of 'busmen and to some cabmen. In acknowledgment of this generous gift he has adorned his whip with a rosette composed of the donor's colours.

At the West-End we notice an old cabman seated on the box-seat of his four-wheeler. There is an air of contentment about him, for he is on a good stand and knows that it will not be long before he is hailed by a "fare." Near by, waiting outside a club, is a hansom in summer array. Cabby looks very cool in his white hat and light coat, and we see that he has also done his best to make his patrons comfortable; for a white awning is spread over the roof of his cab, and inside the hansom is a palm-leaf fan.

On a certain summer afternoon we may find the pensioners of that excellent society the Cabdrivers' Benevolent Association mustering at Westminster Bridge for their annual summer treat—a river trip to Hampton Court. Many of these weather-beaten old fellows (some are very feeble) have their wives with them, and a happy day is always spent.

The cabmen's shelters are filled with drivers enjoying their midday meal. The accommodation is small, and the men have little elbow-room, but the good quality and cheapness of the food more than atone, in the cabmen's opinion, for limited space. It is while having a meal in a shelter that cabmen discuss matters of interest to themselves. One describes the personal appearance of a well-dressed man who "bilked" him on the previous day, and another distributes cards announcing that a "friendly lead"—or, as it is sometimes termed, "a select harmonic meeting"—is to be held for the widow and children of a deceased comrade. "Friendly lead" cards are usually drawn up by cabmen, and, as the chairman and other officials are generally advertised by their nicknames, they afford amusement to outsiders.

Between the hours of two and five in the afternoon hundreds of cabbies drive to some of the big yards, such as that of the London Improved Cab Company, where they change horses and have their cabs "spotted," that is, the splashes of mud removed. (The illustration on p. 97 is from a photograph of Mr. Patrick Hearn's well-known yard in Gray's Inn Road.) And in the West End electric cabs, occupied by charmingly attired ladies bent on shopping, are plentiful.

About 9.30 p.m. the first hansom to finish its day's work of twelve hours returns, and soon the washers begin their long night's work, dipping their pails into the tanks and throwing the water over the wheels and bodies of the muddy cabs. One man quickly finishes his first cab, and getting between the shafts pulls it out into the main yard, where some hours later it will be polished.

Standing at the corner of a street, nearly opposite one of the chief theatres, is a thin, shabbily-dressed, dejected-looking cab tout. His eyes are fixed on the stalls and dress-circle entrance, and the moment the earliest of the homeward-bound playgoers appear he hurries across to them. "Four-wheeler, sir?" he calls out to an elderly man, who is accompanied by his three pretty daughters. A four-wheeler *is* required, and the cab tout dashes off to a side street to fetch one. Soon he returns with it, and is rewarded with sixpence. Seeing that there is no chance of another job at this theatre, for his fellow touts are many, he hurries off to a later-closing one, where he earns eightpence—a sixpenny tip and a twopenny one. His night's earnings are only fourteenpence, but he is quite satisfied. The previous night he spent, supperless, on the Embankment; to-night he will have a fish-supper, a pot of beer, and a bed.

The day cabs continue to pass into the various yards until two o'clock in the morning, and by that time the Metropolis, with the exception of its night workers, is asleep. But hansoms and four-wheelers are waiting on the stands, and before the city awakes many a Londoner will have cause to be thankful that, though trams and 'buses disappear from the streets for a few hours, a cab is always to be found.

IN A CABMEN'S SHELTER.

IN A LONDON WORKHOUSE.

By T. W. WILKINSON.

PAUPER'S ADMISSION ORDER.

TO pass in a north-westerly direction through the squares and by the towering flats lying between Langham Place and Northumberland Street, and to enter "York Palace"—no royal palace in fact, but the St. Marylebone Workhouse, and so called because of its palatial appearance and its proximity to York Gate, Regent's Park—is to step from the front door of Dives into the home of Lazarus. Plenty and poverty exist side by side. My lady's boudoir is on the one hand; the pauper's dormitory on the other. Extremes meet in London as they meet nowhere else.

Further contrasts await us at the entrance to this last refuge of civilisation's superfluities and failures, which we may take as a type of the many workhouses scattered over the Metropolis. Tarry awhile at the porter's lodge, and watch the incomers before they lose some of their individuality. Here, with slow, unwilling steps and lack-lustre eyes, comes a man who, worn out with life's struggle, has reluctantly obtained a relieving officer's order for admission. Enter next his antithesis—a London wastrel to the very marrow, shiftlessness stamped on his stubbled face, and with the air of one going through an oft-repeated performance. Who art thou, O unshorn one, that callest thyself a painter? Let him be put down as a painter, but the officials know him as something more—a confirmed "in and out," a man who discharges himself in the morning and is back at night or the next day. A mere neophyte this, however; he has not yet achieved distinction in the professional pauper army. The gap which separates him from the champion "in and out," a supremely gifted genius of the East-End who has been discharged and admitted about two thousand times, is that which separates lance-corporal from colonel.

Another contrast. In through the doorway of sighs comes a typical working man who palpably shrinks from the future, because he knows nothing of the life on which he is entering. When he goes before the Visiting Committee, may good fortune be his! Everybody admitted appears before that body, which is brought into closer contact with the inmates than are the Guardians who, as a board, meet fortnightly; and he is one of those cases which it helps

RECEIVING AN INFIRM PAUPER.

by giving money or finding employment or both. It thus saves men, and does untold good quietly and unostentatiously. He passes; and here is his successor—a man for whom the poor-house has no secrets and no terrors. He was born in the workhouse; all his life—and his hair is white as driven snow—he has lived in the workhouse; and he will die in the workhouse.

Could we wait here for twenty-four hours the iron chain of circumstances would show us still stranger juxtapositions. Picture a common scene. It is night. From the

person of a man who has kept want at bay for sixty years or more, and who rolls up easily and comfortably in the official carriage kept for those who cannot walk. Rubber-tyred are the wheels of this vehicle, and it contains every necessary convenience known to medical science.

Leaving the lodge, all these and other types are conducted to the receiving ward, and then they are scattered over the buildings according to age, sex, and other circumstances. To get glimpses of them when they are settled involves some walking.

IN THE AIRING YARD.

Marylebone Road comes no sound save that of a cab bearing a belated roisterer homeward. Tap! tap! from the knocker, loudly, imperiously. The door is opened to admit a policeman carrying in his arms the familiar bundle. No need to ask what he has got. Another little mite has been found on a doorstep, nestled, perhaps, in an improvised cradle, and with a note from its despairing mother pinned to its clothing—a note that adds to the poignancy of the tragedy. "Oh, pray," wrote one poor creature from the depths of a sorrow-laden heart—"oh, pray somebody be kind to my little darling. I have to work very hard for six shillings a week, or I would look after her myself."

This is how tender, budding youth often comes to the workhouse gate. Age is represented not many hours afterwards in the

Where shall we begin? In an institution known to one section of the community as "the grubber," one thinks first of the kitchen. Let that, then, be our starting point.

A large, lofty room, lined with white glazed bricks, and with a score of steam-jacketed coppers, tea coppers, roasting ovens, and the like, it seems to have been designed and fitted for a regiment of Brobdingnagians. Here they make sixty-gallon milk puddings, have three teapots of eighty gallons capacity each, cook a quarter of a ton of bacon and a ton of cabbage at an operation, and steam potatoes by the ton. Fixed in the middle of the kitchen is a mincing machine, one of the uses of which is artificially masticating the meat supplied to old and toothless paupers. On a large cutting-up table to the left the joints (always of good quality) are carved, and then, with other food, passed through two trapdoors into the great hall.

What was the menu to-day, Tuesday? Roast mutton and potatoes, with bread. The young men and women each had four-and-a-half ounces of meat, twelve ounces of potatoes, and four ounces of bread. For breakfast the ration was four ounces of bread, one-pint-and-a-half of porridge or one pint of cocoa; and for supper it will be six

measured out in doses at stated times. Adjoining is one of the four special day wards, which introduces us to the classification system. Formerly paupers were lumped together, as "casuals" are, outrageously enough, to this day; now the best of them are isolated and made comparatively comfortable. As the superior men are discovered they are drafted into one or other of these rooms, which are much more bright and attractive

THE KITCHEN.

ounces of bread and one-pint-and-a-half of broth.

Through the great hall—a fine building capable of seating twelve hundred, and affording an infinitely suggestive scene at dinner-time—out into the airing yard again, past the beds of flowers that fringe it and make it bright and cheerful, by seat after seat occupied by paupers reading in the sun, and presently we reach one of the general males' day wards, of which there are four, all exactly alike. It is full of men, some standing in groups talking, some sleeping, some reading, some playing dominoes on the long table. On another table to the right stand huge bottles of medicine—stock mixtures for coughs, indigestion, and other common ailments of the race—ready to be

than those for the lower grade. The one we have just left is bare, rather noisy, and full of movement; this is hung with steel engravings, the table is strewn with books and adorned with plants, and all is still and quiet. In the other room the men, of a rougher class, wear their hats and like to sleep and play dominoes; here the inmates are bareheaded, and spend much of their spare time in reading. Separate dormitories are also provided for these select paupers, and they enjoy, therefore, a degree of privacy which used to be quite unattainable in a workhouse. In addition there are, of course, rooms exclusively for infirm males, who spend hours sitting apart in silence, as if listening for Time's oncoming footsteps.

More tacking and turning bring us to a

doorway from which pro-
ceeds a monotonous
"ger—er—er." Inside
are a number of men, each
bent over a crank, which
communicates with a
huge, overgrown coffee-
mill. Able-bodied un-
skilled paupers, they are
literally fulfilling the
primeval curse, and earn-
ing, as well as making,
their bread by the sweat
of their brow, since they
are converting wheat into
whole meal, which, mixed
with a proportion of white
flour, they will eat later
on in the great hall. Two bushels of grain
form the daily task.

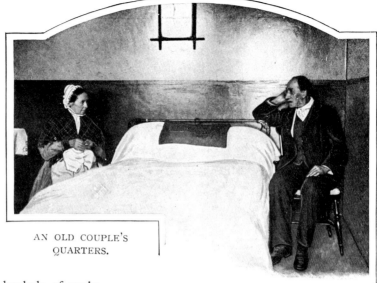

AN OLD COUPLE'S
QUARTERS.

Chop! chop! chop! with the buzz of
a saw, from another shop. It is, of course,
the firewood manufactory. The eye takes
it all in at a glance. At the far end four
men are turning a crank that supplies the
motive power to a circular saw, which is
fed by a fifth inmate. Scattered about the
room other paupers are chopping and
bundling the wood. They are all old—
mostly too old and too unskilled to do
heavier or more
profitable work. No
fixed output is

exacted. The men, in fact, are here more
that they may kill time than anything else.

In other shops pauper "tradesmen" are
variously employed. Piled up yonder,
awaiting the attention of the cobblers, is a
heap of boots about the size of a hayrick.
These seats in the corridor, fit for any gentleman's lawn, are home-made, and are for
the garden. And now the odour of methy-
lated spirit reaches the nose. We have
arrived at the French-polishing shop, concerning which the indefatigable Master of
the workhouse could tell
a story. Once it had an
inmate who too freely
supped the potent but
nauseous spirit used for
polishing. To make the
stuff still more horrible,
the officials dosed his
supplies with asafœtida,
and there is every reason
to believe that that elo-
quently noisome drug
proved too much for even
his palate. But the ex-
periment was only a
qualified success, because
the offensive product
spoiled the spirit for the
purposes for which it is
generally employed. Over
the remaining shops we
need not linger. Enough

IN A
WOMEN'S
WARD.

AT DINNER.

that employment is found for all except the physically unfit, and that all the work of the house is done by its inmates. There are only two salaried artisans in the place.

Now let us pass to the female side, which differs little, except in obvious details, from the male side. One feature, however, has a pathetic interest, and that is the number of aged inmates. Included in the population of this microcosm—two thousand, the full roll of many a country town with a mayor and corporation—are no fewer than two hundred octogenarians, of whom the majority are women. Veritable dear old creatures many of them are! The feeling they produce must needs be one of sadness, and yet there is something pleasing in the spectacle they present when hob-nobbing over their tea in the afternoon. Many of them have their own teapots—presents, in some cases, from the kindly matron—and they get the delicious leaf from visitors and in other ways. Sometimes one of the less infirm women, having no proprietary rights whatever in such a utensil, puts a screw into a pot belonging to a more fortunate companion, and in virtue of that contribution is entitled to a cup of the brew. So there you shall find them all at their accustomed hour, drinking tea as of old, and perfectly contented with things as they are, judging from the nodding of caps and the smiles and the whispered confidences. If they are not happy, appearances belie them. It is certain, at all events, that most of them will gradually rust out, and die at last of the workhouse complaint, old age.

And now we reach the aged married couples' quarters. Consisting of ten little tenements for as many Darbies and Joans —one room, one couple—and a general room at the end for meals, the "private apartments" form a sort of miniature model dwelling that overlooks the Paddington Street Recreation Ground. Admirable is the only word for this division. The brightly-painted walls, the pictures, the official furniture, including a chest of drawers and a table, the photographs and knick-knacks belonging to the inmates, who are allowed to bring in such property and arrange it as they choose—all this makes a "private apartment" home-like and a

delight to the eye. If an old couple must spend their last days in the workhouse, one could wish them no brighter or more healthy quarters.

A final pause at the nursery, and then to another gate—that of the casual ward. The infants' room is, perhaps, the saddest side of any workhouse, though everything possible is done for the helpless little mortals in "York Palace." Some little sufferers are in bed; the rest seated together at the end of the room, close to a table where food—milk, bread-and-milk, bread and butter—is always kept in readiness. They are always eating, but they cannot exhaust the supply, for that is illimitable. Though they have not been cradled in the purple, they bear no trace of hardship. A chubby-cheeked girl, who never takes her eyes off your face, came from a doorstep in a neighbouring street, and some of her companions have identically the same history. Where are their mothers—alive or dead? Others are known orphans, and two or three are the children of women in the house. But they all look well and robust.

Five o'clock. The casual ward opens at six, and already there is outside it a mass of the human wreckage that the irresistible tide of London life is ever casting up. Nearly two-score pitiable figures—broken-down professional men, artisans out of work (some of them "too old at fifty"), women with innocent children clinging to their skirts, whole families even, from the head to the suckling at its mother's breast—are waiting for admission. One of the women is eyed curiously by her fellow "casuals." She is decently dressed and—here is the cause for special wonder—wearing kid gloves. What strange decree of fate has brought her here?

At six o'clock prompt the door opens, and the tramps enter the refuge in single file. Listen to the answers they give to the usual questions. One is repeated again and again till it sears itself on the brain. It is " Nowhere." "Where did you sleep last night?" asks the porter. " Nowhere." Nowhere! The key of the street; dropping asleep on a doorstep, or, worse still, while still walking, and being rudely wakened by the shock of stepping on a paving-stone that was not there —dropping, that is to say, off the kerb—or running into a lamp-post or a brilliantly-lighted window; dodging about in the cold, grey dawn to get a wash at a street fountain when a policeman is not looking—these and a score of other miseries are summed up in the pregnant word.

Beyond the office the stream of destitute humanity divides, the women and children going one way, and the men another. The males are next searched to see whether they possess more money than is allowed (the limit here is 4d.), and also whether they have pipes, tobacco, or matches concealed about their persons. All pass muster, and, having had a compulsory bath, sit down to supper, which consists of one pint of gruel and six ounces of bread. The meal ended—and be sure that it does not last long—they retire one by one to their separate cells, each of which contains the unusual luxury of an ordinary bed.

To-morrow morning, after breakfast—which is a mere repetition of supper—the inmates will be set to work, the women at cleaning and washing, the men at cleaning and oakum picking. All day, with only a break for dinner—bread and cheese—will they be thus kept employed. Then will come supper again, then bed; and on the following morning, about thirty-six hours after entrance, they will be discharged, turned on the streets once more.

This is the life of those who by the vicissitudes of things are undermost, temporarily or permanently. It is practically the same all over Pauper London, for, as already stated, "York Palace" is a typical Metropolitan workhouse. Vastly as it has been improved of late years, it can be still further bettered without putting a premium on laziness, and it lies with us who are now on top to see that this is done.

CASUALS WAITING FOR ADMISSION.

READING ROOM, AMERICAN EXPRESS COMPANY.

AMERICAN LONDON.

By ELIZABETH L. BANKS.

THERE was a time when American tourists who came to London returned to their native land and informed their compatriots that there was "nothing fit to eat over there," meaning that all the food was cooked and served in English style, and that benighted Britishers knew nothing of the delights of the products of American culinary skill. That Great Britain could exist, and even wax strong and fat, under such adverse conditions was an ever-increasing puzzle to the visiting American who went from restaurant to restaurant, and boarding-house to boarding-house, with his eyes full of tears and his pockets full of money, seeking, always seeking, for what his appetite craved, yet never finding it.

But those melancholy times are past—it was before the Americanising of London that such tragedies were enacted; and now there are few special American dishes which one cannot find at various eating-places in London if one will but inquire for them. Here is a case in point. I was one of a little American party at a restaurant in the neighbourhood of Charing Cross, where pork and beans, Boston style, and salted cod-fish

"picked-up" (i.e. shredded into fine bits and prepared with thick cream gravy) were served to us as the merest matter of course when asked for—and, I may add, to the astonishment of a certain facetious member of our party, who had ordered these "specialities" of Yankeeland with no other purpose than that of dumbfounding the waiter.

That individual, however, only answered, "Yes, sir; certainly sir!" and straightway brought us our cod-fish; after which we had such a beautifully browned bean feast, with crinkled roast pork in the middle and all, that we could proceed with little effort to fancy ourselves in Boston.

But it was London!

It was London, too, into which we penetrated when we left the restaurant to make our way towards Piccadilly Circus; and the semi-circular street down which we looked, to see dozens of star-spangled banners floating from the tops of the business houses, was Regent Street. It was difficult to believe that we were not in New York or Chicago, walking along a street decorated with flags for some extra-special gala occasion. What did it mean? Nothing, except that the month was July, and the shopkeepers, knowing that the "American Invaders" had descended upon London to the number of many thousands, paid them the pretty compliment of hoisting the Stars and Stripes instead of the Union Jack. To be sure, one could not positively affirm that the shopkeepers were wholly sentimental, and gave no thought to the probable increase of trade that the hoisting of the flag might bring! London shopkeepers are human. Nevertheless this Americanising of Regent Street has always seemed to me an exceedingly graceful thing.

And speaking of shops and shopping, let us hasten along Regent Street, past the Circus, into Oxford Street to see another device in the way of American baiting. A very kindly, clever bait it is, that sign in the window of a large Oxford Street draper's establishment— "To our American Lady Customers : Messrs. Blank, having noticed that their American customers seem often to have difficulty in determining the exact value of English coinage, have prepared a table of money equivalents, by which ladies may see at a glance the American value of the articles exposed for sale. Messrs. Blank will also be pleased to

receive payment for their goods in American currency, if more convenient to their customers. They also present, with their compliments, a Guide Book of London, which they are sure will interest and assist American ladies visiting the Metropolis."

"American Rocking Chairs for Sale Here!" "American Shoes!" "American Desks!" "American Pickles and Catsup!" "American Cut Glass!" "American Soda Water and Other Iced Drinks!" "American Bar—Gentlemen, Try our 'Whiskey Sour' and 'Manhattan Cock-tail!'" "American Candies—Made Fresh Every Day!"

Everywhere and hundreds of times a day our eyes are greeted with these and other signs of American London.

Having eaten our American luncheon, and shopped in American fashion with American money with which we have bought American things, let us to Victoria Street to pay our respects at the American Embassy, which has the distinction of being unique in its unpretentiousness and inconveniences among the various embassies of London. We find the Ambassador, who is at the head of American London, receiving numbers of his countrymen and countrywomen, assisted by the different

IN THE COURTYARD, HOTEL CECIL.

than at the Embassy, and the inconveniences arising from lack of space are proportionately greater. Into the Consulate, to pour all their troubles into the ears of the sympathetic and genial Consul-General, go hundreds of Americans daily during

secretaries. During the "Invasion Season" it is computed that about one hundred Americans daily apply at the American Embassy for the two tickets which the Ambassador has the privilege of giving away each day for entrance to the House of Lords. This means that ninety-eight Americans daily leave the Embassy disconsolate and disappointed, declaring that the only fault they have to find with London is the fact that the chamber of the House of Lords is not so convenient of access as is their own Senate chamber at Washington.

If it happens to be a Fourth of July, the Ambassador is found at his private residence, shaking hands, shaking hands, always shaking hands, with thousands of his countrymen and countrywomen who are resident in or passing through London ; and after the hand-shaking, in which the Ambassador is, of course, assisted by his wife, there is a descent to the dining-room for the strawberries— which every honest American will admit to be better than any strawberries eaten in his native land — ice-cream, cake, and punch. There was a time in years gone by when only Americans attended these receptions, given to celebrate the breaking of the chain which bound the American Colonies to England ; but in these later years a great many Englishmen and Englishwomen go to the American Ambassador's house every Independence Day. Great Englishmen of title bring their American wives to shake hands with the Ambassador, and jestingly refer to the "Anglo-American Alliance."

At the American Consulate, in St. Helen's Place, the scene is sometimes even busier

OFF FOR THE DAY : I. BY COACH.   II. BY CHAR-A-BANC.

the "Invasion Season" ; and to the American tourist unaccustomed to the people and manners and ways of English life the Consul-General is expected to act the part of guide, philosopher, and friend. Among these callers are not a few ladies who seek his advice in connection with matters of all kinds.

Also into the Consulate go the "stranded" Americans in London, asking for help to "get back to God's country" ; and then the Consul-General and his assistants must kindly but firmly point to a framed legend on the wall, which runs : "This office is not provided by the United States Government with any fund for the assistance of needy Americans in London."

The Consulate is besieged by English as well as American visitors. It is to the Consulate, in the private office of the Deputy-Consul-General, that hundreds of British merchants and others go to make what is known as their "declarations" before shipping goods to America, that is, they "declare" the value of the goods they are exporting.

To the Deputy-Consul-General also go the Americans to get advice upon notarial, legal,

A FOURTH OF JULY RECEPTION AT THE AMERICAN AMBASSADOR'S RESIDENCE

and other matters of various kinds. There, too, go the many Yankee inventors, who, arriving in London with what they term a "mighty handy device," yet knowing not what to do with it, proceed to St. Helen's Place to seek information from the always good-natured Deputy-Consul-General concerning where to "place" their inventions on exhibition to attract the attention of Londoners.

But the Embassy and the Consulate are only two of the places where Americans in London foregather. Go to the Reading Room of the British Museum, and watch them hunting up their ancestors, diving deep into the records of the Harleian Society, turning page after page of peerage books and works on county families. Observe the smiles when they discover that there was a live lord in the family away back in the centuries agone ; see how they chuckle if they can discover connection, however distant, with a dukedom. They like the British Museum for other reasons than that it enables them to discover the secrets of their ancestry. They particularly like the place, because in the summer it is cool and in the winter it is warm, heated after the American manner and sometimes to the American temperature. Thus is the British Museum one of their favourite haunts.

Round the bust of Longfellow, too, in Westminster Abbey, frequently gathers American London, with kindly thoughts of the England that has thus honoured America's poet. Then from the Abbey, on the top of a 'bus, talking with the driver and giving him such tips as are calculated to turn him into the most voluble and interesting of encyclopædias, go the Invaders to the Tower, to St. Paul's, and other resorts which any American after a visit to London of even two days would blush to say he had not seen. In the afternoon at tea-time, or later in the cool of the day, again comes the foregathering, this time in the courtyard of the Cecil, the Palm Court of the Carlton, and the lounges of the other hotels that welcome Americans to the neighbourhood of Trafalgar or Russell Square. Notes are compared while teaspoons click against cup and saucer. There are calls for ice, ice ;

and there is such a volume of American accent, American vivacity, and American dressing as would be apt to convince a foreigner dropping suddenly into the scene that London was the chief city of America.

The two classes that go to make up American London are the Settlers and the Invaders. I have so far been writing of the Invaders. It is they who spend their days in sight-seeing, who fill the coaches and char-a-bancs going to Hampton Court and other places of interest. They gather in the shipping offices to purchase tickets to their native land. They haunt the bureaus of information, they go in their dozens to the office and reading-room of the American Express Company in Waterloo Place to see the American papers and inquire if there are any "express packages." Those who cannot afford the high-priced hotels betake themselves to boarding and lodging houses, with a preference for those over Bloomsbury way, and a particular and especial liking for such as are diplomatic enough to display the American flag or the American Eagle shield over the fanlight.

For the benefit of the Invaders, to make them pass their time profitably and pleasantly, the Settlers, assisted in many instances by Englishmen and Englishwomen, have started clubs, societies and unions, and leagues. The first of these societies was probably the American Society in London, which gives American dinners and receptions on such holidays as the Fourth of July, Thanksgiving Day, and Washington's Birthday. Then comes the Society of American Women in London, with its beautiful rooms and its wonderful luncheon parties at Prince's. The Atlantic Union, though it numbers among its members many Colonials, makes a specialty of American members and devising means of entertaining American visitors and bringing them into contact with British subjects ; while the Anglo-American League is, as its name indicates, a combination of inhabitants of both countries in the interests of peace, good-will, sympathy, and for the strengthening of the international ties. The fact that membership in this society is open to all British subjects and American citizens, on the payment of a subscription of not less than a shilling or more than a pound, will

in itself show how broad
are its aims and how
wide-reaching should be
its influence.

The American Set-
tlers in London number
about twenty thousand.
Those who make up this
twenty thousand belong
to all sorts and conditions,
from the American society
woman entertaining not
only her own countrymen
and countrywomen, but
members of the English
royalty and nobility, to
the humble American
negro, who elects to reside
in London because of what

MAKING " DECLARATIONS "
AT THE AMERICAN
CONSULATE.

he thinks is the greater degree of " liberty,
equality, and fraternity."

There was a time when to hear the
American accent on the English stage
caused smiles and comments. Now upon
the boards the " American language " is heard
almost as frequently as the English tongue,
while theatrical companies made up entirely
of Americans come to London with the
expectation of remaining the whole year
round.

American journalism, too, with its good
points and its bad ones, has come to London

to stay, not for a year, but probably for the
century. Some papers being " run " on the
American plan, it, of course, follows that the
importation of American journalists has
become a necessity, so all along Fleet Street
American journalists can be seen at any hour
of the day, and almost any hour of the night
as well, flying hither and thither. I myself
have a keen recollection of the time, only a
few years back, when, calling at the office of
a London newspaper, I would feel and express surprise at finding one of my own
countrymen in the editorial chair, ready to discuss with me plans for my
work. Now my journalistic
work constantly brings me
into contact with my own
countrymen as editors of
London papers.

So thoroughly, indeed,
has London become
Americanised, so great is
the influx, both by pre-
ference or by marriage, of
American women into
London society, that it is
really dangerous for the
unsophisticated to discuss
in public American people,
American customs, or
American manners, unless
they are named for the
purpose of praising them.
It was not so very long ago

IN THE DEPUTY-CONSUL-GENERAL'S OFFICE : A MATTER OF BUSINESS.

that a Frenchman, being entertained in the home of a certain Duchess, was discussing at an evening reception the characteristics of American women as compared with those of Englishwomen and Frenchwomen. The Frenchman did not like or approve of American women, and made bold to express his opinion in no flattering terms of certain of their faults and failings. He also ventured to suggest that in point of beauty, charm, intelligence, and morality they were, as a class, far inferior to English and Continental women.

"Do you not agree with me, your Grace?" asked the Frenchman, gallantly bowing to the Duchess.

"That is a somewhat embarrassing question for you to have put to me," answered the Duchess coldly, "since I am an American woman myself, though, of course, I am now a British subject!"

Day by day and year by year this Americanising of London goes on. New "schemes," new enterprises, new inventions —even new customs and manners and new words for the English language—are ever making their appearance in London; and, inquiring whence they come, one is usually informed "From America, of course!" Then down come some of London's old buildings to make room for steam-heated American office-blocks, which their architects would rear to the thirty-fourth storey were it not for the interference of London's building laws.

Through the streets of London roam the German bands and Italian organ-grinders, playing "The Star-Spangled Banner" and "Hail! Columbia," and little English girls follow, keeping time to the music, dancing as only London children can dance.

All this is American London.

AN AMERICAN CALLER AT THE CONSULATE.

BOUND FOR SOUTHEND (FENCHURCH STREET STATION).

BANK HOLIDAY LONDON.

By A. ST. JOHN ADCOCK.

IF you happen to live near any of the great open spaces that fringe the outskirts of London, you know what it is to be wakened before sunrise on three mornings of the year by weird, unwonted noises passing without—clattering of hoofs, rattling of wheels, cracking of whips, occasional shouts, occasional bursts of laughter.

Getting out of bed to peer round the edge of the blind, you see a shadowy, intermittent procession flitting through the ghostly twilight—a donkey-cart laden with sticks and a sack or two of cocoa-nuts, a man perched in front driving, a woman nodding drowsily behind; a slow van top-heavy with painted poles and boat-shaped swings; a sleepy alien pushing an ice-cream barrow; another donkey-cart presently, and another; costers with barrows full of fruit, of nuts, of winkles —all passing dimly like phantoms in a nightmare; but, remembering it is a Bank Holiday, you know you are not dreaming, and that these are enterprising tradesmen racing early for the best places on the adjacent pleasure ground.

By and by you take a stroll out over that ground before breakfast, and find those shadows of the dawn looking solid enough in the daylight. They have lined the roads and paths with their stalls and barrows; the cocoa-nut shies have been prepared, and, pending the arrival of sportsmen, the proprietors are squatting on the grass enjoying an interlude of repose, or sipping at cups of coffee from the nearest refreshment-stand, and assimilating thick slices of bread and butter.

Already, however, the revellers are coming. Here are small boys, bent on missing none of the day and impatient to begin enjoying themselves, tramping in out of the streets clutching newspaper packets of provender. And, supposing the ground of your choice to be Hampstead Heath, and the weather fair, here come other boys, and here, too, come older citizens, who are used to being bleached in City offices on ordinary days of the year, each adventuring forth now with his rod, and a tin can, and a pocketful of worms. Down by the ponds on the Heath, or in Highgate Fields, you shall see them bait their hooks and cast their lines, and settle down to the placid enjoyment of watching their floats.

But they have an hour or more of comparatively peaceful fishing before them yet, for the great mass of holiday-makers are only just getting dressed, or sitting down to breakfast. A small minority are approaching in trains and 'buses and trams, or afoot, but, generally speaking, those who are up so early as this have promised themselves a day at the seaside, and are hurrying to the big railway stations, such as London Bridge or Fenchurch Street, to catch excursion trains to Brighton, Southend, or elsewhere, or—especially on the August Bank Holiday—are pouring down the stone steps on to the Old Swan Pier, and fighting a passage through the increasing throng on to the excursion steamers for Clacton, Margate, and other resorts.

Many who could afford it went away by rail or river on Saturday afternoon, and will not return until to-morrow morning, but the multitudes scurrying now to the railway termini or seething and struggling on the pier will come back to-night weary with too much happiness, with the sea-voices lingering in their ears, and in their eyes a memory of lovelier horizons, to make the jaded city seem, by contrast, dingier than it really is.

Except for such as these, and for the ardent cyclists who are setting forth at this same hour on a long spin into the country, the average Londoner is not inclined to get up unusually early, even to make holiday; in fact, he more often allows himself the luxury of an extra hour's sleep, as if it were a Sunday, and does not

emerge into the open till noon, after a premature dinner.

Nevertheless, by nine o'clock Hampstead Heath is alive and growing livelier every minute; after noon the ceaseless flow of new arrivals quickens and swells and spreads itself out over the landscape, until you can scarcely see the grass for the people on it. Up the road from the railway station and the tram terminus the crowd sweeps, closely packed, and as if there would never be an end to it—a jovial, motley crowd, in which very gorgeously arrayed young ladies and dapper young gentlemen mingle with artisans and navvies in working habiliments, and dowdy, draggled women, who are equally happy in the dresses they wear at the wash-tub; and decent, impecunious shopmen and master mechanics and their trim wives and daughters rub shoulders with embryo Hooligans and pallid, grubby urchins fresh from the slums and alleys they rarely care to escape from except on such a day as this.

Up the road tramps a party of callow youths, singing and

TWO SCENES IN WHITECHAPEL.

A CHILDREN'S PICNIC (WENTWORTH STREET, E.).

marching to a tune one of them is playing on a mouth-organ. Up the road come half a dozen similar youths, with half a dozen maidens in dresses of bewildering brilliance: each pair have changed hats, as a token of affection, and walk droning a plaintive ballad, with their arms round one another's necks.

Up the road comes a small middle-aged father of a large family, wheeling the youngest but one in the perambulator, while his wife carries the youngest, and the five elder children straggle after them eating sweets or apples; the smallest boy creating excitement at intervals by loitering and getting lost, when they have to go back, calling wildly, to look for him, and, having found him, to cuff him in a paroxysm of affectionate thankfulness, and dare him to do it again.

Up the road, in a word, come boys and girls, men and women, old and young, in rags and in finery, married and single, with babies and without; and all the way by the roadside vendors of "ladies' tormentors," long feathers known as "ticklers," penny bagpipes and tin trumpets, stand contributing to the general uproar. In a side street, opposite a public-house, a piano-organ is rattling out a lively waltz, and a bevy of girls are setting to each other, bowing and swaying, or catching each other by the waist and whirling round ecstatically; while their male escorts wait for them, doing impromptu breakdowns, or looking on and grinning, with their hands in their pockets.

But all this is almost Arcadian peacefulness beside the hubbub and riot now in full blast on the Heath itself. Every man at the stalls and the cocoa-nut shies is bellowing his loudest; and as you make what progress you can along the uproarious, congested roadway you are startled by sudden crisp reports from a shooting-gallery on your right or the blunt thud of the hammer being vigorously brought down on the try-your-strength machine to your left. At every step you are embarrassed by invitations to try your weight, to have a swing, to undergo shocks at galvanic batteries, and bewildered by the allurements of stalls that offer you ices, jewellery, tarts, fruit, whelks, pigs' trotters, and inexpensive toys; and suddenly the crowd scatters, laughing and shrieking, to make way for two soldiers and their sweethearts, who are jolting downhill in the heat of a donkey race.

Here and there among the stalls is a side-show. You pay a penny at the door of a

ON BOARD A RIVER STEAMER: PASSING THE BOX FOR THE BAND.

canvas castle, and within view through a series of holes a pictorial representation of the career of a celebrated criminal. For other pennies you witness an unsensational boxing-match in one tent, and in another contemplate waxwork models of the very latest murderer and his victim. In a small open space amidst the dense throng, beyond the stalls, a troupe of acrobats is performing to a packed and appreciative audience. And near by, in a smaller space, the proprietors

head in bandages. There has been an accident; the man has been knocked down by a swing, and he is preceded and followed by men, women, and children who have quitted less exciting games to see him conveyed to the ambulance tent. In like manner there are groups who spend hours in the immediate neighbourhood of the police-tent for lost children, keeping count of the number of the lost, and ready to place their information and their philosophical deductions

A STREET FAIR (BATTERSEA).

of a skipping-rope, who have placed a board on the earth for the use of customers, and are turning the rope for an imaginary skipper shout, " Now, then, lydies! Skip as long as yer like for a penny!" And while they are calling an answer comes from the surrounding thousands, and the imaginary skipper materialises in the shape of a buxom factory girl, who skips with such agility, quickening her pace as the rope goes faster and faster, that it is looking as if the men's arms must tire before her feet, when an interruption abruptly ends the competition.

The crowd warps and splits and bursts in, right across the skipping board, and marching smoothly and swiftly through come two ambulance officers carrying a pale-looking man on a stretcher with his

at the service of any unsophisticated straggler who will lend an ear to them. " Here's another of 'em!" observes a bleary, ruminant man, who leans on the railing drawing hard at a short pipe. " This makes the sixth what's been brought in since I've been 'ere. They ain't all lost, don't you believe it! Their people nips off an' leaves 'em, an' watches till they sees 'em brought in 'ere safe, an' then goes an' enjoys theirselves, an' just calls for 'em on their way 'ome." It does happen now and then, however, that a distracted man and woman rush up and disappear into the tent, and presently emerge with one of the lost infants, masking their agitation from the onlookers under an affectation of wrath or flippant laughter.

But the centre of all the gaiety and noise

ON HAMPSTEAD HEATH.

I. SKIPPING.   II. ACROBATS.   III. THE VALE OF HEALTH.   IV. LOST CHILDREN'S TENT.   V. AMBULANCE TENT.

on Hampstead Heath is in the Vale of Health. There the roundabout calls and calls all day, siren like, and lures the mob down into its tumultuous whirlpool, and will not easily let them go again. Round and round giddily go its wooden horses, each with its rider, man or woman, boy or girl, with such a shrieking of the whistle and rolling of the organ, and singing and giggling and screaming, as no words can give any idea of.

Right and left of the roundabouts boat-swings are rising and falling, full of passengers; across the road, on the green under the trees, young parties are playing at kiss-in-the-ring, and old parties are picnicking sedately. Here, too, are the famous tea gardens where so many generations of holiday Cockneys have refreshed themselves; and within the primitive enclosure, at the primitive bare tables, representatives of the present generation are refreshing themselves now.

Whether it is Easter or Whit Monday or the first Monday in August makes little difference, except in the state of the weather. There may be a cold snap at Easter, or on any of the three days a rain that will drive the merrymakers home depressed, or send them early to whatever entertainments may be had under cover. On Boxing Day, of course, there is practically no provision for out-of-door amusements, unless the ice is strong enough for skating; moreover, most of us who remain in town are occupied with Christmas festivities at our own firesides or, in the evening, swarming to the pantomimes. But on the other three Bank Holidays of the year the joys of Hampstead Heath unfailingly repeat themselves and are simultaneously reproduced, with modifications, along the approaches to Battersea Park, in Wembley and Victoria Parks, in Greenwich Park, on Blackheath, in fact, in and around every park and common and open space to which working London resorts when the time has come for it to play.

They are reproduced at Epping Forest without any modification at all. When you struggle from the overloaded train at Chingford you see and hear the jolly revellers before you get your first view of the forest. Organs are clattering and rippling universally: three are playing different tunes simultaneously on the grassy patch skirting the forest opposite a big and busy hotel; and behind and before each organ boisterous couples are dancing, light-footed and light-hearted, as if, like Sidney's shepherd-boy, they "would never grow old." While you pause for a moment in the road your limbs are suddenly imperilled by the passing of ladies and gentlemen on unruly donkeys, of children in erratic goat-chaises, of select parties arriving in their own donkey-barrows; in the thick of the hubbub a group of evangelists hold an inaudible meeting; and the inevitable photographer is in evidence with a wheedling insinuation of appeal that a young man with a sweetheart finds difficult to resist.

Meanwhile London's great waterway is almost as lively as its dustier highways. There are gay boating parties putting out from Richmond; and up to Kew, and down to Greenwich, or, further still, to Gravesend, steamers are gliding through the river, with laughter aboard, and music, and even dancing when there is room enough on deck for such diversion.

In a word, everywhere to-day where there is any entertainment to be found a crowd is there to find it. The parks that tolerate no stalls or roundabouts have extra allowances of select and strictly orderly visitors placidly taking the air. Wherever there is a green space sufficiently uninvaded boys and men are playing at cricket; while on the Serpentine, on the lakes at the Welsh Harp, "which is Hendon way," and on every other suburban sheet of water available for the purpose, there is boating as long as the light lasts.

Not one of the public-houses in any district is deserted; most of them are continuously bubbling and boiling over with customers— good-humoured folk in the main, though you may look for a rumpus here and there before the day is over. There are few, if any, vacant seats at this afternoon's matinées, and to-night the theatres and music-halls will be full to suffocation, and turning hundreds away from their doors.

But it is too early to be talking of night yet awhile. The fact that thousands have gone out of town for the day is fully compensated for by the other fact that thousands have come into it for the day from easily accessible provincial towns—strangers and pilgrims who help to swell the hosts that flock to see great cricket matches at Lord's or the Oval, or cycle and foot races and miscellaneous sports and shows at the Crystal and Alexandra Palaces, and the hosts that are attracted to the Zoological Gardens or, during the season, to the latest exhibition at Earl's Court. They mingle also with homelier Cockneys who are turning their leisure to account by making the acquaintance of the Museums, the Art Galleries, the Tower, and the Monument.

Judging by the myriads that have gone out and are still going by road and rail and river, you might expect to find practically all London disporting itself away from home. But, apart from the well-to-do or the sedate, who are superior to Bank Holidays, and prefer to avoid their tumult by remaining within doors, even the poorer quarters of the town are far from being depopulated.

South and east, in Walworth, in Whitechapel, and elsewhere, though most of the shops are shut and the air is strangely peaceful, children are swarming in many of the streets playing every-day games in quite their every-day manner. There are maturer people who like a stroll through their native streets better than the fun of the fair, or who find all the recreation they desire no further away than the public-house at the corner. There are elderly people, glad of the quiet their more rollicking neighbours have left behind them, seated in the sun outside their doors, sewing, smoking, gossiping, dreaming maybe of earlier years, when they were more disposed to exert themselves and found less pleasure in rest. Some of the children in the streets are the offspring of roistering parents, who have bribed them to contentment with certain pence, and gone off, leaving them in charge of their grandmothers, who thankfully give them liberty to wander off with small companions to invest their unwonted wealth at a suitable shop and hold informal banquets on the pavement outside.

They have a quiet, uneventful time, these and their stay-at-home elders, all day; all day until evening. Then the returning tide of pleasure seekers begins to come in, and goes on coming in till midnight and after, with sounds of discordant singing, groanings and whimperings of concertinas, and buzzings of mouth-organs. And everyone is tired, and nearly everyone is satisfied to be home at last; and to-morrow, for the most part, the workaday world will turn from playing to its old humdrum workaday ways again.

"LOOK PLEASANT, PLEASE!"

OUTSIDE THE ROYAL EXCHANGE.

THE CITY AT HIGH NOON.

By CHARLES C. TURNER.

OVER our heads the traffic of the City rolls on, the roar of it coming down to us in the subway at the Bank of England, whither we have travelled by rail, in a bewildering confusion of deep, discordant tones. Let us ascend, choosing for our exit the steps leading to Princes Street. As we mount the steps the noise presses round us, the horses' hoofs ring on the asphalt close by our heads. On the top step we secure a foothold on the eagerly contested pavement space. We set our backs to the wall, and regard a scene which in many respects has no parallel in the wide world.

It is midday, and London's business is at high tide. Those whose working hours commence at eight o'clock, nine o'clock, and ten o'clock have all by this time got into the swing of the day's work. Shoppers and leisurely sightseers add to the throng. At innumerable stages, up to four, five, and six miles away, towards every point of the compass, omnibuses have filled at their cor-

ductors' cry, " Bank ! Bank ! " Through great stress of traffic have they come, and hither in long, uninterrupted processions do they continue to come. Of all colours are they, and so closely ranged together that they blot out of view all but the upper portions of the buildings. At the will of traffic-managing policemen, now this stream of vehicles, now that, holds the field.

The hubbub of it ! Underlying all is the incessant rumble of wheels; but high above that rings the clatter, clatter of hundreds of horses' hoofs on the smooth, hard road. The rustling footsteps of thousands of men and women make a light accompaniment. And this babel of sounds goes on incessantly —a continual hum, and roar, and clatter; till you wonder that the hardest pavement does not wear through in a day, that the toughest human nerve can sustain it for a couple of hours. Venture into the stream of people. If you are in a dreamy mood, inclined to philosophise as to the meaning of this tumult of seething life, you will soon be rudely awakened, you will be jostled by a crowd which has not time for day-dreaming. You will find it best to have an object in view. On your left hand is the Bank; opposite the loftier but less impressive Mansion House. Between the two, but set far back, stands the handsome pillared front of the Royal Exchange, sur-

coats, nearly every one of which supports a gold watchchain, the generally well-groomed look about most of the people, may impress you. Cornhill and Lombard Street, its neighbour, are both thronged with streams of hurrying men. Both ways are narrow, absurdly so, a contrast to stately Queen Victoria Street which, close by, makes so busy and impressive a junction in

QUEEN VICTORIA STREET (JUNCTION WITH CANNON STREET).

mounted by the campanile with its gleam-ing gilt grasshopper, which strange device indicates the direction of the wind. Let the Royal Exchange be your objective, and proceed to cross the roads which separate you from it.

You are now in the money region, the land of stocks and shares. Close by are the Stock Exchange, the Royal Exchange, and a remarkable gathering together of banks. Here the throng, representative of the dis-trict, contains a big proportion of men who deal on exchanges or are employed in the banks. The glossy hats, the well-conditioned black coats and trousers, the expensive waist-

Cannon Street. Both are fed by and connected by an astonishing number of narrow alleys, bearing the oddest names, and lined with banks and offices. At every few yards one of these busy lanes leads off in the most ramified and unexpected fashion, and if you leave the main route and explore them it is like entering another world. The superficial observer sees only the great, im-posing rivers of traffic, which certainly cannot be said to be unsatisfying to the most exact-ing country visitor, but in alleydom we get a more intimate view of the City. There is an unending patter of footsteps, a continual passing hither and thither of people who evidently know whither they are bound, and mean to get there as soon as possible; though to the observer their movements are like the bewildering mazes of a swarm of May flies.

Cornhill is a shop street; Lombard Street is a street of banks, and is almost restful through its freedom from 'buses and much wheel traffic. One can stand in the roadway and observe the worldwide character of the banks. Every country that has a vestige of civilisation appears to be represented.

the Bank. Within a stone's throw from the City's "seven dials" are traffic torrents independent of it. Where Gracechurch Street separates Lombard Street and Fenchurch Street, is one of these; and less than a furlong away, at the junction of Cornhill, Bishopsgate, and Gracechurch Street, is another, just as crowded as the Mansion House corner. The Gracechurch Street stream is one that avoids the Bank, connecting London Bridge and the Liverpool Street quarter.

CORNHILL (CORNER OF GRACECHURCH STREET).

Through the great glass doors you see rows of busy clerks. Across the street dart young men carrying account-books or a bag secured to their person by a heavy chain. If the thousands of busy feet do not actually tread on gold, you have a feeling that underneath are vaults and strong rooms guarding fabulous hoards. But it is seldom more than a step to the ridiculous—Lombard Street is the heaven of the kerbstone toy-seller. Mechanical bicyclists, tin horses and carts, run across the road, pedestrians indulgently making way for them. Where the golden chains of the commerce of the world are gathered together in a great knot you can buy cheap toys from ragged street merchants.

Here it is forced upon your attention that all the great thoroughfares do not lead to

The Fenchurch Street crowd is slightly different from that of the great Bank corner. It lacks both the banking and the sightseeing element. These are made up for by a marketing crowd from Leadenhall Market, which is situated among a network of crooked streets on your left hand, and a shipping element from the offices of the shipping companies which here abound. Handsome offices bearing names, devices, and pictures which tell of the world's ocean routes arrest your attention. Each side of the way has its hurrying concourse; faces of every conceivable type pass you in bewildering medley. There is a certain voyageur element, which is, however, more noticeable as you get further east; a cab or two laden with sea-going trunks; a group of Lascar seamen perhaps. But the traffic is mainly of a general character. On either hand there is a continual glint and twinkle of swinging office and restaurant doors, common, of course, to most City streets. The doors of the latter are obtrusively glazed, and of such establishments and of tea-shops there are uncountable numbers. Moreover, it is past twelve o'clock. The City dinner or luncheon hour lengthens out from twelve to three, and the restaurants are besieged by workers in vast throngs. The noise and flash of the swinging doors add appreciably to the confusion of sight and sound.

As you near Mincing Lane the character of the busy, eager crowd again undergoes a change. You are in an Exchange neighbourhood again—the Corn Exchange, the Baltic, and the Commercial Salerooms are in this quarter. Brokers and salesmen and their clerks leaven the throng. If you turn down Mark Lane, you will find the hatless variety in evidence, groups of them conversing round the entrance to the Exchange. The crowd consists almost entirely of men —the chief exceptions being wives of barge skippers, who sometimes come in connection

with matters of freight ; and in these lanes few vehicles are to be seen.

The business of the Exchanges overflows into the street, and however negligent the attitude of some of the dealers may appear, it is business they are after. So sacred are these particular lanes to the broker interest that the outsider almost feels as if he were committing trespass by venturing into them. In the great hall of the Corn Exchange the din of voices is deafening. Merchants crowd round the pillars, at the base of which are samples of grain. Mark Lane, Mincing Lane, Billiter Street, and the ways leading to them are a city within the City—a crowded, strenuous hive, living to itself, cut off from the surrounding districts by definite peculiarities. And that is like London. Crowded to intensity throughout, there are defined districts in it each with a character of its own.

From Billiter Street to Leadenhall Street is like coming out of a close room into the open air, yet for its traffic Leadenhall Street is absurdly narrow. There is little more than room for one stream of vehicles each way, and such an incident as the fall of a horse delays a long stream of 'buses, cabs, and waggons. There is a sudden scramble, clatter, crash ! and a horse is on its side ; then a tugging at the reins all along the line, and a swerving towards the centre to avoid telescoping. No shouting is heard, and for the most part people pass on without a pause, too busy to take heed. Yet there is a brief thicker congregating of human atoms. Suddenly, with an alarming scramble of hoofs, the horse is on its feet, perplexed and trembling. A kindly pat, and the cause of the obstruction moves on, the thick knot of people dispersing.

Where St. Mary Axe leads out of Leadenhall Street is the

ST. PAUL'S CHURCHYARD   (CHEAPSIDE END).

IN THE CORN EXCHANGE.

ancient church of St. Andrew Undershaft. As you pass its clock strikes "One." It may be that the hour will be followed by some of the nursery-rhyme-like peals of the bells, which have a quaint, old-world sound about them. They clang out over the tumult of the street with singular effect. Also they add to the tumult; and as the queer chimes ring out a stream of men pours from Great St. Helen's, a few yards up the street. They are from the great hive of offices there. All around are indications that to-day the chimes time a great human institution. The streets were crowded before, now they are full; and instead of soberly hurrying, many are in precipitous haste to secure their favourite table.

Through the turnings and squares of Great St. Helen's we come into Bishopsgate Street, one of the mightiest City thoroughfares. In Bishopsgate Street, Old Broad Street, and London Wall we get the modern system of great blocks of offices, such as Gresham House, Winchester House, and Palmerston Buildings. These are cities in themselves, with a maze of streets on every floor. The great name-boards, with numbers up to and over 250, and the continual hurrying to and fro bespeak the huge commerce they represent. They even have some pretensions to being self-contained—some of them boasting a restaurant, a barber, a tobacconist, and even a collar and tie shop.

It is hopeless to try to get more than a passing glimpse of the heart of the City in one day's wanderings. Those who imagine that the scene by Bow Church, Cheapside, marvellous as is its press of people and vehicles, represents the varied life of the City are out of their reckoning. Day after day could you go there and find unsuspected centres of business in quarters that have a curious way of hiding themselves from the superficial sightseer. And each centre you would find represents an aggregation of allied interest. Of such are the banks of Lombard Street; the shipping offices of Leadenhall and Fenchurch Streets; the accountants of Old Jewry; the clothes and clothing interests of Wood Street and the network of narrow ways just east of St. Paul's Cathedral; the curious excrescent growths from the great Bank district to be found in the extraordinary maze of irregular, narrow lanes and *culs de sac* of Austin Friars and Copthall Avenue, where you see an overflow of hatless brokers from Throgmorton Street; and, again, the Tokenhouse Yard and Telegraph Street region, which is different from any other. Each one of these is the scene of the labours of a multitude of busy men; and if we cannot examine them separately we can, at any rate, look at them in mass from the top of the Monument. Climb up its long spiral staircase, and look down. The section of London that is within easy range of vision is the heart of the City. The roar of it comes up to you from all sides. You see countless streets, every one of which is crowded with quick-moving people. Great streams of traffic creep along in every direction. They appear to be endless. It is one continual strenuous movement. You turn away dizzily. You resolutely fix your at-

CHEAPSIDE (SHOWING BOW CHURCH).

tention on other matters for half an hour; thinking by that time the tumult will have ceased. But when you look again it is just as it was before. Hour after hour, and every day, is the mighty, throbbing life renewed.

No picture of the City of London, no matter how hurried and incomplete it is, may neglect St. Paul's Churchyard. Here, in close proximity to the Cathedral railings, is a row of handsome shops, beloved of the fair sex. Along the greater part of the roadway no wheeled traffic is allowed — a fact which secures its patrons from the splash of mud in bad weather. Here, for the first time in the City, we find a crowd of ladies. It is the only place where there is a collection of shops for their benefit, and the shops are of an excellence which has earned for "St. Paul's Churchyard" fame throughout Britain. As a contrast to the congregations of men we have been among, St. Paul's Churchyard is singularly striking. Men there are, of course, but the bulk of the people are ladies, crowding round the shop windows. Into the roadway do they extend, and only near the railings is progress easy. Any attempt at rapid walking in busy City streets only leads to exasperation; and in Cheapside and St. Paul's Churchyard only the slowest progress is possible.

But the City levies a heavy toll on nerves and physical endurance. Let us go for respite into the calm Cathedral, where London's mighty voice is only heard as a subdued but strangely distinct murmur, and faint, echoing footfalls and the lisp of distant whispering fall drowsily on the ear.

SEWERMEN GOING BELOW.

UNDERGROUND LONDON.

By ERIC BANTON.

LONDON has long been to a very considerable extent what one may call "a two-decked city," and it is tending every year to become more so. You cannot be thoroughly familiar with a ship if you confine your attention to the main deck, and you do not know the Metropolis till you have learned something of its strange and fascinating underworld. For here, beneath the stones of its streets and the foundations of its houses, are some of the most remarkable phases of London's life, and some of the most striking examples of skill and ingenuity devoted to the service of its citizens.

To turn on a tap in order to obtain water, and another to obtain a light, to let soiled water run off into a drain, to receive a telegram, to ascend in a hydraulic lift, or answer a summons at the telephone—all these are the commonest acts in the business and domestic life of Londoners. They are performed mechanically, with little thought of the skill and labour that helped to make them possible. Yet they all call into play some part of a vast underground economy

that is not the least of the wonders which London can show to the curious investigator.

Not that she does show these things to all and sundry. You may travel to your heart's content on the underground railways of the Metropolis, you may get glimpses in places where the road is "up" of the great gas and water mains that lie beneath the roadway, you may happen upon a workman sitting on the pavement with coils of wire around him mending the underground electric wires, or upon a sewerman descending a manhole and disappearing apparently into the bowels of the earth. Yet these are but suggestions of the great underground world of London. In order to investigate that world thoroughly special arrangements will have to be made, and special permission obtained from the various authorities.

How many Londoners know that in various parts of the capital there are underground streets extending for several miles, in which the workmen of the gas, water, and electric lighting companies are constantly busy ; or that the sewerman, when he reaches the bottom of the manhole, is in a perfect labyrinth of underground passages in which he might wander, if he chose, almost all over the Metropolis without ever coming to the surface?

The usefulness of the subways is undeniable, as they enable pipes and wires to be repaired and new ones laid without the necessity of tearing up the roadway, and it is not surprising to learn that the London County Council are largely extending the system. The existing subways, whether

With so many services concentrated in a small space, it may be supposed that the City subways are at times scenes of considerable activity. The workmen of all the companies whose mains run through the subways have, of course, access to them, and the staff employed by the City Corporation act practically as caretakers. At one point, as we pass through the subways, we may meet the gas company's official testing the gas mains —a daily task the importance of which is at once realised when one reflects on the serious consequences that might result from a leak in

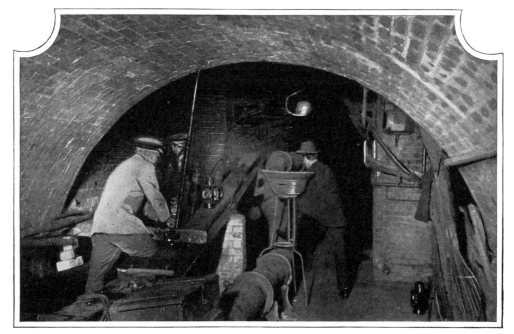

REPAIRERS IN THE SUBWAYS (NEAR HOLBORN CIRCUS).

under the control of the City authorities or of the County Council, are by no means unpleasant places in which to work. They are clean, dry, well ventilated, and well drained, and though, of course, hardly any daylight struggles through the ventilators, they can be well lighted by gas jets at any point where the work requires it. There is nothing in the least degree gruesome about the subways. On either side of the stone-paved gangways are the water mains, gas mains, electric lighting and power cables, hydraulic power mains, telegraph and telephone wires, and the pneumatic tubes of the General Post Office through which written messages in carriers are forced by compressed air.

a 48-inch main; at another point the workmen of the General Post Office are giving attention to the telephone service; here the water main is being connected up with a new building, and there the gas is being cut off from the house of someone who is in arrears with his payments.

But how, it may be asked, do the workmen know with which house they are in connection? This is one of the most interesting features of the subways from the visitor's point of view. Each subway is named to correspond with the street under which it lies, and the numbers of the houses are painted on the mains. It is curious to find in these subterranean regions such familiar names as Shoe Lane, Charterhouse Street, and others, but still more curious is it to come here and there upon certain names of places which in the upper world were swept away years ago.

There is considerable sameness about the subways, but now and again the even tenour of their way is broken, as, for instance, at the junction of Charterhouse Street and Holborn Circus, where two sets of mains unite, and a light wooden bridge affords access from one underground

JUNCTION OF CHARTERHOUSE STREET AND HOLBORN CIRCUS SUBWAYS.

thoroughfare to the other; and again at the point where Holborn crosses Shoe Lane. Here there is a vertical descent from the subway under the one street to that under the other, and the mains, of course, have to be bent accordingly. Standing in the lower subway at this point, we have Shoe Lane above us, with the Viaduct above that, while six inches beneath our feet is the main sewer, and below that again is the Central London Railway. This is only one of many spots in London where the City is not merely a "two-decker" but a "three-" or "four-decker." The typical "scenery"

of the subways, however, is shown in our photographic illustration of Charterhouse Street on this page.

For the greater part of their length the subways are arched brick structures from 7 ft. to 11 ft. in height, so that one can easily walk upright in them. But at Snow Hill, where the subway crosses the South Eastern and Chatham Railway, the height is only 5 ft. Here there is only just sufficient room for the subway to pass between the footway above and the railway below. The position necessitates a different kind of structure from that elsewhere adopted: an iron girder construction, with an iron roof covered with concrete, takes the place of the usual brick vaulted passage. It is a queer place to work in —this 5 ft. square iron tube — and not, one would suppose, a very comfortable one. But the workmen whose duty calls them to this spot are no doubt proof against the nervousness the chance visitor might feel from the knowledge that only a few inches above his head are the flagstones of a busy thoroughfare, while

A LONG STREET IN THE SUBWAYS (CHARTERHOUSE STREET).

EMERGING FROM A SEWER.

he was to the end quite prepared to go down if called upon to do so. No doubt the comparative immunity of the workmen from disease is largely due to the care that has been bestowed on the underground ventilation. The City sewers, have, in fact, quite a high reputation for their excellence in that and in other respects, and, though not exactly show places, they have frequently received in their gloomy depths visitors interested in sanitary work at home or abroad

The first thing a visitor does is to array himself in a sewerman's slouch hat, blue smock, and great waterproof boots ; he then arms himself with a lantern or a rough wooden candlestick, and lights his pipe or cigar. Thus equipped he descends the manhole, and begins his tour of inspection in these strange regions, which prove, in fact, scarcely so loathsome as his imagination had probably depicted them.

In the larger sewers, where it is possible to walk upright and where there is a continual flow of water, one's chief impression is likely to be of the utter monotony of the journey—a monotony broken only by an occasional scurrying

nothing but the $\frac{1}{4}$-in. iron plate on which he stands separates him from the gloomy abyss at the bottom of which lie the platforms and rails of Snow Hill Station.

Very different are the conditions under which the sewermen carry on their peculiarly unpleasant but most necessary work. In the single square mile of London which constitutes the City there are forty miles of main sewers, along which the sewermen can, and habitually do, walk or crawl in the performance of their duties ; while the main sewers of Greater London extend for many hundreds of miles. In order to keep the great drainage systems in the perfect working order on which the health of the city in great measure depends, large staffs of men are constantly employed, some in making structural additions, alterations, and repairs, others in regulating the flushing arrangements and preventing obstructions.

Eight hours of daily toil in the sewers, varied by occasional spells of duty above ground, would inevitably in a short time, it might be thought, tend to undermine the health of the strongest. But experience has shown that the work is not specially unhealthy. For instance, there was one old sewerman engaged in the service of the City Corporation for forty years, and, though for the last few years of his life he was not employed actually in the sewers,

CLEANING OUT SEWERS.

rat—and one's chief anxiety to avoid slipping on the slimy bottom of the channel.

When the passage narrows to 5 ft. or 4 ft. 6 in. in diameter one begins to realise more vividly the drawbacks of the sewerman's calling, and there are very few visitors who are so consumed with curiosity as to wish to worm their way through the 3 ft. or the 2 ft. 9 in. spaces.

There are some places, however, in Sewer-land that are distinctly impressive in their grim way. One of these is just beneath Ludgate Circus, where two main sewers discharge themselves into a larger one, 12 ft. in diameter. This great sewer is none other than the historic Fleet River, which, once a clear and sparkling stream, degenerated into a foul ditch, receiving the refuse from houses on its banks, and was at last arched over and used as a main drain. Here one has to wade with caution, for the current flows with considerable force; in times of heavy storms the Fleet is quite impassable. A few yards beyond the junction of the two sewers there is a flight of stone steps down which rush the contents of the Ludgate Hill sewers, to mingle with the waters of the Fleet—a veritable underground waterfall. The iron gate at the top of the steps, and similar gates elsewhere, prevent any possible backflow from the main sewers in times of flood.

One section of the City sewers is arranged after the style of those in Paris, the sewage flowing through an open trench; for the most part, however, it passes through circular conduits. Just beneath Farringdon Street the sewer is, as our illustration at the foot of the opposite page shows, quite a spacious under-

AN UNDERGROUND WATERFALL (LUDGATE CIRCUS).

ground chamber; and here the rake work, which prevents accumulations, is carried on with comparative ease. But similar work has to be done even in the narrowest passages.

As to the sewer rat one has to confess that neither in point of numbers nor of size does he quite come up to his reputation. Yet is he not lacking in enterprise, and has been known to snatch from a man's hand a lighted candle held in front of a drain.

Curious finds are sometimes made in the sewers, the most common being purses and coins. But let no one suppose that London's drains are mines of wealth, for the purses are invariably empty, and the coins are of base metal—the explanation being, of course, that pickpockets and coiners sometimes find the sewers useful for hiding the traces of their guilt. A small collection of these coins, duly nailed to the wall, may be seen in the City sewermen's room under Holborn Viaduct.

Of underground travelling we can only speak very briefly here, reserving for another article the important subject of underground railways. Few things are more striking in the recent history of London than the extent to which facilities for this mode of travelling are being extended. Apart from the railways, there is little doubt that London will in the near future be provided with a considerable number of underground thoroughfares for horse and foot traffic. Already there are a few of these, by far the most important and interesting being the Blackwall Tunnel, which, however, is not strictly speaking under the ground, but under the bed of the river between Greenwich and Blackwall.

The constant stream of traffic which all day long passes through the Blackwall Tunnel shows how great was the need of a link between the northern and southern parts of the city beyond the region served by the bridges. The traveller through the tunnel scarcely experiences the sensations that are usually associated with tunnelling; there is no steep descent, no darkness or stuffiness, no want of space. The roadway is 16 ft. wide, and on each side of it is a 3 ft. path; while beneath the surface of the roadway is a subway for gas and water pipes—a subway within a subway. Few, perhaps, who pass over this broad, well-made, and well-lighted road realise that they are in a great iron tube consisting of 1,200 iron rings, each composed of fourteen segments weighing over a ton apiece. The tube is 27 ft. in diameter, and is rendered water-tight and rustproof by an outside coat of liquid cement, being lined inside with white tiles.

When we have spoken of all the underground arrangements for travelling and for the public services we have by no means exhausted the subject of Underground London, for in numbers of unexpected places people have burrowed under the surface for their private business purposes, and you can hardly go anywhere in the Metropolis and be sure that men are not at work a few feet below the spot on which you stand. As you cross the Royal Exchange, for example, you are on the roof of a busy printing office; under the south-eastern corner of St. Paul's Churchyard is a much frequented restaurant; and in many places throughout the great city are large storage cellars containing millions of pounds' worth of goods.

ENTRANCE TO BLACKWALL TUNNEL.

AT THE CAFÉ ROYAL : A SATURDAY AFTERNOON SCENE.

FRENCH LONDON.

By PAUL VILLARS.

THE time is past when Leicester Square and its immediate neighbourhood were the only regions frequented and inhabited by Frenchmen. Leicester Square is still a French centre, but it has lost its character as headquarters of the French colony. The French are now to be met in almost every London district, and some of the most influential French business men, having their offices in the City, reside in Croydon, which rejoices in quite a colony of Frenchmen.

The French colony, unlike the German or the Greek, is on the whole anything but wealthy. There are only two cases on record of Frenchmen having made large fortunes in London. The first was a cloth merchant who left some £400,000, the whole of which ultimately went to his nephew, now dead, who was a member of the Chamber of Deputies ; the other was a well-known *restaurateur* who, it was said, made in a comparatively short period three times as much.

The French in London form a sober, well-behaved, industrious and law-abiding community. They give very little trouble to the police and law courts, and it is seldom that the name of a French *resident* obtains an unenviable notoriety in the newspapers. There are about 21,000 French sojourners in England, and about 11,000 of them live in the Metropolis.

From 1850 to 1875 the number of genuinely French firms in Bond Street and Regent Street was very large ; the French names on the shop fronts were almost as numerous as the British ones, and in every one of these houses the *employés* were almost exclusively French. Most of these names have disappeared and the few that remain are only a tradition, a reminiscence of former days. The founders of these establishments are dead, and it is rare to find a second generation of French residents in London. The *animus revertendi* is sometimes stronger in the sons and daughters of French people established here than in their parents. This

PUBLISHED IN LONDON.

explains why we find so few French names among the West-End tradesmen and why the French colony, although more numerous now than formerly, is also less important from the business point of view.

The French residents, the members of French London, are not to be found loafing in the neighbourhood of Leicester Square and Piccadilly Circus. They are to be found in City offices and warehouses, in banks and factories, in workshops and studios, in West-End establishments and shops, in schools and in private families. In all art industries they occupy a prominent position, on account of their skill and ingenuity and of the fine training they have received in their native land. In illustrated journalism the names of French artists resident in London are too well known to need their being mentioned here; and it is also to French residents that the School of Sculpture of the Victoria and Albert Museum and the Slade School are indebted for so much of their success.

Unlike the London residents of other origin, the French Londoner, if the expression may be used, remains above all else a Frenchman, and retains all the feelings, characteristics, and customs of his race. He does not, like many a German, for instance,

transform himself rapidly into an Englishman. He seldom applies for letters of naturalisation. He adopts, when in this country, British customs, but he adapts them to his wants. The French residents have not succeeded in establishing and keeping up a club of their own. In London, as in France, they use the café as a club; and on Saturday afternoons a large number of them are to be found at the Café Royal, which in some respects may be said to be the favourite club of French London. But if the French colony cannot boast of having a club in the ordinary acceptation of the word, it may justly take pride in its benevolent and charitable institutions.

The first and foremost of these is the French Hospital and Dispensary in Shaftesbury Avenue. It was founded in 1867 by three French residents, M. Louis Elzingre, M. Eugène Rimmel, and Dr. A. Vintras. Thanks to their efforts and the support they received from their countrymen, this hospital whose beginnings were very modest is now second to none in London for the skill of its medical, surgical and nursing staff, and for the efficiency of its management. Although the French Hospital is essentially a French institution, it is by no means an exclusive one, for with characteristic generosity it opens its doors to all French-speaking foreigners. Once or twice a year an entertainment is given to the patients, and the Christmas concert especially is a very interesting event to those who are privileged to be present. It must be said that the benefits conferred by this eminently useful institution on the poor foreign denizens of the centre of London cannot possibly be overrated.

It was Count d'Orsay, that brilliant wit, that distinguished gentleman, that artist of merit, who founded the French Benevolent Society. In his rambles through London the Count was struck with the number of poor Frenchmen he met in the streets, and in order to save them from distress and misery, to rescue them from the workhouse, he planned and established the Society which is now in Newman Street, Oxford Street. The French Benevolent Society has several objects. It first gives immediate relief to necessitous French people, whose numbers increase from year to year, and who flock to London in the hope of obtaining work as craftsmen, clerks, or in any other capacity ; it also gives alms in the form of money or of " bread tickets " or of clothes ; it sends back to France, at its expense, those who can hope to get help in their own country from their relatives or friends, and, finally, it gives small annuities to a number of aged and infirm poor refugees.

Sad are the scenes witnessed every Thursday, when applicants for relief present themselves before the committee. Men and women, old and young, but all in the direst straits, ragged and famished, with hunger and privation depicted on their wan and thin faces, look wistfully at the chairman and tell their tale of woe. Every tale is patiently listened to, every case is investigated, no one is turned away without a little help and a few cheering words of comfort.

As we mentioned before, the French Londoners are too conservative, too fond of preserving their national characteristics, even in the midst of London, not to have thought of teaching their own language to their children. The poorer French Londoners have good schools to which they can send their little ones. We refer to the schools near Leicester Square (Lisle Street), managed by sisters of charity, and founded by the Marist Fathers. Since the year 1865 the schools have been giving a very fair French and English elementary education to the children of working men of the neighbourhood of Leicester and Soho Squares.

These three institutions play a considerable part in the organisation of the French colony in London, as most French residents are interested in one or in all of them. A link is thus established between men who live far apart, and it is, one may say, on the basis of charity, benevolence, and national education that the intercourse between the French residents really rests.

But there are other institutions, not of a

A BALL (SOCIETY OF FRENCH MASTERS) AT THE ROYAL INSTITUTE OF PAINTERS IN
WATER COLOURS.

charitable kind, which flourish in London, and are of great service not only to the French community but also to the general public, as they tend to promote trade and intercourse between France and England. The French Chamber of Commerce, which was established in 1883, is now a very prosperous body. It has taken for its task the improvement of Anglo-French commercial relations, and its efforts have more than once succeeded in obtaining concessions from the Customs, postal and railway authorities, and the abolition of several useless and vexatious formalities.

The Society of French Masters, founded in 1882, has done much to increase the efficiency of French teaching in this country. Its success has been great, and it has obtained a most flattering recognition of its efforts in the City of London, for every year the distribution of prizes in connection with the examination of pupils of all schools takes place at the Mansion House, under the presidency of the Lord Mayor.

For many years now the Society of French Masters has organised periodical dinners and balls. The balls take place at the Royal Institute of Painters in Water Colours, and usually bring together a large number of members of the Society and of their English friends, who are always given a warm and hearty welcome.

The most characteristic trait of the French Londoner is his intense attachment to his country, his national language, habits and customs. It would be possible to name numbers of French residents who, notwithstanding a long sojourn in London, are quite content to possess a smattering of the technical terms in use in their special profession or business. If you happen to call on them, a French servant, innocent of English, will open the door, usher you into a room the furniture of which is French, and in which you might fancy yourselves in any French town. For those French residents the daily paper does not grace the breakfast but the dinner or supper table, when the postman has brought the Paris paper of the morning. For news of what goes on in the French Colony they have *La Chronique*, a bright little paper published in London every Saturday.

As to their sons, if born in England, they

OUTSIDE THE FRENCH EMBASSY: I. THE AMBASSADOR ENTERING HIS STATE CARRIAGE. II. AWAITING HIS EXCELLENCY'S DEPARTURE.

have been registered at the French Consulate, and by the time they are twenty-one they are duly made to figure on the list of the young men who have to draw lots for military service at the *mairie* of the First Arrondissement of Paris. For it may be news to the English reader to know that every French subject born abroad and registered at a French Consulate belongs *ipso facto* to the First Arrondissement of Paris. There are about fifty every year who thus draw lots and, according to the number they draw, join the Army,

APPLICANTS WAITING TO GO BEFORE THE COMMITTEE (FRENCH BENEVOLENT SOCIETY).

after undergoing a medical examination at the Consulate. As to residents who have served in the Army, they are registered at the Consulate and are liable to be called to the colours in time of war. Not to tax them unnecessarily and interfere with their career or occupation, they are, under certain conditions, exempted from the periodical twenty-eight or thirteen days' service.

Mixed marriages are not infrequent in the French colony, but, as a rule, French people marry among themselves. And here it must be said that, French plays and novels notwithstanding, it is extremely rare to find French or mixed couples appearing before the Divorce Court. This is a fact to be pondered by those who have been brought up in the idea that the French look upon marriage ties as made only to be loosened or even cut at pleasure.

It will, no doubt, surprise many people who look upon the French as unbelievers, agnostics, atheists, or what not, to be told that the French churches in London are very well attended, on Sundays, by men and women, old and young. Of course, the most numerously attended is that of Notre Dame de France in Leicester Square. But more interesting, perhaps, on account of its old associations, is the tiny chapel in a little mews off Portman Square, known also

as the Chapel of the French Embassy. This little chapel, which is about the size of an ordinary drawing-room, was founded at the time of the French Revolution by the *émigrés* who had fled to this country. The registers of births, marriages, and deaths of this place of worship contain most interesting and valuable records, for the most aristocratic names of France are to be found mentioned therein.

There are two annual gatherings of the French colony which bring together its best elements, the French Hospital dinner and the French Chamber of Commerce dinner, at both of which the French Ambassador usually takes the chair. The former is the more popular and the more representative of the two. At this banquet, invariably honoured by the presence of the Lord Mayor, the first toast is that of the Sovereign and the Royal Family of these realms, a very natural thing, no doubt. But what is to be particularly noted is that on this and every similar occasion a very interesting fact is brought home to every Englishman present, and that is the intense loyalty of the French colony in London. It can be asserted, without fear of contradiction, that at no purely English dinner or meeting are the loyal toasts received with more respectful and sincere sentiments of enthusiasm than at a gathering of French residents in this country. The French had the greatest reverence for Queen Victoria, and they entertain the same feeling towards the present King who, when

situated at Albert Gate, and on Levee days there is usually a great crowd to see the Ambassador getting into his state carriage, an imposing looking vehicle, drawn by splendid horses.

A CHRISTMAS CONCERT AT THE FRENCH HOSPITAL.

Prince of Wales, gave to the French colony so many proofs of interest and of kindly patronage.

Once a year, on the day of their National Fête (14th of July), the French residents in London gather at the French Embassy, where the Ambassador, surrounded by his secretaries and by the Consul-General and his staff, holds an open reception to which all Frenchmen are invited, and which most of them make a point of attending. There is thus a link between the official representative of France and the French residents in London. The French Embassy, since its enlargement, is the finest in London. It is

As a French Ambassador said once at a 14th of July reception, the French colony in London is an honest, industrious, law-abiding community, and it may be added that by the trades and industries which they carry on, by the skill of those who are engaged in artistic pursuits and the ability of the professional men among them, by their efforts to promote good feeling between their native land and this country, they play a by no means unimportant part in the life of this great Metropolis, and repay the generous hospitality extended to them, which they highly appreciate and gladly acknowledge.

LONDON'S POLICE COURTS.

By E. BUXTON CONWAY.

AS the forenoon hour of ten strikes, the day of the London Police Court begins.

The big folding doors of the building, outside which men and women have been assembling on the footway for the past half-hour, are flung open by the burly young constable on duty within; and instantly, despite his remonstrances, the crowd elbows and jostles its way inside with the impatient eagerness of a gallery audience entering a Shoreditch music-hall.

It is evidently not upon pleasure, however, that this crowd is bent. A bedraggled and dingy-looking throng it is, for the most part,

court, it may be seen that the prevalent expression is one of anxiety or gloom, and that blackened eyes, bandaged heads, and scratched faces are much in evidence, as though some weird epidemic which marked its victims thus were prevalent in the district. For these are the applicants, each of whom has come to seek the law's redress for some real or imagined wrong.

"Silence!" calls an usher, and the police and pressmen rise to their feet as the magistrate of the court enters and takes his seat. The foremost of the queue of applicants— a sodden, unshaven law-writer whose bed

APPLYING FOR PROCESS AND ADVICE.

in whatever quarter of the great city the court may be situate; for the fashionable West-End of London, no less than the squalid East, has its slums and alleys, its haunts of lawlessness and vice, from which the *clientèle* of the police court is largely drawn. And as the members of this assemblage are ranged in a long line inside the

and bedding have been improperly seized for rent—enters the witness-box and relates his story.

Clearly and courteously, though with a rapidity bewildering to his drink-muddled brain, the law-writer's case is disposed of He stumbles out of the box, to be followed by another, and another—a seemingly endless

Police Court

In the Metropolitan Police District.

To

of

INFORMATION ———————— has been laid
this day by
for that you, on the   Day of
in the Year One Thousand Nine Hundred and
at

within the District aforesaid, did *unlawfully maliciously and feloniously send to the said knowing the contents thereof, a certain letter threatening to kill and murder him the said Contrary to the Statute, etc*

YOU ARE THEREFORE hereby summoned to appear before the Court of
Summary Jurisdiction, sitting at the   Police Court
on   day tha   day of
at the hour of   in the   noon, to answer to the
said information.

Given under my Hand and Seal this   day of
One Thousand Nine Hundred and

* SCH. I.—2.
SUMMONS
GENERAL FORM INDICTABLE
AND SUMMARY CASES.

One of the Magistrates of the Police Courts of the Metropolis.

10000-12-00. M.P. (96)

SUMMONS.

stream of complaints and dilemmas, as to which the advice of the "poor man's lawyer" is anxiously sought and freely given. Questions of law and questions of fact; pitiful tales of violent husbands and intemperate wives, foolish tales of doorstep quarrels and scandals; applications for process and requests for assistance and counsel, are poured forth into the magisterial ear. Garrulous women are there, whose eloquence upon their burning wrongs cannot be checked; pale, faded gentlewomen in rusty black, speaking of their troubles in whispers, lest the rest should hear what is meant for the magistrate alone; landlords with defiant tenants, anxious parents whose children are missing—the queue seems a summary and epitome of human woes.

Here is a "crank," long-haired and snuffy, with a working model (that will not work) of a patent that should have made his fortune but for an infamous conspiracy against him, "with the Home Secretary at its head, your Worship!" An elderly lady follows, smoothing out a fat bundle of crumpled, dog's-eared papers as she relates a vague story of a hundred pounds that ought to have been left to her under a will — "if you'd please peruse these few documents, sir." A young man whose former "young woman" will not return his engagement ring and the knifeboard he had given her as a contribution toward furnishing a home; a tradesman who has been victimised by means of a worthless cheque; a workman dismissed without notice; a khaki-clad trooper who has overstayed his leave; so the tale goes on.

To each in turn the magistrate gives such advice and assistance as his legal training and his wide experience of the darker side of London life suggest. For lesser breaches of the law summonses are granted, a warrant is issued for the arrest of the cheque swindler, and another against the husband of that pale, timid-looking woman with the cut lip. The widow beside her receives a grant from the Poor-Box to help her to purchase a mangle; and so at last the lessening line of applicants melts quite away.

Now comes the hearing of the "night charges" against persons who have been arrested since the prior afternoon, charged with offences of every imaginable kind, from playing pitch-and-toss in the streets to burglary, highway robbery and even graver charges. Every police station within the

WARRANT.

district of the court has contributed, by police van or on foot, its quota of prisoners for trial; and these, whilst the applications were proceeding, have been marshalled in the chill corridor at the rear of the court, where they now stand awaiting the ordeal of an interview with the magistrate.

A strange and motley assembly they form, each prisoner confronted by the officer who has him or her in charge. The vagabond is there in his foul rags, charged for the twentieth time with begging; the dandy who has dined not wisely but too well; the worthless, brutal "corner boy," who took part last night in a game of football with a young constable playing the *rôle* of the ball, jostles against his neighbour—a lad whose heavy eyes tell of a sleepless night in the cell to which some dishonest juggling with his master's accounts has brought him.

One by one, as their names are called by the inspector in charge, the prisoners appear in the dock and are dealt with. The less serious cases are disposed of first—charges of intoxication and misbehaviour, street betting, reckless driving, assaults and affrays with the police, small larcenies, and so on. For the most part these are adjudicated upon straightway, with care and judgment, yet with a celerity that strikes the onlooker as amazing —for the magistrate's trained observation helps him vastly in discriminating between the loafer and the honest toiler, the professional thief and the new recruit of crime. The young embezzler, after a stern warning, may perhaps be handed over to the care of his friends; the unhappy girl who has attempted her own life is left to the good offices of the missionary, who will find her honest work; but the hardened shop-lifter and hopeless drunkard return from their brief interview the recipients of a sharp and salutary sentence. Convicted offenders will be detained by the gaoler in the police court cells until they pay their fines or are removed to prison by police van in the afternoon.

Charges of a graver nature follow. The burglar, taciturn, resolute-looking and light

of build, may be succeeded in the dock by the vicious, undersized wielder of the knife, the cunning old convict who has turned coiner, or the spruce, well-groomed advertisement impostor, for whose talents London always offers a tempting field of operations. Such cases are only investigated and sorted out, as it were, by the magistrate. Those in which the evidence is inadequate are

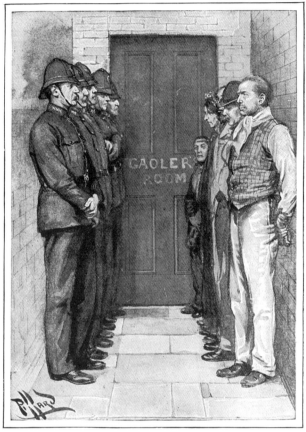

AWAITING THE ORDEAL.

either remanded for further proof or are dismissed; the rest are committed for trial before a jury, either to the London County Sessions or to the "Court of oyer and terminer and gaol delivery," known and dreaded of London's criminals under its familiar name of the Old Bailey.

Although the procedure we have described is the same for every London police court, yet each of these, owing to the special character of its district, has its own particular type of case in which it differs from all the rest. This huge London of ours, less a city than a collection of unlike towns, varies

INVESTIGATING A CHARGE AT A POLICE COURT.

according to locality in its crimes no less than in its fashions and pleasures.

Let us then, by the aid of the flying carpet of fancy, visit in turn—were it but a brief glimpse—some of the score or so of police courts to which detected breakers of laws in London are brought.

Whither shall we first wend our way ? A report in the morning's press of a stabbing affray among the Lascars aboard a steamship in the East India Dock determines us, and we reach the dingy little Thames courthouse at Stepney as the two prisoners enter the dock. Yellow-skinned, barefoot, clad in some thin cotton fabric, they stand before the magistrate with eyes upcast and hands uplifted piously, while the interpreter repeats the oath to the first witness called. This is an almond-eyed Chinaman, whose glossy black pigtail sweeps the floor as, in obedience to a gesture from the interpreter, he kneels in the witness-box. A saucer is handed to him by the usher of the court and he holds it whilst the official says aloud, the interpreter repeating the words in Chinese, "You shall tell the truth and the whole truth." There is an instant's pause as the witness, still on his knees, raises the saucer and dashes it into fragments on the hand-rail before him. Then the oath is completed with the words, " The saucer is cracked, and if you do not tell the truth, your soul will be cracked like the saucer."

A Turk and two Krooboys are to give evidence next, but we do not stay. Leaving the polyglot charge to drag on its slow length, we hasten westward to the little pseudo-classic Temple of Justice at Great Marlborough Street, a stone's throw from Oxford Circus. Here a fresh-coloured young gentleman dressed in the height of fashion, and clearly one of the gilded youths of the West, listens with a slightly wearied air whilst the magistrate points out that excess of spirits, whether animal or otherwise, can scarcely be accepted as an excuse for breaking street lamps in Piccadilly last night and "bonneting" the sergeant who ventured a remonstrance.

The young exquisite having bowed himself out of court to pay his fine, the investigation is resumed of a remanded charge against a handsome Bengali of "deceiving divers of his Majesty's subjects by professing to tell

fortunes," and his appliances are spread out before the magistrate by a stolid official with the air of one preparing a meal. Two silk sheets inscribed with curious hieroglyphics, a skull, a pair of daggers, a crystal sphere and a hammered bowl full of some black fluid : then the officer steps back as if to announce that dinner is ready. Meanwhile, the fortune-teller, whose Indian robes contrast oddly with his fluent English, has elected to give evidence in his own defence. He is sworn in a strange and impressive fashion. A copy of the Koran (the Mohammedan Bible) being laid on the ledge before him, he places one hand on the volume and the other on his forehead, then slowly bows his head until it rests on the book.

Let us hasten now across the river to the grey, crowded southern bank. There is a throng of the "great unwashed" about the entrance to the Tower Bridge Police Court as we pass through—sure sign that a local vendetta is being investigated. And so it proves. The ruffianly-looking trio in the dock—two scowling men and a hard-voiced slatternly virago—have headed a mob armed with pokers, pitchforks, and iron railings in their attack on the O'Shaughnessys of Dove-and-Pigeon Court, in the course of which affray not only Mr. and Mrs. O'Shaughnessy but also some half-dozen innocent passers-by were beaten and thwacked unmercifully, as their bandages and wounds attest.

A flying visit to the Guildhall—where a dreary charge of falsifying accounts is occupying the court and apparently boring the gentlemanly prisoner to extinction—ere we cross the northern border of the City proper and peep into the court at Worship Street. Here a "railway fence" is on trial— a receiver of goods stolen from various goods stations ; and a diminutive Jew, hairy and uncleanly, who has taken part in the robberies, is giving evidence against his old associate. As he leaves the witness-box there is a sudden sensation in court. The burly prisoner makes a desperate attempt to spring upon the accomplice who has betrayed him. He is dragged back struggling and cursing, and the little Jew, deathly white beneath his grime, and shaking like a man with the palsy, escapes from his sight.

At Bow Street an extradition case is proceeding, and proves to be unconscionably

MOHAMMEDAN TAKING THE OATH.

Of the summonses which occupy the afternoon at most police courts there is no need to speak at any length. To be present at their hearing would make most people cynics for life. The brutality of husbands, the trickery of the fraudulent shopkeeper whose butter is margarine and whose milk is freely watered, the stories of parental cruelty, and of the hardships and ruin wrought by the drink fiend in numberless London homes, make up a daily chapter of wrongs at once pitiful and terrible.

At five o'clock all is over for the day and the great doors are shut again. A little knot of men and women gathers at the corner, waiting for the departure of the prison van with their friends in its keeping. Presently it rattles out of the police court gateway, over the flagstones into the street. The mob fires a volley of hurried salutations: "Goo'-bye, 'Liza!" "Cheer up, 'Arry, I'll raise the blunt for yer," and so on. A dishevelled woman rushes wildly down the street in the van's wake, screaming hoarsely, "Good luck, old man—keep yer pecker up!" till the vehicle disappears round a bend in the road. The crowd disperses in quest of refreshment, and another day in the London Police Courts is ended.

dull and tiresome. At Clerkenwell the police court is bright with gay colours—head-dresses of blue and old gold, crimson silk scarves and orange kerchiefs; for there has been yet another desperate affray with knives among the Italians on Saffron Hill, and the colony has come down almost *en masse* to hear the evidence. Olive-visaged, chestnut-haired, their bright brown eyes and white teeth flashing, these children of the South have come to the dingy court-house as to a *festa*, and now eagerly await the performance.

Meanwhile, a small English offender is on trial—a boy of thirteen charged as the ringleader of a gang of young rascals who levy blackmail on solitary boys going on errands, and on the shopkeepers of the neighbourhood. Meek and timid enough he looks as he stands in the dock, though it is said that he is known among his admiring satellites as "Dashing Dick," and a loaded pistol was found in his pocket when he was arrested. The case completed, this youthful highwayman is ordered to receive a dozen strokes with the birch. At this his fortitude gives way, and "Dashing Dick," the hero of a hundred street fights, is led away howling to receive punishment.

CHINESE FORM OF OATH.

ON PARLIAMENT HILL.

IN THE STREET.

CRICKET LONDON.

By EDWIN PUGH.

"CRICKET extry! Latest scores up to close of play!"

The hot-faced, husky-voiced newsboy, with a bulky bundle of pink papers under his left arm, distributes his sheets at lightning speed, taking money and giving change with the dexterity of a juggler. A clamorous crowd of men and lads, all feverishly anxious to ascertain how their favourite teams have fared, hustle him and bustle him on every side. As each gets his paper he opens it, turns to the third page, and walks slowly off, reading. The street is splashed with moving patches of colour, each patch testifying eloquently to the popularity of the national game in London. Nor is this popularity the outcome of a merely vicarious interest. He who reads to-night will probably to-morrow afternoon (to-morrow being Saturday) don flannels, and fare forth to exhibit his own prowess at the popping-crease. Indeed, so keen is he that, passing a narrow paved street on his way home, he stops to watch a crowd of ragged urchins who, with improvised bats, wickets formed of heaps

67

of jackets, and a penny composition ball, are batting and bowling with a tremendous earnestness that more than counterbalances their lack of skill. The looker-on sighs for the morrow.

The morrow comes. On every open space in and about London there is a green tract set aside for cricket. In all the parks and in each suburb—north, south, east, west, from Walthamstow to Putney, at Blackheath and at Parliament Hill alike—the sleek turf is dotted with white-clad figures and massed with darker groups of interested onlookers. The quick, staccato cries of the players, the pat, pat, pat of bat on ball, the frantic handclappings and applauding cheers—all these brisk, healthful sounds mingle pleasantly with the whispering of the breeze and the song of birds. Here, on this level sward, all linked together in a common fellowship, are tiny little chaps from the Council schools learning the priceless lessons of fair play, strengthening their bodies, and expanding their souls; here are artisans, labourers, factory hands, clerks, shopmen, who but for this weekly respite from their sedentary toil might grow up weedy weaklings, vicious and mean-spirited. All sorts and conditions of leagues and alliances are in existence to promote a stimulative rivalry between the various clubs. In addition to these public playgrounds, there are the private grounds of the great banks and business houses and such classic meadows as that of St. Paul's School in Kensington.

But it is not only on Saturday afternoons that this aspect of Cricket London obtains. Every evening, in the public playing fields, nets are set up and practice is indulged in. The scene then presented, though often quite as crowded with figures, is not nearly so picturesque, since most of the players, being engaged during the day, have no time to go home and don their flannels, but must be content to turn out in their ordinary garb. On Thursday afternoons, too, there are always matches in progress between teams of shop assistants.

All this, however, reveals but one phase of our subject, and not the most momentous. There is now to be considered spectacular cricket—the cricket, that is, which depends on popular favour for its support. Lowest in this scale is "Komik Kriket," so called, though usually the only humour displayed is good-humour. In this class of cricket the teams are, as a rule, composed of actors or music-hall artistes, who meet to clown away an afternoon in the sweet cause of charity; while higher come the matches between county "second elevens" and strong local teams. And then, to pass from the general to the particular, we have organisa-

Photo : Russell & Sons, Crystal Palace.

DR. W. G. GRACE AT THE NETS (CRYSTAL PALACE).

tions such as the London County C.C., formed by the sempiternal W. G. Grace, technically a first-class county, with head-quarters at the Crystal Palace.

But genuine first-class cricket is played at only three grounds in London—Leyton, the Oval, and Lord's.

Leyton, home of the Essex County C.C., is the newest of these. It lacks the great traditions of its two mighty rivals, but its supporters are none the less enthusiastic on that account. To realise this one has only to hear the roar of welcome that goes up when the players take the field.

But, when all is said and done and written, Cricket London only finds its supreme expression at the Oval and at Lord's. Within the borders of these two historic grounds you shall find, on high occasions, types representative of all

TAKING THE FIELD (LEYTON).

who have delight in the summer game—from tattered, grimy *gamins* playing truant to members of the House of Lords. It is, however, on a public holiday that the Oval shows at its truest. Half an hour after the gates have been opened every free seat is occupied; already the stone galleries are thickly thronged; whilst away over at the remote end of the ground a large, devoted band is watching the practice in the nets. On the smooth

the toss!" and a mighty, exultant shout goes up. An instant later the players come out, carelessly flinging a ball from hand to hand.

The day is slumbrously hot; many of the spectators tuck handkerchiefs or newspapers under their hats to protect their necks from the rays of the sun. A long-suffering old gentleman in the front row puts up his umbrella, but it is so hotly reviled for obstructing the view that he instantly closes it again. The spectacle of that intent multitude is impressive: the serried lines of pink faces set in the dark mass of the people's bodies, with here and there a red

THE SURREY POET AT THE OVAL.

A CORNER OF THE CROWD (OVAL).

turf hundreds of men and boys are strolling aimlessly about, waiting for the first bell. Experts inspect the playing pitch critically. At last the first bell rings. The strollers on the grass scuttle toward the ring of spectators and search distractedly for seats. The practising players leave the nets and make for the pavilion at a brisk walk, each surrounded by a knot of admirers. Small boys point out their particular heroes one to another; the playing space empties slowly; there is an expectant buzz. Then from the pavilion gates the flushed, grey-headed figure of the Surrey poet emerges. He goes loping round the ground, crying out excitedly, "Gentlemen, Surrey has won

military tunic or a light frock to relieve the sombre effect. The surroundings are not beautiful: a huddled sordidness of commonplace houses, and at one end of the ground the huge, dull-red cylinders of a monster gasworks. But what cares any man for extraneous details? A hum of approval or appreciation, that breaks sometimes into a shout, runs round the ground; or a peal of merriment rives the air, or a groan of disappointment.

Two o'clock, and the players adjourn for lunch. Many of the spectators adjourn also; but the majority, fearful of losing their places, stay on. Packets of provisions are produced, and bottles containing ginger-beer or other less innocent beverages. There is a merry time of hearty feasting; and whilst this goes on out comes the Surrey poet again to amuse the crowd with his evergreen drolleries and, incidentally, to sell his rhymes.

In three-quarters of an hour the match

LUNCHEON UNDER THE TREES (LORD'S).

is resumed. By this time the crowd has swelled to such unwieldy proportions that the playing pitch itself is invaded, and all along the edge of the turf, at the feet of the foremost row of sitters, the spectators lie crouched and huddled together in every conceivable attitude of discomfort.

And so the long, hot afternoon passes. The shadows lengthen; the weary players move a little less jauntily to their places at the end of each over; the crowd grows more and more restless and fidgety. There is occasional inattention; a slight waning of interest; a disposition to mild raillery and horse-play. At last the final over is completed; the umpires pocket the bails; ropes and stakes are set up to protect the pitch; the

flushed, perspiring spectators pour out into the street again, chopping impressions as they hurry homeward.

Turn we now to Lord's. On ordinary occasions it has much in common with the Oval. The crowd, however, is less demonstrative; a more leisurely state of things prevails; the surroundings are infinitely more beautiful. This is in consonance with the stately traditions of the place; for Lord's is, as the home of the M.C.C., which governs and directs all cricket, essentially the historic, classic ground. The splendid pavilion, the belt of fine trees rising benignly on one side above the white awning which shades the seats, the perfection of order that exists, and the absence of rowdyism all conduce

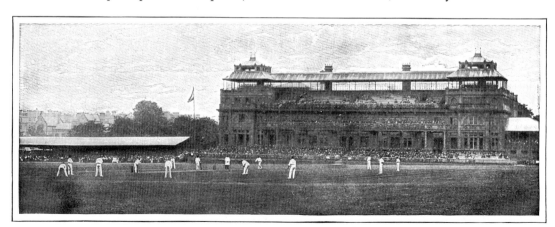

ENGLAND *v.* AUSTRALIA (LORD'S).

to a prevalent tone of dignity and repose. The enormous seating capacity also tends to eliminate any appearance of discomfort or overcrowding. Each spectator cannot but have an uninterrupted view of the field of play, no matter where he may be seated— as well on the mound as in the pavilion itself. But, after all, these are minor differences. It is on the occasion of some great match, such as Oxford *v.* Cambridge, Eton *v.* Harrow, or England *v.* Australia, that Lord's rises to its highest point of glory. Then the crowd of onlookers is a vastly different one from

beginning to end by the actual participants themselves, is followed by the majority of the more aristocratic visitors with only a feeble interest. Here and there excited groups of boys dance up and down, cheer madly, frantically clap their hands, and call their indifferent elders' languid attention to the splendid doings of a favourite chum. Old Boys—bald-headed and eminent Old Boys some of them—follow the game with glistening eyes, recalling their own youth, and clap their gloved hands softly, murmuring, " Played, sir ! Played, indeed ! " But, for

LUNCHEON INTERVAL AT ETON *v.* HARROW MATCH (LORD'S).

that which fills the benches when Middlesex or the M.C.C. are in possession of the field. Demos is in a minority for once. The plebeian billycock or cap shows itself infrequently amid bobbing rows of silken headgear and bewildering millinery confections. The umbrella and gay parasol, that the hardiest of mortals scarcely dares to raise on ordinary occasions, flaunt themselves everywhere now, innocent of any solecism. There are almost as many women as men. Wherever a vacant space is available, commanding a glimpse of the pitch, there you will find carriages ranged in rows, with liveried flunkeys in attendance. The match, played keenly and thoroughly enough from

the most part, the whole affair partakes of the nature of a society gathering. This is apparent when the luncheon interval arrives. The meal under the trees at an end, the lawn is invaded by a brilliant throng of promenaders. The first and the second bell ring. Still they remain in possession. In vain the policemen endeavour urbanely to herd them back to their seats. They complacently ignore these blandishments ; and it is not until the teams are actually on the field, and the re-start has been delayed, perhaps, a quarter of an hour, that they consent to let the match go on. It is only on the last day, when the issue hangs in the balance, that there is any general pervasion of enthusiasm. Then, sometimes, all dalliance will suddenly cease. The most frivolous cannot escape the infection of the universal excitement. There is a hush as each ball is bowled; and finally, when the result is beyond question, a tumultuous outburst of pent-up feeling, in which treble and bass mingle harmoniously.

All this, however, is as nothing compared with the heats and chills, the qualms and fervours, that prevail among the spectators at Lord's when England and Australia meet there in a test match. Early in the morning, before even the screever outside the walls has finished his pavement studies of cricket celebrities, the crowd has begun to assemble; by noon there is not a vacant seat to be had. There is nothing lukewarm in the temper of this crowd; there is nothing slack or careless in the play of the rival elevens. As the fortunes of the game fluctuate a sympathetic ripple seems to run through the watching multitude. A catch is muffed, and a mighty roar batters on the welkin. A hero is dismissed, and a murmur goes up like the growl of a disappointed beast. The ball is hit to the boundary

thrice in succession to a crescendo of ecstatic cheering. Now one of the batsmen approaches his century. He has made many centuries during his career; but, veteran though he be, the fatefulness of his position overbears him a little. He plays with a caution that is infinitely trying to our overwrought nerves. Once he scrapes forward at a ball . . . misses it. There is an appeal. "Not out!"

A minute later, and our hats are in the air. The scoring-board labours, and up goes "100." Strangers shake hands with one another; even the Australians themselves applaud; and the din of our voices must surely set the wild beasts roaring half a mile away.

At the cessation of play the crowd rushes on to the field. The heroes of the day walk to the pavilion through a lane of frenzied worshippers, salvo on salvo of applause thundering in their ears.

And, as we turn away from that scene of rapturous excitement we realise for the first time fully, perhaps, how large a part cricket has come to play in the daily life of London.

HEROES OF THE DAY.

KITCHEN IN THE FARM HOUSE, SOUTHWARK.

"DOSSER"-LAND IN LONDON.

By T. W. WILKINSON.

WHEREVER there are particularly mean streets in London the signs of hotels for the poor hang high over the causeway—by day mere "bushes," by night beacons for the guidance of wrecked humanity. Boys' lodging houses, men's lodging houses, single women's lodging houses, "couples'" lodging houses, lodging houses of the rural type, open to all comers, irrespective of age, sex, or condition, are scattered all over the Great City to the number of about 1,000, sometimes alone, sometimes in twos and threes, sometimes in groups of a dozen, but in general, whether solitary or clustered together, off the beaten track, in the heart of seething, sordid slums.

The "doss"-houses for men only are most numerous and, perhaps, most varied, ranging as they do from the dwelling which is registered for only about half a dozen to the barrack-like building in which some 600 weary heads are laid down nightly, and from the den reserved for thieves and other "game

'uns" to the admirably conducted hostels of the Salvation Army, Father Jay's institution in Shoreditch, the Farm House in Southwark, and the many homes for particular sections of the "dosser" army.

For a typical lodging house for men we cannot do better than go to the district of which Spitalfields Church is the centre. Dorset Street, with its squalid air, its groups of "dossers" scattered over the pavement, as well as Flower and Dean Street—of little better repute, and having the same characteristics in a minor degree—are almost under the shadow of that edifice.

And as to the time of our visit, let it be eight o'clock in the evening. Here we are, then. There is no need to knock : the door is open. At four a.m. it swings back to let out the market porters and a whole posse of lodgers who carry under their arm the mark of their calling—a roll of news-papers, yesterday's "returns." It closes about one in the morning, though belated "dossers" straggle in afterwards.

Through the ever-open door, along the passage, a sharp turn to the right, and—phew! Never mind; it is only oil of "sea rover," which adheres to the "doss"-house as the rose to the broken vase. You may scrub, you may whitewash, the place as you will, but the odour of bloater will cling to it still.

This is the kitchen, the common room of the house, the loafing place of the idle,

A COUNTY COUNCIL INSPECTOR'S VISIT.

and the workshop of the industrious. Opposite us as we enter, taking up nearly one-half the length of the wall, and framed in dull, dead black, a huge coke fire glows and crackles, diffusing to the remotest corner an oppressive warmth. It burns like a sepulchral lamp, continuously, from year's end to year's end. Above, a serried line of tin teapots, battered and stained with long use, and above that, again, the "Rules of the House," one of which stands out in aggressive capitals: "No Washing on Sunday"—meaning that laundry work is for purely social reasons prohibited on the Sabbath.

In the corner beyond the fireplace a buxom female figure is eyeing the depleted collection of cracked crockery ranged on the shelves, her sleeves upturned over massive biceps. She is the "deputy," the domestic ruler of about 200 men. Her office is, even in hotels of this class, open to both sexes, each of which has qualifications for it denied to the other. Woman's strong point is the celerity and dispatch she displays in carrying out certain very necessary operations connected with bed-making. Hence the comfort of a house where females are entrusted with that work—which is axiomatic. Man's superiority lies in quelling disturbances and "chucking." Generally the male deputy is more or less of a bruiser, though it is a mistake for him to be an expert pugilist, else his whole time will be divided, in unequal proportions, between fighting and lying in hospital. All the Maces in "Dosser"-land will flock to vanquish or be vanquished.

Distributed over the kitchen three or four score men are having tea, or, as they would call the meal, supper. And a grim, picturesque assemblage they make. Yonder a seedy, frock-coated failure, on whose black, glossy curls Time's hand has not yet been laid, is sopping some bits of bread — manifestly leavings begged from a tea-shop—in a decoction made from a "halfpenny tea and sugar mixed," his eyes wandering now and again to a pair of kippers which a market porter tossed from a frying pan on to a plate a few minutes since. At his elbow an old man, whose snowy beard is plainly, when viewed sideways, his shirt front, mouths a greasy ham bone like a decrepit dog. In front of the fire is another figure that arrests the roving eye. A pallid youth has his meal spread before him on an evening newspaper, which is his tablecloth. It consists of tea, bread and margarine, and that delicacy of which the "dosser" never tires, the humble bloater. The cup which the youthful lodger has before him is an old jam pot, his only article of cutlery is his pocket knife, and he conveys the food to his mouth with Nature's forks. Artificial ones are not provided, nor is it customary to supply either knives or spoons. Too portable—that is the explanation.

And now mark the men with tea only before them—tea which represents the waste of the "doss"-house table, since it has come from the abandoned pots of other and more fortunate lodgers. All have that haunting expression—that dull, despairing look in the eyes—which hunger and buffeting engender. Judged by even the low standard of the fourpenny hotel, they are wretched in the extreme, and in comparison with them most of the other inmates of the kitchen are prosperous. Half their nights are spent in the street, considerably more than half their days in this common room, where they doze by the fire, "bull" or "milk" teapots, pick up odds and ends from the table, and, if happy chance serve, share the meals of acquaintances who may themselves, for aught they know, have to postpone the next morning's breakfast indefinitely. They live, in fact, largely on the charity of their own class. "Dossers'" dependents are certainly an un-

CUBICLES IN A "COUPLES'" HOUSE (SPITALFIELDS).

scheduled section of the community; but they exist in hundreds, and constitute one of the many mysteries of London.

Endless other phases of the underworld can be studied in the kitchen of the fourpenny hotel. The vagrant industries alone afford an unlimited field for investigation. Paper flowers, sand bags, toasting forks, miraculous corn cures, "novelties" of all kinds—such as the walnut thimble case—are made before your eyes. Old, worthless seeds are converted in a twinkling into the "sweet-scented lavender" of commerce. A penny-worth of scent from the chemist's effects the transformation. You can watch the pavement artist doing "all my own work" by deputy, the begging-letter writer studying his private directory and drafting a condensed tragedy on the back of a music-hall handbill, the broken-down journalist racking his brain for ideas that obstinately refuse to come at his bidding, the old soldier—'rejuiced," as Mulvaney used to say in another sense, "but a corporal wanst"—coaching a comrade in the art of cadging from officers of his former regiment. Occasionally even a singing lesson may be witnessed in a kitchen. Not that "griddlers" practise their hymns in a "doss"-house; they learn them at the "ragged churches" on

OUTSIDE A LODGING HOUSE
(FLOWER AND DEAN STREET, SPITALFIELDS).

Sunday. It is the waits who sometimes rehearse at home.

Next, the sleeping chambers. It is midnight. The door at the foot of the stairs is locked, but for all that many men are in bed. At intervals the "deputy" has opened it, and taken from each lodger as he passed the numbered metal check given to him by the proprietor earlier in the evening as a voucher for his fourpence. Until the "dosser" is going to bed he is not required to show if he has paid his lodging money.

About a couple of yards up the staircase, and we reach the first landing, from which there are openings to the right and left leading into small bedrooms, and those into other rooms, and so on till the stranger thinks he is rambling half way up the street. Here a number of small, domestic-like chambers occupy the upper part of the house. In others the system is different, there being only two or three rooms, in which beds stretch away in a long line on each side of the door. This associated arrangement is in force at some houses where sixpence per night is charged.

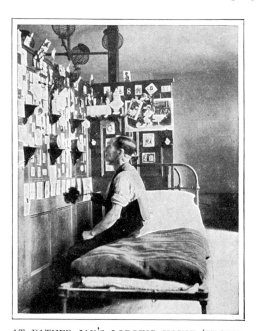

AT FATHER JAY'S LODGING HOUSE (SHORE-
DITCH): A PRETTY CORNER.

But here is the first room. Bareness is its key-note: no curtains or blind to the window, no covering of any kind on the well-scrubbed floor, no pictures on the walls, which are unrelieved whitewash except for a County Council notice and a number at the head of each bed corresponding to that of a room in an hotel. That notice sets forth for how many beds (six) the apartment is registered, and exactly so many does it contain. One more, if discovered—and the inspector drops in occasionally about half-past two in the morning—would subject the owner to a heavy penalty.

On going higher, and seeing room after room of exactly the same character as the

first, you discover that most beds in the house are occupied. From the foot of one a dark mass protrudes. A man has turned in without undressing—that is all. If the rule of the American hotel keeper, "Guests found in bed with their boots on will die that way," was suddenly enforced in common lodging houses, the rate of mortality among "dossers" would be appalling.

Blacker still is an object under another bed. It is a saucepan containing the remains of a stew, the property of him who sleeps above it. The reason it is stored here is not obscure. Look at the waistcoats peeping out from under pillows, or turn down the coverlets on that empty bed and read the legend stamped boldly on the lower sheet: "Stolen from ——." There is the clue. The prevalence of theft in these places — mean, paltry, contemptible theft—accounts for the presence of the saucepan under the bed. Many a man has woke up to find his boots gone, and occasionally a lodger is robbed of all his clothing — coat, waistcoat, trousers, shirt, everything—while he is asleep.

Now there is a rush of feet on the stairs; a babel of voices rising higher and higher. The "last train" is coming up; the laggards who are always loth to leave the kitchen have been turned out. Soon the whole house will be silent save for the chattering of two cronies who have tarried overlong at the "Pig and Penwiper." Then there will be a howl from somebody whom they have wakened, and then, perhaps, a fight.

Of exceptional "doss"-houses for men there are many. A hurried survey of two or three will modify the impression that the typical fourpenny hotel has produced. First, Father Jay's hospice in Shoreditch. Here we are in a different atmosphere. A light, well-appointed kitchen, cubicles above, some of them very

KITCHEN IN A SINGLE WOMEN'S LODGING HOUSE (SPITALFIELDS).

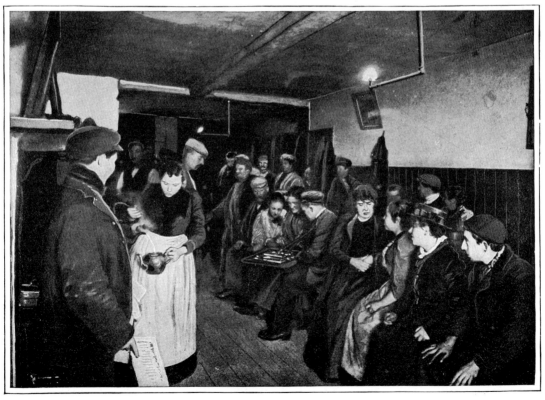

KITCHEN IN A COMMON LODGING HOUSE (SPITALFIELDS).

WASHING AND COOKING AT THE
FARM HOUSE, SOUTHWARK.

Let us now visit a typical women's lodging house. Upstairs, it differs in no way from one for men. Downstairs, the kitchen, with its ruddy coke fire, its overpowering aroma of bloater, its heated atmosphere, as before. Never does it vary very much. Though it is between three and four in the afternoon—a time when a house for men is almost deserted—the room is full of females young and old, some eating, some talking, some at work. One is making paper flowers, another knitting, and a third mending a rent in her skirt.

At the outset the mixed and motley group stirs the imagination profoundly, and still more so when one comes to analyse it. How many of the women bear marks of brutality—swollen lips, cut cheeks, black eyes! And what tragedies has outraged Nature written on some faces which have not been " bashed "—lately ! You can see faint traces of the finer feelings and aspirations in a mass of male wreckage, but here, if they survive at all, the dim light fails to reveal them.

Study, for a moment, that group near the fire. A young woman with dishevelled hair and open bodice (she has apparently yet to make her toilet) is frying steak and onions. By her side a companion equally untidy is also preparing a meal, breakfast maybe, despite the hour. She drops her " halfpenny tea and sugar mixed " into a pot, cautiously lets two eggs sink on the heap, and then pours boiling water on the lot. This is a wrinkle in "doss"-house cookery. The process saves time and trouble always, and in some establishments is compulsory, by reason of the absence of small saucepans. Behind these lodgers a wrinkled old crone is hutched up over her pipe and basking in the heat. Like many of her class, she is intolerant of

tastefully decorated by their occupants, and still higher the ordinary rooms, split up to a certain extent by fixed wooden screens, one of which is covered with brackets, busts, looking-glasses, pictures, and odds and ends innumerable, the property of the man whose bed is beneath—such are the memories one carries away from the place. All is in striking contrast to the bareness and gloom of the typical East-End " doss "-house.

Secondly, the Salvation Army's institution at Paddington, mainly remarkable for its sleeping side. At night one of its rooms is an eye-opener. To right, to left, in front, beds, beds, beds, in seemingly endless number. There is a whole acre of them, all tenanted as far as can be seen. Two hundred sleepers are contained in this one huge chamber, most of them men in fairly regular work—bricklayers' labourers, navvies, and the like. Ask such a man why he stops here rather than in private lodgings, and his reply is prompt and emphatic. " Oh, give *me* company," he says. And, indeed, that is the principal reason. It strikes some people as strange ; but the same thing is met with in higher strata of life.

Finally, there is the Farm House, in Southwark, another very good specimen of the better class of "doss"-houses. It is one of the few establishments of its class where cooking by gas is practicable.

cold, because she cannot feed her bodily fire and produce natural warmth.

If you fill in the details it is not a pleasing picture. Look back. Long, long ago— twenty years, thirty, forty in some cases —numbers of these women came here or to a neighbouring house as girls. And now look forward. You can see them all going to the workhouse or the hospital gate. That is their well-nigh inevitable end, unless they meet a worse fate. They will not, they cannot, rise to a higher level.

One other kind of lodging house looms large in some parts of London, and that is the establishment for " couples." The difference between a place of this class and one for men or women only lies solely in the sleeping accommodation. There is more privacy in the former, though not much in some cases, for the cubicles are like stable stalls. In general, however, they are similar, only smaller, to those boxed-off spaces which the coffee-shop keeper dignifies with the name of bedrooms.

In these places, as in most other " doss "- houses, no questions are asked and no names taken. A man or woman may live in a four- penny hotel for years, and yet be known to the " deputy " by the number of his or her

bed. The majority of the lodgers in hotels for the poor, too, are casuals, not regulars. While one man has had the same " kip " for forty years, and thousands have not changed their quarters for five or ten years or longer, numbers of men and women do not stop many days anywhere. One week a " dosser " may be in the Borough, the next in Spitalfields, the next in St. Clement's, Notting Hill. So that some phases of life in cubicle houses are not so exceptional as the circumstances sur- rounding certain murders which have been committed in them have led many to assume.

On the whole, " Dosser "-land is a squalid, depressing region. Tragedy, then comedy fitfully, then tragedy again—such is life in it. Yet, if its people make the social reformer despair, who shall say that their environment is not better now than ever it was? Of a truth, since the County Council obtained con- trol of lodging houses the improvement in them has been remarkable. The inspectors not only prevent overcrowding, but insist on cleanliness (no more sheet-changing once a month), ventilation, and other sanitary requirements ; and as a result the " dosser " now enjoys a degree of comfort of which formerly he had only heard.

SCENE IN DORSET STREET, SPITALFIELDS.

ON THE STONES, ISLINGTON CATTLE MARKET.

EQUINE LONDON.

By CHARLES DUDLEY

TILL London is conquered by the motor car it will remain both the Purgatory and the Paradise of horses. It is the Purgatory because the work thrown on the heavy brigade knocks up the strongest in a few years; the Paradise because the aristocrats of the equine race live in unwonted luxury, and the aged and the ailing nowhere else meet with such kind and skilful treatment.

Let us ramble through the horse world of London, and we shall see both sides of it. And, first, we will visit Rotten Row this bright, lovely morning. Half-past ten. We are rather too late to catch the "liver brigade." But stay, here is a belated member, mounted on a fine chestnut, which he keeps at a steady gallop; he is pounding up and down in a fashion that will make him go to his club a new man by and by. Near the rails a sleek pony, led by a groom, is taking Master Reginald round for an airing, and eye-

ing his bigger brethren as who should say, "Ah! you'd see what *I* would do if they would only give me a chance." Two fair maidens with their escorts pass by; and then three sisters come cantering down the middle of the Row abreast, their cheeks glowing with robust health, their long hair flowing behind— fine types of Britain's daughters. Still more in the background a mounted policeman, whose like you may meet at night in far-off suburban solitudes, keeps watch over this world-famed stretch.

And now a flash of scarlet catches and holds the eye. In the road bordering the park a string of Guards, their white plumes nodding gently with the steady motion of their horses, whose backs are hidden from saddle to crupper under the voluminous top-coats of their riders, pass along at a walk. They are on their way to Whitehall, there to take turn in standing statuesquely in the sentry-boxes at the Horse Guards—the admiration of nursemaids and the wondering delight of children.

Later in the day the Row is empty, but, on the other hand, the pleasure horse monopolises the circle, now comparatively deserted. Singly, in pairs, tandems, and fours, he draws the family carriage with a lozenge on the panels, the brougham of the fashionable

SHUNTING RAILWAY
TRUCKS.

sessions in the Royal Mews in Buckingham Palace Road—we stroll to Albert Gate, and pass Tattersall's — now, like Aldridge's and the repositories in the Barbican and elsewhere, given up to the sale of horses and carriages. To one class of purchasers it is what the Cattle Market is to another. Small traders mostly look for their horseflesh on the stones at Islington—where there is a scene as much like a horse fair of the rural type as London can show—while gentlemen to whom expense is no consideration betake them in like circumstances to Tattersall's, whose reputation for straight dealing gives them an enormous business. There is no Flying Fox to be sold to-day for 37,000 guineas, or it would be worth while to step inside and witness the event. Smart "steppers" for the Park usually represent the class of business done at the weekly sales nowadays.

doctor, the coupé of the popular actress, the man about town's smart dog-cart.

If we want a contrast to the picture in the Park, the East-End will supply it. High Street, Whitechapel. Gone the high steppers ; gone the glossy carriages ; gone the splendidly impassive footmen. Down the road comes the "general utility" of the equine world and the nearest approach extant to perpetual motion. A shopkeeper's horse more used to the markets and main streets than any other part of London, he is, for the time being, in the service of Pleasure. He is bringing along with a rush a neat little trap, on the front seat of which is the owner, proudly conscious that he can "do it" when he likes, his hat at a knowing angle, a cigar tilted heavenwards between his teeth. Behind an elderly lady lolls in a self-conscious pose; and the rear is brought up, so to speak, by the end of the parlour hearthrug, which dangles behind. Most obviously, the radiant driver is taking the "missus" out for the afternoon. Well, let us hope that they will enjoy their drive.

Returning westwards — not forgetting his Majesty's equine pos-

A short walk farther brings us to one of the numerous

IN ROTTEN ROW.

jobbing establishments that are scattered over London. Enter the yard. A number of carriages with a festive look are in readiness to go out, and we arrive just in time to see a procession of greys led from the stables. "Wedding greys" are they. And what a strange lot in life is theirs—to be the despised of cabby, the rejected of the omnibus owner and the carrier, and the delight of marrying London! The livery master must have them, because they are indispensable for a wedding. Yet their use is almost, if not quite, as restricted as that of the sensitive Flemish blacks, which are reserved for taking us our last drive.

But it creates no exceptional stir in the place, this preparation for a wedding. The firm gets about twenty or thirty of such orders every day. In addition it will,

A BIG STABLE AT WALWORTH (SOUTHWARK BOROUGH COUNCIL).

and does, furnish horses and carriages for every conceivable purpose. Some of its stud have as many different jobs in a day as a boy messenger. They trot placidly with a gigantic boiler behind them in the morning, a lady's bonnet box in the afternoon, and a set of theatrical scenery at night. And it is only one of many firms doing a similar business. Even Messrs. Pickford—who keep more than four thousand horses and frequently engage other three or four hundred by the day—are job masters on a large scale as well as carriers.

A considerable proportion of the horses one sees in the street are, in fact, hired. The hairy-legged members of the heavy brigade that sluggishly drag along the vans

belonging to a certain firm which moves everybody, from the Marquess of Gaunt, of Berkeley Square, to Mr. Thos. Tittlemouse, of Acacia Villa, Peckham; the dashing "tits" of innumerable butchers, bakers, and other tradesmen; the smart equipages which take many doctors on their rounds, ladies to Bond Street or the theatre, music-hall artistes to their engagements, and are met at every turn in Central London; the superb "goers" in the service of the Metropolitan Fire Brigade, on which every eye is turned as they dash through the streets to a constant accompaniment of "Hi-hi-hi!"—all are jobbed at rates varying according to their value and other factors.

Perhaps the only kind of horse which is not hired, except the stolid animal which acts as a shunting engine on the iron road, is the plunging beauty of the Hippodrome, that intelligent creature which can be trusted to look dashing and full of fire and at the same time to work with the regularity of a steam-engine. Every other variety is jobbed. One firm will horse any business for a fixed sum per year, while another is able to supply a horse, brougham, and man at a total inclusive cost of about £225 or £250 a year. At this rate it is cheaper and more convenient to hire a carriage than to keep one; and consequently private stables are becoming fewer and fewer.

Cross the Thames now to the stable of the Southwark Borough Council in Walworth. Here we are at a typical home of the

municipal horse, than which there is no better animal of its class in the equine world. Well-lighted, adequately ventilated, provided with every necessary convenience, it presents an animated spectacle by reason of a number of men being engaged in polishing the brasses on the harness, the suppleness of which attests the attention it receives. About the fine animals in the stalls there is nothing remarkable except their capacity for backing. At that the

municipal horse is easily first and the rest nowhere. He will push a dust cart into any opening, and, what is more, run no risk of having his legs injured, for he will keep them well under him the while.

The apotheosis of the cart horse ! Not the May-Day procession, though in that he has the whole stage and all the limelight to himself, but his principal festival, the show in Regent's Park on Whit-Monday. It is ten o'clock, and right round the inner

AT THE CART HORSE SHOW AND PARADE, REGENT'S PARK.

I. JUDGING.   II. DRAYMAN (FORTY-ONE YEARS' SERVICE) WITH PRIZE HORSE.   III. A FAMILY PARTY.

circle are extended more tnan one thousand fine specimens of the heavy brigade, attached to nearly every kind of business vehicle, some singly, some in pairs, and some in teams.

Here is a typical turn-out. A sleek, well-groomed horse, no rib or pin bone visible, newly-shod, with blacked hoofs, and gaily decked with flowers and ribbons, stands in the shafts of a coal delivery van, in which a family party has been brought from a distant suburb. In front is the driver,

all quarters of London, and it will be late when some of them reach home.

Before we leave the park let us learn the result of the long-service competition. The winner on this occasion—the man who takes the money bequeathed by Miss Isabel Constable—is a veteran who has held the same situation for over 41 years, and the four drivers who have been awarded the premiums of one guinea offered by the Cart Horse Society have severally been in the employ of

TATTERSALL'S.

temporarily oblivious — under the subtle excitement of the moment—that he has been working all night on his horse. Behind him is his wife, beaming and happy, and in the rear are grouped the children, and others all in their Sunday best.

Meanwhile, the judging has been going on. It lasts some time, for not only have the horses to be passed under review, but prizes awarded for length of service. It is over now, and a queue is formed, the winners taking the lead, and all the horses parade once right round the outer circle. Then the procession breaks up. For hours hence its component parts will be returning to

one master for nearly as long a period. And yet cynics say that the race of faithful Adams is extinct!

With a rapid survey of two unique institutions our tour round Equine London may end. Much—very much—must for one reason or another be ignored. 'Bus, tram, and cab horses receive attention in another article in this work, while the "knacker's" industry, important though it may be, smacks too much of the shambles to be pleasant.

The first of the two institutions is the Royal Veterinary College in Camden Town. It is three o'clock in the afternoon, and the free clinic is taking place.

Drawn up outside one part of the buildings are the out-patients—a score of sorry-looking hacks—attended by their owners, who mostly belong to the costermonger class and are all too poor to pay for the doctoring of their ailing workers. Through the opening, and we are in the out-patients' ward. It is a covered yard. In the middle is a thick bed of clean straw, on and round which are scattered groups of surgeons and students.

"Look out!" To the right is a horse, which is about to be cast—to be thrown on its side like another patient which lies on our left. "Capped elbow; the largest I ever saw," says the surgeon, pointing to a huge excrescence on the inner side of one of this poor brute's forelegs. Presently somebody comes up with a leather bucket, fixes it over the captive's nose, and tucks a cloth round the top to keep in the fumes. Chloroform! The unfortunate owner, who is holding down the horse's head, looks as if he himself were about to be operated on, since he is ghastly, with restless eyes quick to see every movement. A moment, and the prostrate brute struggles convulsively; but the anæsthetic quickly overpowers him. Then a student drags a bucket of disinfecting fluid nearer the patient, makes a selection from a number of pretty little instruments, and—but we will not stay longer.

What a boon is this free clinic to the indigent horse-keeper! Any afternoon he can bring an ailing steed to it and have it attended to gratuitously.

The other institution at which we will make a call is Friar's Place Farm—otherwise known as the Home of Rest for Horses—at Acton. This is the most pleasing feature of the equine world of London, for it is a sort of combined hydro and retreat for man's faithful friend. Some of the inmates are resting temporarily or undergoing treatment at the hands of skilled surgeons; but many are pensioners, and have been in retirement for years. They are maintained either by ladies and gentlemen for whom they have worked hard and well or by the supporters of the institution.

The farm consists largely of row after row of stables, from one line of which a dozen heads and necks are craned out as we approach. The inmates heard us coming. They are all great pets. Each has a house of his own, and in it he lives comfortably, even luxuriously, with nothing to do but eat and enjoy life. Every New Year's Day the pensioners are specially favoured, for, by the kindness of a benevolent lady, they are provided with a special dinner of apples, carrots, brown and white bread, and sugar.

Vast and many-sided is the horse world of London; and yet it is all to disappear —stables, institutions, pretty customs, everything—before the noisy, ugly, but decidedly convenient and economical motor vehicle! Perhaps—and perhaps not.

A ROW OF PENSIONERS (HOME OF REST, ACTON).

HOSPITAL LONDON.

By R. AUSTIN FREEMAN.

NURSE (WEST LONDON HOSPITAL).

AMONG the multitudes of way-farers that throng the streets of the Metropolis there are probably few who, as they pass one of the great hospitals, do not glance up at the massive building with some curiosity, and with, perhaps, a passing thought as to the strange scenes that are being enacted within. Yet by few of these are the significance and importance of these institutions fully appreciated, or the scope of their relations with humanity at large understood.

For the great hospitals of London are not only the refuges of the sick and suffering poor; the agents through which the benevolent minister to the necessities of the indigent; the retreats to which the struggling worker can retire in seasons of adversity, to receive relief in his own person and in the removal from his family of the burden of his helplessness. They are all this, indeed; but, in addition, they are the battle-grounds upon which is fought that never-ending contest in which the intelligence of man is arrayed against those invading forces that ever tend to shorten the period of individual life and to augment the sum of sorrow and suffering for mankind at large.

With a view to getting some insight into the inner life of a hospital, let us present ourselves at the out-patient entrance about nine o'clock in the morning. A considerable crowd has collected, and, as the doors are just opened, the earlier arrivals are beginning to pass through. The crowd is at present a very miscellaneous one, for its constituent units have not yet been sorted out and classified. The pale consumptive jostles a sturdy labourer whose bandaged head furnishes an illustration of the momentum of falling bodies; patients with rasping coughs and panting breath; patients on crutches; patients in splints, with limbs swathed in bandages; men and women, old and young, strong and feeble, are here mingled into an

OUT-PATIENTS' WAITING ROOM (MIDDLESEX HOSPITAL).

BOTTLE - SELLING OUTSIDE ST.
BARTHOLOMEW'S HOSPITAL.

indiscriminate assembly. On the outskirts of the crowd an itinerant bottle merchant has set up a little stall (for the hospital does not supply bottles gratis); but most of the frugal patients have furnished themselves from home, and we may see marmalade jars converted into ointment pots, while the jovial whiskey bottle is degraded into a mere receptacle for cod-liver oil.

Inside the doorway a porter and a nurse are engaged in sorting out the patients by means of their cards or letters; and very soon the lobbies outside the various out-patient rooms become filled with groups of patients who, as they sit on the benches awaiting their turn, inspect with an expert and critical eye the new-comers who continue to pass in.

From time to time the door of a consulting room is opened, and an attendant admits the patients in parties of about a dozen, while those who have seen the doctors emerge with their prescription cards in their hands, and go to swell the little crowd that is gathered round the dispensary.

As a batch of patients is admitted we enter a spacious room, round the sides of which are a number of electric lamps fitted with bull's-eyes. At one of these a clinical assistant is examining, with the aid of a reflector fastened to his forehead, a patient's throat, while at another a student is exploring an obstructed ear. The surgeon sits near the window, with a semi-circle of chairs occupied by students behind him, and the patient seated in a good light before him; and as he examines the latter he directs the attention of the students to the salient points of the case, and explains the train of reasoning by which he arrives at his diagnosis.

Of course, the different departments have their own special characters. In the medical,

PORTER (WEST LONDON
HOSPITAL).

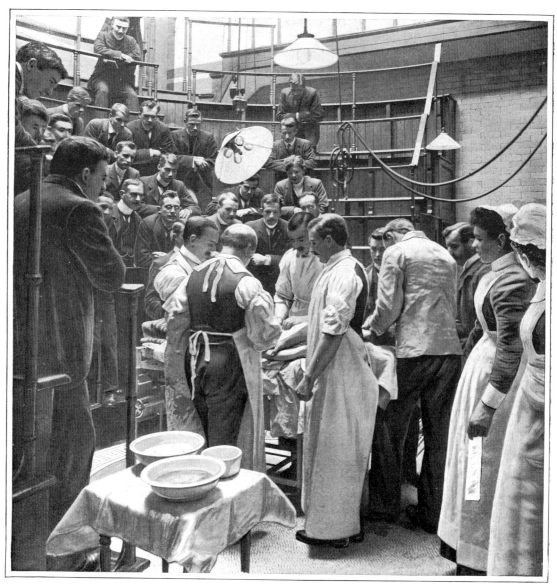

AN OPERATION AT CHARING CROSS HOSPITAL.

stethoscopes abound and coughs prevail; in the surgical, bandages, dressings, and antiseptics are in evidence. In the eye department the air is filled with a droning sound of "E, T, B, D, L, N," as the patients read aloud the letters of the test types through the trial glasses, and students, working out "refractions," are seen in dark closets, throwing from their ophthalmoscopes bright, dancing spots of light on to the eyes of their patients. But we must not linger among the out-patients. We have just seen from the window a couple of policemen wheeling a covered ambulance up to the entrance, and thither we now hurry.

Each of the policemen has embroidered on his sleeve a Maltese cross within a circle, a device which indicates that he has gone through a course of instruction in "First Aid to the Injured," and received the certificate of the St. John's Ambulance. This useful Association not only gives instruction, but furnishes stretchers and ambulances for use in street accidents, and, moreover, owns a number of admirable covered waggons or horse ambulances, which may be hired for the conveyance of invalids or helpless persons.

The stretcher is detached from its carriage and placed upon a cushioned trolley, which is wheeled noiselessly along a corridor to a small room where the house-surgeon with his dressers are waiting. The patient, a respectable working man, has been knocked down by a van which has run over one of his legs ; and to the injured limb the policemen have attached a temporary splint. This being now removed, and the patient's trousers slit up, a jagged wound is revealed, through which a sharp splinter of bone protrudes. The leg has sustained a compound fracture.

The wound is now carefully cleansed by the house-surgeon, who covers it with a dressing of gauze or tissue that has been subjected to heat in a closed chamber to destroy any germs that might lurk in it. Well-padded splints are next applied to the limb, and the patient is then wheeled off on the trolley to a large lift, which carries him and two porters to an upper floor ; where, after traversing a long corridor, the trolley at length brings up alongside an empty bed in one of the great surgical wards. Trolley and bed are now surrounded by screens, and the patient, being lifted on to the bed by the two stalwart porters, is by them undressed with sur-

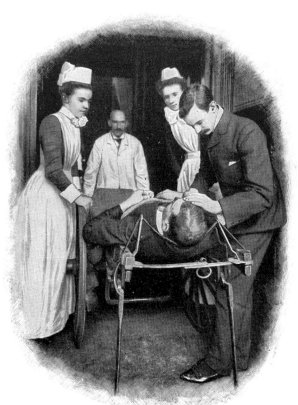

RECEIVING AN ACCIDENT CASE (POPLAR HOSPITAL).

prising care and gentleness and covered with a blanket. Finally, the screens are removed, and a nurse proceeds to trim up the bed with sheets and counterpane to the required standard of neatness.

Let us glance round the ward into which we have followed our patient. It is a lofty apartment of great length and relatively narrow—somewhat like a very large corridor. The spaces of painted wall between the large windows are hung with pictures and framed

texts, and the floor is of polished oak, elegant in appearance and easy to keep clean, but very slippery. Down the middle of the ward is a range of long tables, supporting flowers, ferns, and palms, as well as basins, ewers, and other appliances.

Each side is occupied by a row of beds extending the whole length of the ward, most of them occupied by patients, whose red flannel bed-jackets contrasting with the white counterpanes impart a very bright and cheerful aspect to the place. Indeed, a general air of cheerfulness and comfort is the most noticeable feature, even of a surgical ward. In most of the beds the patients are placidly engaged in the perusal of newspapers and books; convalescents with crutches or arm-slings are play-ing draughts at the tables or doing such odd jobs as their condition allows, amid much animated conversation and many lively sallies of cockney wit from the occupants of the beds; while the busy nurses flit from patient to patient, making the building resound with the clatter of their so-called " silent ward shoes."

But the graver side of hospital life is in evidence too. The patients are not all convalescent, nor are they all cheerful and happy. Here, for instance, is a silent, motionless figure, the pallid face surmounted by an ice-cap, and the half-closed eyes singularly ghastly and death-like — a bad case of concussion of the brain. In the bed hard by, the clothes of which are raised by a " cradle," like the tilt of a waggon, a man lies staring fixedly at the ceiling ; and when the sister has told us that " 23 had his leg amputated above the knee yesterday" we can read in the sad, dejected face the sorrowful thoughts that are passing through the sufferer's mind. We know that he is thinking of the wooden pin on which he is to stump through life, of the struggle for existence made tenfold more bitter, of the sports and pleasures that he enjoyed in the past and will enjoy no more!

While we are looking round the ward one of the house-surgeons, with an attendant squad of dressers, makes his appearance, and forthwith a glass table running on rubber-tyred wheels is brought out to accompany him on his round. The glass shelves of the table are filled with air-tight cases of sterilised gauze, tissue, cotton wool, and bandages, sealed glass tubes of sterilised silk and cat-

solutions of carbolic acid or corrosive sublimate, and the dressings would have been impregnated with iodoform or other germicide substances; but the "antiseptic" surgery which wrought such marvels in the past is disappearing in favour of the still more perfect "aseptic" system of the present day.

The introduction of this new aseptic system —by which it is sought to exclude all microbes from the neighbourhood of wounds, instead of applying to them "antiseptics," or microbe poisons, as was formerly done—has not only produced a great change in the materials and processes used in the dressing of wounds, but has rendered the daily round of the dressers a much less important proceeding. For under the older system a considerable portion of the surgical cases required to have

Photo: Dr. E. H. Harnock.

SINGING TO PATIENTS (LONDON HOSPITAL).

gut for closing wounds, and porringers or little basins for the sterilised water from the Pasteur filter with which the wounds are cleansed if necessary. A few years since these porringers would have contained

the dressings renewed daily; whereas nowadays wounds are commonly sealed up immediately after an operation with germ-proof dressings, which are left undisturbed until the wounds are completely healed. Should some mischief-

VISITING DAY AT A
CHILDREN'S HOSPITAL
(GREAT ORMOND STREET).

working microbe find its way in through the dressings, despite all precautions, and set up suppuration in the wound, there is not a little grumbling on the part of the surgeon, and a strict inquiry is made into the history of the faulty materials with which the wound has been covered.

But, although the daily dressings are now much reduced in number, there is still in a large hospital ward plenty of occupation for the house-surgeons and dressers, and their morning's work will hardly have been completed before the appearance upon the ward tables of mounds of bread, neatly cut into symmetrical "doorsteps," announces the dinner-hour, and as they leave the ward they are met in the corridor by a waggon or large trolley piled high with the smoking materials for the meal, and diffusing a savoury aroma as it passes. Drawn up alongside the table, it disgorges its freight, and volcanic mounds of potatoes, verdant stacks of cabbage, ribs of beef, fried soles, plump chickens, and seething mutton chops attract the expectant regards of the patients and receive the attention of the sister and nurses. Then comes the rather unequal distribution of the delicacies. No. 4, who is recovering from the effects of a blow on the head, is on a

very restricted diet, and, as he wolfishly devours a diminutive sole, glances avariciously at his right-hand neighbour, an emaciated "hip joint" case, who is demolishing half a chicken with the gusto of a South Sea Islander. No. 8 is taking light refreshment through an india-rubber tube with the aid of a funnel, while the street arab in the corner bed assaults a mutton chop literally with tooth and nail, gnawing at the bone with chuckles of cannibalistic glee.

The meal concluded and the ward tidied up, an air of restlessness and expectancy becomes evident in the demeanour of the patients, which is presently explained when we discover that this is a visitors' day. Soon the patients' friends make their appearance, the men holding their hats gingerly and stepping on tiptoe, with immense strides (by which means it has been shown that the maximum amount of sound can be extracted from a pair of creaky shoes), and the women particularly attentive to the conduct of their offspring. Sometimes a visitor goes down with a thump on the slippery floor, to his own unspeakable confusion and the undissembled joy of the regular inmates. The bedside greetings run the whole gamut, from the half-sheepish

"Wot-O! Bill! How goes it?" of the male visitor, to the passionate embrace of the anxious wife or mother.

The unconscious "concussion" is visited

her blinding tears or hear her sobs as she hurries away through the echoing corridor.

In the Children's Hospital visitors' day

THE LUPUS LIGHT CURE (LONDON HOSPITAL).

by a pale, frightened-looking woman, who sits by the bed and gazes disconsolately at the silent figure. No. 23 brightens up somewhat as a quiet, trim-looking little woman, leading a sturdy boy of six or seven, approaches up the ward; and when she has seated herself by his side and holds his hand in hers as she chats of the doings outside he grows quite cheerful, although when his boy breaks out into joyous anticipations of the fun they will have "when father comes home" he has to turn away hastily and fumble in the locker by his bedside. The street arab has no friends to visit him, and consoles himself for the fact by putting out his tongue at a juvenile stranger and watching malignantly the little parties round the other beds. The allotted time quickly runs out, and the warning bell rings all too soon. Amidst a clatter of chairs the visitors rise to take leave of their friends, and then slowly troop out of the ward. No 23's wife is the last to go, and she turns at the door to wave her handkerchief and throw him a kiss; and he, poor fellow, greatly comforted by her pluck and cheerfulness, turns over with a sigh of contentment, for he cannot see

is especially a season of rejoicing; for then anxious mothers, who have, perhaps, gone away heart-broken at having to leave their little ones alone among strangers, experience the delight of seeing them again, bright, happy, tenderly cared for, and in the enjoyment of luxuries undreamed of in their own homes.

On days other than visiting days the wards are enlivened by the visits of the physicians or surgeons and the students, who, here at the bedside, receive the practical part of their professional education. Frequently a popular surgeon will be accompanied by twenty or thirty students, who form a semi-circle round the bed while the case is discussed in all its bearings and a *vivâ voce* examination is held upon the points involved in its history, diagnosis, and pathology, and any anatomical or physiological questions arising out of it.

From the wards we may proceed to the operating theatre, where one of the surgeons is already at work. The building is roughly horseshoe-shaped, and consists of a central area surrounded by tiers of platforms, rising one above the other in the manner of a Roman amphitheatre, for the accommodation of students who have come to watch the operation. In the area precautions against the ubiquitous microbe are everywhere in evidence. The group of surgeons, dressers, and nurses around the table on which lies the unconscious patient, all dressed in white sterilised over-garments, and in some cases even guarded by sterilised gloves; the seething trays in which the instruments are boiling, and the air filters that supply the ventilators: all testify to the importance of the great principle underlying modern surgical methods—the exclusion of micro-organisms. But that when the micro-organism has actually effected an entrance into the body he is not at all times secure against the warfare waged by means of modern appliances is made evident in the lupus cure department. For here the bacilli that give rise to this intractable and disfiguring disease are killed by the application of light from an arc electric lamp, the rays being brought to focus upon the diseased tissues, which are rendered more translucent by pressure made upon them with a water lens.

We might continue our ramble through the immense building of a London hospital indefinitely. We might explore the spacious garden where convalescents are taking the air, and where in summer time open-air entertainments are given to the patients; we might examine the dispensary with its multitudes of great bottles and Brobdingnagian jars; we might look in at the kitchen and marvel at the huge gas ovens like bankers' safes, the frying stoves as large as billiard tables, and the rows of cauldrons for cooking vegetables or making soup, each balanced on trunnions and inverted by means of a windlass; or inspect the incubators in which tiny, doll-like, prematurely born infants are reared in an artificially warmed atmosphere. But our time has run out, and, with a final glance at a bright-looking ward where, to the cheerful strains of a musical-box, a number of children are revelling in the enjoyment of toys that will make their recollections of hospital life a dream of bliss, we pass out of the building and mingle with the crowd that surges at its gates.

WAITING FOR MEDICINE (WEST LONDON HOSPITAL).

THE ROYAL MINT.

By CHARLES OLIVER.

BY a singular irony of Fate the building in which the nation's money is made is situated in one of the poorest districts of London. Close by the Mint the hungry docker passes rich on a few pence an hour, while from the wharves adjacent there pours a stream of ragged immigrants, which, percolating into every hovel of the east, sweeps on and on northward to Whitechapel, westward to Saffron Hill and Soho, emptying itself finally into the outlying districts.

There is little in the external appearance of the Royal Mint to attract attention; nothing to indicate the stupendous wealth that reposes within its walls. But as we stand outside there is evidence that something of special interest is about to take place. There are several burly-looking policemen on the spot, and, if we judge them correctly, they are watching for suspicious characters. The fact is we are in luck's way, for the great gates of the Mint are suddenly thrown open, and a van is driven in at a sharp pace. It is a very ordinary looking van—for aught a stranger could say to the contrary it might belong to a caterer—nevertheless its contents are worth a king's ransom. We could not have arrived at a more opportune moment.

Having received permission of the Deputy-Master to visit the Mint we are admitted into the courtyard, and, on reaching the lobby, are severally requested to register our names and addresses in a book provided for the purpose. At the door are a number of officials—a representative of the Mint, a clerk from the Bank of England, together with a constable and a couple of porters. They are going to unload the van, and as our presence is not objected to we notice that its precious freight consists of several large chests securely padlocked. A trolley is wheeled forward, and presently one of the clerks produces a bunch of keys, and a case is opened. It is full of silver ingots. Many a hard-working man has to toil for a whole year to earn one of those ingots, while before he can become possessed of a trolley-load the clerk in charge of them has to labour possibly for a lifetime, and be a favourite of fortune as well; but there is no envy in the clerk's breast. His face is as expressionless as the stone flags on which he stands.

RECEIVING SILVER INGOTS.

Out they come one by one until a hundred ingots have been counted—£13,000 worth of solid silver. The metal is the property of the Bank of England, and will soon be converted into money.

MELTING AND POURING GOLD.

The van having disgorged its wealth to the last ounce, we follow the ingots far into the interior of the Mint, first into the Weighing-room, where they are weighed in the presence of the Bank officials, who remain until each ingot has been placed upon the scale, and then into the Strong-rooms. At every turn a dazzling hoard of gold confronts us. We brush against three trolleys on which are stacked a hundred small bags, and our guide observes with characteristic nonchalance that £40,000 would not purchase them. They are full of worn sovereigns—old stagers *en route* for the melting pot.

And now to the bullion stronghold to realise the magnitude of the work performed at the Mint, for there is not a coin bearing the King's head that has not come out of this chamber. The massive steel door is shut against us, and to turn the lock three keys are necessary. These keys are in the hands of three trusty officials, and their kindly aid having been obtained the doors swing heavily back, revealing to our astonished gaze a stock of gold and silver representing a million pounds. Hundreds of millions—enough to pay the National Debt twice over—have filtered through this stronghold of gold. Ranged upon shelves in admirable order are ingots of gold and ingots of silver,

each one duly marked and numbered so that its identity can be established on the instant. These ingots—those of silver are worth £130 and weigh 1,100 ounces—have been carefully tested by the permanent staff of analysts in the Assay Department and are ready to be sent to the Melting-house.

There are two strongholds at the Mint to make a poor man's mouth water. The second is for coined silver, and it harbours £200,000 of coins packed away in neat bags. Five shilling pieces, half-crowns, florins, shillings, and sixpences are done up in £100 bags; threepenny pieces in £25 bags.

We will now proceed to the Melting-house to gaze upon the pleasant spectacle of £20,000 worth of gold melting like butter. There are twenty-two furnaces in all—eight in the gold Melting-house and fourteen in the silver. The eight men dressed in blue serge employed in the former have melted in their time enough gold to fill a small pond. With as little concern as a cook puts bones to stew over the kitchen fire they place each ingot with its proper proportion of copper alloy into a crucible and plunge it deftly into the red-hot furnace, where it remains until it is reduced to a liquid state. The melting done, the crucible is withdrawn from the furnace by means of hand tongs, and the contents—a white molten fluid—are poured into an iron mould, the result being that a number of narrow bars are produced each worth between four and five hundred pounds.

From the Melting-room we step into the busy Rolling-room, where the bars go through the various mills until eventually they are rolled down to the required thickness. Every man is in full work, and each one is touching gold in the form of beautiful yellow strips from one to two inches thick that would suffice to support him and his family in luxury for a good twelve months. More gold passes through the hands of these humble workers in a year than a millionaire sees in a lifetime.

The average visitor to the Mint cudgels his brain in vain to understand how a check can be kept on all this wealth, for there is scarcely any waste, and theft is unknown. The explanation is simple, however, for, contrary to general supposition, nobody is searched when

employés in that department have to find it before they go home. Several other precautionary rules have to be observed, not because there is any doubt as to the honesty of the workers, who bear the best of characters —the greed of gold is not for them, familiarity with the precious metal having removed all temptation—but in order to prevent the ingots from going astray.

Each department is kept locked throughout the day, and no man can visit a room other than his own without the sanction of the officer who is over him. Further, the metal is weighed as it is passed from room to room. The head of each department knows by his books the weight of metal that was given out to him in the morning, and consequently has no difficulty when work ceases for the day in ascertaining the exact amount of gold and silver, after allowing for waste, that should be in his hands. Even the dust

THE ROLLING-ROOM.

he goes home at night, and there is no system of espionage; but no employé engaged in the making of money is allowed to leave the building until the day's work is done— the men must take their dinner on the premises—and until every particle of metal has been weighed. If a valuable piece of metal is missing from any department, the

on the floor is taken into calculation. Before the bells sound for the nightly exodus each room is carefully swept, and the particles that have accumulated during the day having been collected they are put into water, with the result that any gold or silver that may be present soon separates itself from the dust by dropping to the bottom of the pan. It is interesting also to observe that the gold pieces are counted as well as weighed as they are carried from room to room.

But the Mint is a large place, and a personally conducted tour occupies an hour and a half, so we must get on. Leaving the Rolling-room we proceed to the Cutting-room, where perspiring men of all ages are occupied in putting into machines the bright clean strips of gold out of which are punched blank pieces the size and shape of the coins. The "blanks" are afterwards placed into marking machines and reappear with a raised edge.

CUTTING-ROOM.

From the Cutting-room the "blanks" are despatched to the Annealing-room, for the rolling has rendered the metal so hard that before it can receive the impression it must be put into the oven to be softened

The next process takes place in the Blanching-room. Here myriads of gold and silver blanks are treated with acid, the silver to obtain the desired whiteness, the gold to remove the black surface which has been

RINGING THE COINS.

caused by the annealing. Two men are at work here. Their joint wages do not, perhaps, exceed more than a few pounds a week, but during their careers each one of them has fingered his million. One of them has just finished blanching a couple of thousand silver "blanks," and to rid them of the acid he has poured them into a pan and is holding them under a running tap. With so little fuss does he clean his blanks that we inquire how many he loses in a week, and the startling reply is "None." Nothing is lost at the Mint.

It is now necessary that the blanks should be dried, and for this purpose they are shaken up in revolving drums containing warm sawdust. This drying process cleanses the "blanks."

By far the busiest place in the Mint is the Coining Press-room, which we enter after quitting the Drying-room. Here are engaged the livelong day—from 8 a.m. to 5 p.m. —eighteen presses turning out money at the rate of 110 coins per minute apiece. The Coining Press-room of the Royal Mint is Britain's Klondike, for within its four walls every gold and silver coin in general circulation in the United Kingdom is made.

The machines, to each of which there is but one operator, stand side by side. The blanks flow in from a receptacle one by one, and, behold; in the twinkling of an eye they fall into a little tray below, a finished coin of the realm.

Our final visit in our walk through the Mint is to the Weighing-room. In this extraordinary hive of industry from three to four hundred thousand pounds' worth of money is weighed in a day by machines which are not to be found in any other part of Great Britain, save at the Bank of England, for they not only retain the good coins, but they throw out the light and the heavy. Faulty coins are re-melted. Having been weighed, the gold money goes to the "ringers"—boys who test each coin by throwing it down on a steel block. Boys are also utilised for overlooking the silver coins.

The gold is now put up into £1,000 bags and stored in the Strong-room. The following day a van arrives from the Bank of England, and the money is quietly taken away. With silver and bronze the case is different. Coins made of these metals are counted by a wonderful machine, which in one way is a good deal more than human, for although it sometimes counts a ton of bronze

coins in the brief space of sixty minutes, it never makes a mistake. It is only on silver and bronze coins that the Mint earns a profit. On gold there is considerable loss; but on silver and bronze the profit is large silver being coined into any denomination at a fixed rate of five shillings and sixpence per ounce.

It is important to note that none of the gold in the Royal Mint belongs to the Government. It is the property for the time being of the directors of the Bank of England, who, whenever they require an addition to their stock of sovereigns and half-sovereigns, send a supply of bullion to the Mint, where it is turned into coins at the expense of the Government. The Bank pays nothing for the manufacture of its gold money.

Thus are the King's coins brought into the world. It may be remarked, in conclusion, that a high wall surrounds the Royal Mint, and that inside the wall there is a military path where sentinels—soldiers quartered at the Tower—are posted night and day.

IN THE COINING PRESS-ROOM.